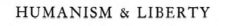

HUMANISM & LIBERTY

Humanism & Liberty

WRITINGS ON FREEDOM FROM

FIFTEENTH-CENTURY FLORENCE

•

TRANSLATED AND EDITED BY

Renée Neu Watkins

UNIVERSITY OF SOUTH CAROLINA PRESS

LIBRARY OF CONGRESS
CATALOGING IN PUBLICATION DATA

Main entry under title:
Humanism & liberty.

Includes index.
CONTENTS: Aretino, L. B. The history of
Florence.—Alberti, L. B. Happiness. The conspiracy of Stefano Porcari.—Bracciolini, P. On
nobility. [etc.]
1. Florence—History—1421–1737—Addresses,
essays, lectures. 2. Humanism—Addresses, essays,
lectures. 3. Liberty—Addresses, essays, lectures.
I. Watkins, Renée Neu.
DG737.4.H85   945'.51   78–6588
ISBN 0–87249–360–1

Thus any animal caged and subjected to others never ceases to try to be free again to make use of its own self, its wings or feet or other parts, not at another's will but with liberty, at its own behest.

Leon Battista Alberti
Della Famiglia

Contents

Introduction	3
Leonardo Bruni Aretino	21
The History of Florence	27
Preface	27
Book One	30
Book Four, Speech of Giano della Bella	69
Book Twelve	74
Chronological Guide	92
Leon Battista Alberti	97
Happiness	103
The Conspiracy of Stefano Porcari	107
Poggio Bracciolini	117
On Nobility	121
Lorenzo de' Medici	149
A Memoir and a Letter	157
Angelo Poliziano	167
The Pazzi Conspiracy	171
Alamanno Rinuccini	185
Liberty	193
Girolamo Savonarola	225
Treatise on the Constitution and Government of the City of Florence	231
Index	261

MAPS

1. Italian Peninsula around 300 B.C.   94
2. Italian Peninsula around 264 B.C.   95
3. Major northern Italian powers, 1390–1433   96

HUMANISM & LIBERTY

Introduction

HUMANISM AND LIBERTY?

Humanism and liberty are two words that attract and that are bound closely in meaning. Today we occasionally describe an intellectual or political orientation as "humanistic." We mean a way of thinking which leaves room for humanity by respecting the will —the conscious or even the potentially conscious will of groups or individuals. A humanistic architecture, for instance, implies an architecture not only concerned with the basic needs of the inhabitants, but with their freedom. Though it may consist entirely of functional parts, it presents to the eye openness beyond the functional, to the imaginative mind possibilities beyond the foreseen functions. The same is true of humanistic religion, philosophy, psychology, or practical policy: whatever the specific content, there is openness to self-initiated activity from all parties. This contrasts with systems requiring only activity based on the plans of an authority. Humanism in this sense is more than humane—but unfortunately sometimes less.

WHO AND WHY

This anthology presents seven Renaissance writers on political issues. All enjoyed the patronage of the sixty-year Medici regime

(1434–1494) under which Florence experienced considerable prosperity and fame. Yet whether that regime was good for the city or not was a subject of controversy. At least some of these authors express bitter anger with the Medici usurpation of power and mourn the Republic's loss of liberty.

Perhaps variety is the chief attraction of this group—variety along with skill in the art of writing. Eloquence was their word for it, and they all took pride in their eloquence. Leonardo Bruni, in the first book of his *History*, elegantly describes to us a thousand years of Roman history, rich in heroes and traditional anecdotes. He makes clear and thoughtful assessments of the upheavals that mark this era. Later, in Book Twelve, which is also translated here, he describes the most recent history of Florence: her external danger and her political machinations in the struggle to survive. Another author, Leon Battista Alberti, comments on the ideal of happiness and the fact of slavery. Poggio Bracciolini discusses the ideal of nobility and the fact of ruling classes. Making use of dialogue form, both Alberti and Poggio handle profound ideas lightly. In the deft manner of sensational journalism, Angelo Poliziano describes an attempted assassination of the Medici. Lorenzo de' Medici himself gives a sober account of his reign, and his letter to his son combines moralism and humor. The dialogue *On Liberty* by Alamanno Rinuccini speaks to us like many a novel of protest. And the terse political theorizing of Savonarola soon turns, as one might expect from that greater preacher, into a bloodcurdling diatribe.

For these authors the meaning of liberty shifts: it is more perceived by its absence than by its presence. The concept seems to point in a general direction rather than toward a clearly defined goal. These seven writers help us to understand what sort of impulses are combined in the fundamental human quest for liberty.

HUMANISM

Renaissance humanism was an intellectual movement of the mid-fourteenth to the mid-sixteenth century. Its inspiration was the classical world. For the Italian humanists, who led the movement, the pagan Romans were identified, despite their paganism,

4

as "our ancestors." Certain Romans were models of patriotism and wisdom, and Roman writers were models of style. Since the Romans themselves had acknowledged the Greeks as their teachers, Renaissance humanists tried to read the Greeks and to understand what the Greeks had done and believed. This interest in the ancient world was not without all sorts of practical applications.

It changed the very language of poetry and history and moral thought. Most serious writers abandoned Medieval Latin. They strove instead to approximate classical Latin and to include many Greek quotations. The works of Alberti, Bruni, Poggio, Poliziano, and Rinuccini translated here were written in a flowing classical Latin imitating, in each case, the style of one or more ancient authors.

A Florentine bookseller, Vespasiano da Bisticci, sketched some of the lives of fifteenth-century humanists he had known.[1] What he saw in his subjects (who were also his clients) was a common concern with collecting manuscripts, contributing to learning, and living in a morally admirable way. To them learning and moral character were intimately related. The same general picture emerges in Georg Voigt's much fuller mid-nineteenth-century *Lives of Humanists*.[2]

Paul Oscar Kristeller stresses that, aside from belonging to their time, these intellectuals belonged to no distinct school of thought. Their "republic of letters" was an informal guild of those occupationally interested in the classical languages. What these professional rhetoricians shared, he says, was not a philosophy or a political outlook, but mainly pride in their professional activity.[3] As Kristeller points out, western philosophy owes little or nothing to them. To add to philosophy, however, is not a distinction at which they were aiming.

Humanist poetry takes delight in the physically beautiful and the mythologically strange. Humanist history moves between rhetorical amplitude and analysis, between concrete and abstract. While medieval historians generally catalogue the rather stereotyped traits of leaders, the humanists build up portraits in distinctive detail and analyze character for its specificity. Humanists discuss in their favorite form, the philosophical dialogue, all sorts of issues: "Is there free will?" Can one really believe that there is none? Can one imagine asserting in the face of God that there is?—or, "How can one be happy in misfortune? ... and in good fortune?" —or, "Should an old man marry?" Humanists rebelled against systematic philosophy, against abstract propositions organized in syllogisms and separated from any historical context. They accused this kind of thinking, which continued to flourish at the universities, of being jargonized and essentially impersonal, emotionally persuasive to nobody, not even to its authors.

Basing their work on the manner of discourse they found in Plutarch, Lucian, Cicero, and others, they combined literary imagination with a keen interest in interpersonal and social issues. They instituted a kind of writing later carried on by those the French would call *moralistes* and *philosophes*. They observed the vices of their time and sought to correct them. They tried to describe the nature of humankind. They combined subjective sympathy with observation and a dose of advice. The fifteenth-century humanists focused for the most part on the struggle of individual human character (*virtù*) against external obstacles (*fortuna*).[4] Western social criticism owes them a great deal.

Humanism was not systematic; it was antisystematic. Yet the humanists were concerned with a search for general truths. Writings such as those presented in this book clearly intend, for the most part without reference to a Christian framework, to state or suggest universally valid insights. All the diversity of the humanists' eclectic reading was thought to reflect the same light, a moral light not of this world alone. That faith—explicit in metaphysical thinkers of the time like Cusanus, Ficino, and Pico della Mirandola—is implicit, it seems to me, in Bruni and Poggio, Alberti and Rinuccini.[5]

As a quest for ideas, humanism moved beyond the education found at the universities. It grew on the fringes of the universities and appeared early at the Curia. There was even a great humanist who became pope (Pius II). Humanism flourished also at secular schools, at princely courts, and in the administrative offices of republics. Private groups studied under learned individuals and included poets, historians, and some philosophers. Almost all nonscholastic and nonprofessional education was, in fact, humanistic. For over a hundred years before the Reformation, this movement nibbled away from within at the intellectual foundations of clerical power over thought. Humanism was a counterideology that developed within the European ruling class.

FLORENCE IN THE FIFTEENTH CENTURY

Florence (*Firenze*) is in central Italy, 125 miles north of Rome. The Arno flows through the city and meanders westward to the coast. Twelve miles from its mouth, about forty miles from Florence, is Pisa. In the fifteenth century, Florence struggled to conquer and control this long important maritime city, as well as nearby Leghorn (*Livorno*), the other Tuscan port. Florence managed to administer a sweep of control in all directions: Its territory reached north toward Bologna and sometimes included the town of Lucca to the northeast; in the east, Florentine territory rolled across the central hills of the peninsula to a strip of papal territory along the Adriatic shore; Florentine power to the south included the towns of Arezzo and Volterra, which guarded the northern edge of Siena's lands. Within the Florentine state were at least seven towns that had been independent states themselves.

The agriculture of the region was productive and for the most part was exploited by landlords who regarded land as an investment. The government of Florence made sure that local crops were sold in the city, yielded a tax, and were offered at a reasonable price. Florence attracted population, as well as money and goods, from the entire area to work in her important craft industries. Thus, the economic interests of all parts of the territory were subordinated to those of the city.

Having accumulated profits by diversified trade, as well as by lending money to the papacy and collecting taxes for the church, Florentine merchants stood in the fifteenth century among the most prominent wealthy men of Italy. The range of their activity extended from Syria to England, from Sicily to the Netherlands. They imported the raw materials of a cloth-finishing and dye industry and employed large numbers of people in producing luxury goods for sale and export. At home the great merchants competed with each other to be the rulers of the city.[6]

The government of Florence was based on republican forms. Members of the chief legislative and policy-making body, called the Signoria, and many other officials as well, were chosen by lot. Members of craft and professional guilds (men only) were eligible if over thirty years old and free of financial debts. The selection of officials required lists of these eligible citizens, and it was by manipulating these lists in favor of a large body of followers that the Medici, a banking family, actually came to rule the city.[7] In 1434, after a bitter struggle with the opposing faction of the merchant patriciate, Cosimo de' Medici gained power. He used—with a judicious display of moderation—the weapons of exile, confiscation, and discriminatory taxation. He made policies and distributed appointments in the official government as well as in his "party."

Cosimo's son, Piero, who succeeded him in 1464, faced organized opposition to his assumption of power, and for a while the elections were not rigged. Numerous key positions fell by lot to Medici supporters, however, and so Piero, too, was able to take control and to punish his adversaries. When he died in 1469, his son Lorenzo became, at not quite twenty-one, the unofficial chief of Florence. His younger brother, Giuliano, was his associate and assistant. Although in 1478, the Pazzi family with the help of Pope Sixtus IV conspired to kill both Medici brothers, the assault killed only Giuliano, and the revolt failed. At home there ensued a wave of repression; abroad Florence had to fight a war with Lorenzo's enemies. Lorenzo was able to end this war by personal diplomacy, and thereby to win greater prestige than ever both at home and throughout the peninsula. He was able later to gain for his son Giovanni the position of cardinal—which led to that young man's becoming, in 1513, Pope Leo X.[8]

HUMANISM AND THE FLORENTINE REPUBLIC TRADITION

Humanism flourished at courts, and humanists were often writers of propaganda or flattery. Even when they were not actually serving princes, they spoke only to a small group of wealthy and powerful people. Their esoteric interests and profound concern with language could be shared only with the leisured and literate. Nonetheless, being innovators and intellectual pluralists, they tended to complain of tyranny and to like tolerance. Venice and Florence, the great Italian republics of the time, made good centers for some kinds of public controversy. Florence, the more turbulent and unstable of the two, was perhaps for that very reason the main home of Italian humanism—especially of humanist political thought.[10]

Eugenio Garin, a historian of philosophy, has demonstrated the presence of a philosophical premise and dogma in Florentine humanist thought—faith in free will.[11] Both he and Hans Baron have shown that Florentine humanists shared an ethic that called for active participation in the world—and acceptance of property, family, and civic responsibility. Hans Baron has traced the early history of this ethic, which marked a turning away from the clerical tradition, and he has illuminated the role of Leonardo Bruni in helping to formulate it.[12]

At the turn of the fifteenth century, as Baron has pointed out, the Republic of Florence defended her power and her very existence against the imperial ambitions of the duke of Milan. The war reached a military crisis in 1402 that was nearly fatal, but ultimately favorable, to Florence. Ideological controversy concerned the opposition between dictators and republics. Salutati's fourteenth-century arguments against tyrannicide[13] were countered by certain of his friends who defended freedom and even Brutus, the assassin of Caesar. Under the pressure of events and the influence of certain classical authors, Leonardo Bruni, probably the most erudite of those young humanists, began to define and defend the Florentine constitution. In the first four decades of the century he proved himself the outstanding stylist and thinker of "civic humanism."

The parts of his *History of Florence* translated here show how he was able to find inspiration in the history of Rome. Roman history was rich for him in confrontations between the freedom of peoples and the imperialism of the Romans. There was also the

9

question of internal freedom—to Bruni it was a sad decline when the republic became the empire. Bruni also interpreted the Florentine constitutional upheaval of the late thirteenth century. He wrote a classically eloquent speech for Giano della Bella, the leader who organized middle-class Florentines against the local nobles who were oppressing them; Giano demanded that the citizens resist, enforce existing laws, and make some new ones. This was, in the truest sense of the words, a bourgeois revolution. In Book Twelve, the last one he wrote, Bruni described the battle of 1402 with the "Goliath" of Milan. He showed that the ideology of republican Florence was in that crisis used as a weapon in the patriotic struggle.

While Leonardo Bruni was writing his *History of Florence*, he also held the highest bureaucratic office in Florence, that of chancellor, in a state ruled by Cosimo de' Medici. Bruni's *History* expressed what he claimed were the true and traditional Florentine ideals, including that of justice based on full and equal rights to life and safety of property for every citizen. Though in practice Cosimo did not always respect the rights of citizens, he certainly was not offended by the ideals.

Bruni's friend, Poggio Bracciolini, writes about the leading people in Cosimo's Florence. An upstart among men of great inherited wealth, he laughingly but freely discusses the possibility that even money and hereditary status together might not be enough to confer true nobility. They might not even be necessary. Though he thus challenges the thinking of most respectable Florentines, he also shows appreciation of the way aristocratic Florentines offer to men of talent both recognition and freedom of speech. He aims sharp sarcasm at established ruling classes elsewhere; indeed, he excoriates the various ruling classes of Italy and the rest of Europe. Then he grants the ruling class of Florence some credit for good sense and diligence, but casts a little doubt on the dignity of commerce. His wit, like Bruni's wisdom, somehow stands just clear of direct conflict with authority.

Leon Battista Alberti was descended from an eminent Florentine family, long allied with the Medici, and was himself their friend. He wrote to his Florentine correspondents the account of a revolt

10

in Rome. The overt message of this report ("The Conspiracy of Stefano Porcari") is that a disgusting revolt led by an outrageously conceited man has been suppressed. He also reveals Porcari's frustrated Roman patriotism. Even though some Roman aristocrats were among the cardinals, even though young Romans could find positions serving the papacy, it was not mainly Roman in its concerns or in the background of most of its officials. Alberti implies that it is far, far better to be Florence, an autonomous city with a ruler like Cosimo, than to be subject like Rome to the foreign, if benign, government of the papacy.

Some decades later, Alamanno Rinuccini, a member of an old patrician family and an official under Lorenzo, complains that the values of the Florentine aristocracy—the values essential to the republican tradition—are being undermined by Lorenzo's secretly brutal one-man rule. There is no government by citizens, and Lorenzo's foreign policy is reckless. Rinuccini writes from the self-imposed exile of his country home; he has quarreled with Lorenzo and openly regrets the failure of the Pazzi conspiracy. He must not have circulated this manuscript indiscreetly, since he was able to rejoin Lorenzo's government a few years later.

Angelo Poliziano, eminent poet, scholar, and tutor of Lorenzo's children, lived in the Medici palace. He gives an account of the Pazzi conspiracy that amounts to a defense of his patrons. Though he bases his admiration of Lorenzo largely on Lorenzo's popularity, Poliziano's is not the voice of a republican. His is the voice of an observant courtier.

Savonarola was abbot of St. Mark's in Florence, a position he received from Lorenzo de' Medici. Nevertheless, he openly criticized the luxurious style of life that the Medici favored. He denounced not only elaborate feasts and rich clothing, but secular painting and poetry that celebrated the delights of this world. He was very outspoken against sexual freedom, which he saw as pure sin. In the *Treatise on Government* translated here he looks back with indignation to the tyranny of Lorenzo and describes it as associated with greed and lust. He was a monk and not a humanist.

Savonarola was one of the chief spirits in the overthrow of the Medici regime in 1494, but he also struggled to obtain amnesty for its former supporters. He wished immediately to heal divisions and to create a new unified republic that would be capable of leading a program of religious reform in the world. He favored a constitution broadening the base of government and hoped for a revival of the republican faith. His analysis of the tyranny of Lorenzo foreshadows in some detail Machiavelli's prescription in *The Prince* of ruthlessness and hypocrisy. To Savonarola these traits do not appear—as they will to Machiavelli—primarily as expedient for the ruler. Ruthlessness and hypocrisy appear to Savonarola as the result of unbridled greed and pathological fear, immediately harmful to the people and ultimately harmful to the state. Savonarola seems to think that the trickery of the dictator will, as he exposes it, horrify his readers, that such knowledge as he provides will lead them as citizens to oppose future dictatorships, and that he can persuade them to cling to their fraternal unity and appreciate the sanctity of law. He was more independent of patronage than any of our other writers and exercised the greatest immediate influence.

Savonarola was executed by his political enemies, however, less than a year after he wrote the *Treatise*. The government, which continued for fourteen years in approximately the form he had favored, abandoned his moral crusade. In 1512 Cardinal Giovanni de' Medici was able to restore his family to power, overcoming with the aid of Spanish troops the resistance of the Republic.

IDEAS OF LIBERTY

Autonomy of the City

One of the oldest and at the same time most current meanings of "liberty" in the fifteenth century was city-state autonomy.[14] For Leonardo Bruni, as later for Machiavelli, the price of this kind of liberty was military vigilance. Bruni was very proud of the Florentine ability to spend money on good soldiers. He makes it clear that to be truly free a state must know how to subjugate her neighbors in order to become what we might call a "viable unit," big enough to survive. At times a league of similar states must join together to fight for the liberty of each and all, as the Etruscan states should (in his view) have done against the Romans, as the two parts of the later Roman empire should have done against the barbarians, and as Venice and Florence, two republics, could possibly have done to stop the expansion of Milan. Liberty—in the sense of autonomy—rests on self-control, voluntary sacrifice, and power over certain others. The price of liberty—it turns out—is repression.

Imperialism may be the way to stay free, but it involves the very greed which Bruni considers fatal to liberty at home. There is ambition, and—Livy's nightmare—the temptation of luxury. If liberty is seen as a good, moreover, won't conquered neighbors ardently desire it too? Florence, having brutally conquered many smaller strategic places, tried to hold Bologna as an ally against Milan by supporting a dictator there; and Bruni traces the struggles, realignments, and shifts of fortune that result. The Florentine pursuit of liberty, as he presents it, provokes opposition, does not create a stable political situation, and does not promise survival. He does not present the fight against Milan as in fact a conflict of pure republicanism against tyranny.

Alberti, in his book on the family, asserts that Florence loves not only liberty but also rational peace; she conquers only in self-defense. He imagines his older relative, Piero degli Alberti, talking to the duke of Milan and saying, "Our people, being less reckless and foolish than other free states, were naturally more interested in peace than in war. . . . one can only call it justice if men who love liberty defend it."[15] Leonardo Bruni was perhaps, like most Florentine writers, too enthusiastic for Florentine imperial eminence to speak in this way.

Citizen Participation

Citizen participation is one of Bruni's criteria for internal liberty. Rinuccini and Savonarola carry on his thought and add their own elaborations. The three stand as pillars of the Florentine republican tradition. As Donald Weinstein says of that tradition, "Liberty was freedom from arbitrary rule protected by a broad, but not an equal,

13

degree of participation in the electoral and legislative processes."[16] What Weinstein seems to mean by "broad, but not equal" is a chance of participation for all the respectable, prosperous male citizens, with older members preferred over younger members of families. There is no participation for apprentices or laborers who were not even apprentices, and none for women. "Broad" in this tradition means inclusive of all heads of households who were also employers.

For Bruni, Rinuccini, and Savonarola, the enemy of liberty is faction—the self-interest of a group that manages to makes the rest of the elite powerless. These writers would clearly like to limit the freedom of such factions. Savonarola even plans, perhaps unrealistically, to prevent all caucusing in the Signoria. Both Bruni and Savonarola see the rule of a united and stable group as necessary for the rule of law; dissident families, nobles, or other groups within the ruling class must be curbed.[17]

Yet Rinuccini and Bruni stress the importance of freedom of speech. Without that, self-governing councils are broken reeds. As they point out, freedom of speech requires not only the absence of a tyrant threatening violence, but also individual courage to confront majority opinion, which likewise could take violent reprisals. As Petrarch said long before when comparing mid-fourteenth-century Florence and Milan, the tyranny of many can be as oppressive as the tyranny of one.

The silence of Savonarola on the question of free speech, considering his stress on citizen-participation, is interesting; he believed, I think, that the rule of the majority in Florence might be led by the spirit of Christ himself. It seems that his description of a good governing council implies that such a body need not listen to dissenters. These are readily to be suspected of trying to overthrow the government. In this respect he does not adhere to the Florentine civic tradition represented by Bruni and Rinuccini. His model may be partly the old church councils, which involved wide participation but which excommunicated heretics. What seems new in Savonarola, in secular application at least, is the idea that such a body as the Signoria will be more moral than its individual members. Not only will the interest of the whole override the self-interest of factions, but in the Signoria a moral vision will be shared. The vision—the collective spirit—underlies the new constitution; it is also expected to guide Florentines in making laws and policy. Savonarola implicitly thinks of liberty as Christian liberty, the state of high inspiration that enables men to act for the good.

Freedom from Politics

In both Rinuccini and Poggio, "liberty" sometimes means privacy. Speaking through the mouth of Niccolò Niccoli, Poggio echoes the Platonic opposition between public opinion, which reigns in the social and political world, and truth, which may be found by the diligent individual thinker. Such an individual thinker may at times choose to retire from the arena where public opinion dominates—the arena where wealth and status are the prizes. To the sage, truth gives values that he can maintain alone and that will help him inwardly when outer events are adverse. Truth, and the privacy needed to seek it, are his bulwarks against flux and instability. Through Niccolò this theme is cheerfully propounded, for Poggio's hypothetical sage could have chosen politics but has chosen a higher wisdom—and he is probably a writer. In Rinuccini's *On Liberty*, however, retirement and writing appear as a last resort, the way of life open to a man disappointed by politics. Politics, says Rinuccini, is currently corrupted by violence. Attempting to serve has brought him trouble and frustration. He has chosen the refuge of a virtuous, self-disciplined, but almost entirely isolated life on his little farm. His claims to contentment ring a little hollow. What he has gained is the freedom to be just, and that is the form of liberty with which he must be content.

Organic Community

Alberti's dialogue *Happiness* is another exploration of the meaning of personal liberty. Alberti asks the basic question, "What is lost by becoming a slave?" The dialogue he invents, a dialogue of newly captured slaves, does not concern the loss of political opportunities or the diminished chance, if it is diminished, of achieving peace of mind. What is lost fundamentally is membership in an organic patriarchal community where each age-group of men and of women has its dignity based upon its sphere of action. That community is what is lost, those spheres of action are what is lost, when people are captured and sold on the market for their labor. Not long after he wrote this brief but profound dialogue, Alberti wrote his long book *On the Family*. If the family is well led and if its young men respect and learn from their elders, the family provides (he believes) the basis of effectiveness for all its members. It is the source of the individual's ability to act and to find satisfaction.[18]

Under the Medici, however, faith in that family was probably more easily maintained than faith in republican forms, private virtue, or one's own kin. Among our writers, Angelo Poliziano and Lorenzo de' Medici clearly believe in politics just as it is practiced. Poliziano writes that, even at the time of the Pazzi conspiracy, the city was filled with love for Lorenzo. Love for the leader was its unifying principle. Yet he also makes it frighteningly clear how much hate lay smoldering in the city. Thanks to Lorenzo's good leadership, he suggests, this hatred did not flare up to subvert Lorenzo's rule, but most of it fell raging upon the minority that had dared to revolt.

Far less concerned than Poliziano with the play of popular passions, Lorenzo presents his own account of his family's rule in the brief "Ricordi." In a letter to his son, he expresses some of his ideas of political wisdom. Lorenzo stresses, not popularity with the masses, but judicious behavior towards those immediately around you, discretion in the exercise of power, and, as befits a banker, prudence in the management of wealth. Lorenzo combined his power with rhetorical skill, caution, and practical cunning rather than with wide ideological vistas. Except for a certain wistfulness about the fact that he himself had not been able to live free from politics, he simply ignores the issue of liberty within the state. He does not fail, however, to idealize the role of his family in preserving the liberty (in the sense of autonomy) of Florence. For the Medici, he says, used their wealth and wits to help the city. They did not grow richer by ruling; they served the common welfare and the common glory. They built up the city's prosperity, on which its freedom depended.

RADIX MALORUM

These authors all favor and represent a wealthy capitalist ruling group. And all, as if by some law of dialectics, agree on one point: private greed for property is the cause of public misery. Remote by three centuries from the technologically induced delusion that each man's pursuit of his own self-interest somehow serves the general good, our humanists agree with the tradition that runs from Thucydides to Machiavelli: The price of liberty is self-restraint. Self-sacrifice is requisite to individual happiness and to community strength. Bruni is fierce in denouncing luxury as the road that leads a state, like early Florence in his narrative, into disastrous enterprises. Alberti shows horror at slavery, not because of the cruelty of the individuals who shackle and guard the victims, but because of the cruelty of *fortuna*—the vicissitudes inevitable where there is war. He does not blame commerce, but it is obviously implicated. He expresses the feeling that slaves remain mentally the people they were before slavery, and that it is a horrendous evil for them to become property; he expresses it simply by letting the slaves speak for themselves. Poggio, though he shows delight in wealth, throws darts at its arrogance. He mocks at ruling classes who sit in idleness or practice highway robbery. He echoes the Roman idea that commerce is not a very dignified kind of pursuit either, and is no education for ruling others. For Poliziano, the source of every outrage is desperate poverty: Poverty rather than arrogant wealth is the source of evil—yes, but such poverty is brought on, in his analysis, by living among the rich, borrowing from them to spend and gamble until one faces bankruptcy. Lorenzo regrets the fact that his wealth exposed him to so much danger that he felt forced to rule the state, and thus, of course, was not universally loved. Rinuccini celebrates the moderate poverty of his rural life. And Savonarola in his utopian design severely limits private consumption.

17

Against all this stands Poggio's ironical remark, which he attributes appropriately enough, to a Medici: "Though poverty is much praised, we know that both philosophers and other admirable men have preferred to lack that distinction rather than to lack material resources."[19]

MODERN RESONANCES

The Renaissance was a time when every craft was closely organized and when manufacturing depended entirely on craft, when people's work lives had not yet been separated from their private lives, and when, above all, the family—both as clan and as household—was closeknit and powerful.[20] The family as clan was a patriarchal network of kin united under a name associated with wealth and power, and, though there were feuds within and between families, there were binding traditions and hierarchies as well. The family as household was a group usually based on a couple and their children and a number of servants, all bound together in a system of mutual dependence. Everyone performed tasks and had his or her place in a chain of command. Our authors constantly reflect this sense of community by their assumption of passionate loyalty and passionate treason, and by their hopes and fears concerning the state. What a close community might mean continues, of course, to intrigue us. Was the organic community, as Alberti thought, the source of freedom? If so, whose freedom?

Our authors suggest that liberty was communal and private *or* private. When communal, it was attained through direct citizen participation in essential policy-making. When private, it was available to the man of good family in his home. Can it exist within such structures as house us today—our real estate developments, our bureaucracies, our electronic systems of communication? Can these provide for individual independence, citizen participation, state autonomy? Perhaps to read these fifteenth-century humanists is to rediscover some of our own political myths in the matrix of lost institutions and to discard them at last as meaningless for us in their traditional form. If we want freedom, we probably cannot expect it from revolts of the patriciate against tyrannical factions, from withdrawal into privileged seclusion, or from inspired citizen participation in large councils. Perhaps, like the Florentines, we need authors who can point out to us new ways to think of freedom and to assure it.

NOTES

1. Vespasiano da Bisticci, *Lives of Illustrious Men*, translated by W. G. and E. Waters, ed. M. Gilmore, under the title *Renaissance Princes, Popes and Prelates*, New York, 1963.

2. Georg Voigt, *Die Wiederbelebung des Klassischen Altertums*, reprinted Berlin, 1960 from the edition of 1893.

3. See for example Paul Oscar Kristeller, *Renaissance Thought*, New York, 1961, esp. "Humanism and Scholasticism in the Italian Renaissance," 92–119. For further discussion, see Jerold E. Seigel, *Rhetoric and Philosophy in Renaissance Humanism*, Princeton, 1968.

4. Charles Trinkaus, *Adversity's Noblemen*, New York, 1940, presents the moral, and his more recent, *In Our Image and Likeness*, the religious thought of the humanists.

5. Concerning humanist belief in the existence of a single universal truth, see Paul Oscar Kristeller's introduction to Pico della Mirandola's "Oration on the Dignity of Man," (*The Renaissance Philosophy of Man*, eds. E. Cassirer, P. O. Kristeller, and J. H. Randall, Jr., Chicago, 1948). The most thorough study of Renaissance humanist thought on the unity of knowledge and the divine source of knowledge is Frances A. Yates, *Giordano Bruno and the Hermetic Tradition*, New York, 1964.

6. Armando Sapori, *Le Marchand Italien au Moyen Age, Paris*, 1952, 29–61, describes the growth of late medieval commerce and the position attained by Italian merchants. Cf. Harry A. Miskimin, *The Economy of Early Renaissance Europe 1300–1460*, New Jersey, 1969, "Towns and Industry," 73–115. On the capitalist in the country, see David Herlihy, "Population, Plague and Social Change," in A. Molho, ed., *Social and Economic Foundations of the Italian Renaissance*, New York, 1969.

7. Gene Brucker, *Florentine Politics and Society*, 1343–1378, Princeton, 1962, pp. 57–72, clearly describes the system of government.

8. For general narrative, see Ferdinand Schevill, *The History of Florence*, New York, 1936; for precise analysis of political events, Nicolai Rubenstein, *The Government of Florence under the Medici*, 1434–1494, Oxford, 1966. See also Cecilia M. Ady, *Lorenzo dei Medici*, Cambridge, England, 1955, New York, 1962.

9. See Lauro Martines, *The Social World of the Florentine Humanists*, Princeton, 1963, and Lawrence Stone's introduction to William Harrison Woodward, *Studies in Education during the Age of the Renaissance 1400–1600*, New York, 1967.

10. On "intellectual pluralism" in the humanists and on their role in a repub-

lic, see William J. Bouwsma, *Venice and the Defense of Republican Liberty*, Cambridge University Press, 1968, "Renaissance Republicanism . . ." 1–51.

11. A good introduction to Garin's thinking is the chapter, "Logic, Rhetoric, and Poetics," in his *Italian Humanism*, New York, 1965.

12. Some major contributions of Hans Baron are *The Crisis of the Early Renaissance*, Princeton, 1955, and *From Petrarch to Leonardo Bruni*, University of Chicago Press, 1968.

13. The work *On Tyranny* by Coluccio Salutati is translated and discussed in Ephraim Emerton's *Humanism and Tyranny: Studies in the Italian Trecento*, Cambridge, Mass., 1925. The present anthology is intended as a sequel.

14. Nicolai Rubinstein, "Florence and the Despots. Some Aspects of Florentine Diplomacy in the Fourteenth Century," *Transactions of the Royal Historical Society*, 5th series, vol. II (1952), 21–45.

15. Leon Battista Alberti, *The Family in Renaissance Florence*, University of South Carolina Press, 1969, 254.

16. Donald Weinstein, *Savonarola and Florence*, Princeton, 1970, 307.

17. For a discussion of Bruni and factions, see Donald Wilcox, *The Development of Humanist Historiography in the Fifteenth Century*, Cambridge, Mass., 1969, 73–81.

18. Leon Battista Alberti, *The Family in Renaissance Florence*, op. cit., esp. "Prologue."

19. Poggio Bracciolini, "On Nobility," herein.

20. For a succinct statement of the domestic conditions normal in any preindustrial European city, see Peter Laslett, *The World We Have Lost*, New York, 1965, esp. 1–21.

Leonardo Bruni Aretino

Leonardo Bruni Aretino 1370–1444

In 1396, aged twenty-six, Leonardo Bruni took the advice of his friend Salutati, the great chancellor-scholar of Florence, and interrupted his legal studies to learn Greek from a Byzantine visitor, Emmanuel Chrysoloras. In the first four decades of the fifteenth century, but especially in the 1420s and 1430s, Bruni greatly enriched Florentine culture by translating Greek works into Latin. These included Aristotle's *Ethics* and *Politics* (previously rather neglected works) and some of Plato's most important Socratic dialogues, such as the *Apology* and the *Symposium*.[1] His own writings in Latin were considered innovative and wonderful, both for their style and their content.

For the intellectual control which he exercises in the *History of Florence*, giving clear thematic and chronological shape to a mass of inherited materials, Bruni may be considered the first modern historian.[2] Most of his writing is related at the same time to education and to the "active life." Bruni defends statesmanly and military careers as well worthy of an educated man, more worthy than a life of retired contemplation.[3] In his writing generally, and in the *History of Florence* specifically, Bruni strives to possess the virtues that he declares characteristic of the liberal arts themselves: "They [the *studia humanitatis*] have great authority because of their elegance, and they convey a certain kind of intelligence appropriate to free men."[4]

After an early career at the Curia which left him with excellent scholarly and diplomatic connections in Rome, Bruni became chancellor of Florence. He held that office from 1427 until his death in 1444. He weathered the storms of Florentine political life by investing politically as well as financially on both sides of the Albizzi-Medici fence. Although before Cosimo's political triumph in 1434 he was allied with eminent anti-Medici families, Bruni was able to remain a luminary among the learned men admired by the ruling Medici circle and to become a wealthy citizen and a pillar of Cosimo de' Medici's government. He eventually combined his regular administrative office with diplomatic missions and membership in the highest decision-making committees of the Florentine government.[5] His personality combined traits not unsuitable for a self-made Florentine patrician: he was discreet, knowledgeable, aloof, and avaricious.[6]

Bruni wrote the literary and political history of Florence. In the dialogue *Ad Petrum Histrum* he discussed the great poets of the fourteenth century and the educational concerns of the fifteenth-century humanists. He wrote lives of Dante and Boccaccio. Of Florentine government he made a precise constitutional analysis (in Greek), and for Florence wrought a handsome panegyric (in Latin). His letters show that philology and politics were his favorite topics, linked in his eyes by their common value to the fame and glory of the country. His greatest tribute to his adopted city (for he came from Arezzo) and to his homeland, Tuscany, was the *History of Florence*. He worked on it for thirty years from at least 1415 until his death; he never considered it finished.[7]

In the *History of Florence* Bruni praises the valor and cultural eminence of Tuscans, the wisdom and tenacity of Florentine statesmen, and Florentine "liberty" or independence. Through narrative and speeches he makes clear his conviction that Florence ought to rule, as rule she does, over all Tuscany, that this is a political necessity for her and contributes to the glory of the Tuscan people. Since one of the chief lessons of the *History* concerns this imperial role of Florence within Italy, a map showing the growth of her power is appended.[8] Bruni's patriotism is a new secular flower growing out of a veneration for a Florence formerly clad in religious vocabulary.[9] The meaning he gives to "liberty" was consonant with and helped to confirm the concept as used by his fellow Florentines; it consists in state autonomy and the capacity to extend one's power over lesser states.[10]

There may be some debate over the extent and meaning of Bruni's republicanism.[11] The speech of Giano della Bella in Book IV of the *History of Florence*, as here translated, shows some of Bruni's thinking. At a time of crisis wide participation in government is needed to control an over-powerful group of citizens who think themselves not subject to law. The liberty of citizens depends on general respect for persons and property and on the absence of a state of war or anarchy. It is not clear how much participation in power Bruni desired for the mass of citizens at times when the state was

23

reasonably firm. He generally favored wide accommodation of conflicting factions in the state, debate rather than violence,[12] and every political means to prevent the festering discontent of an excluded group capable of returning in arms.[13] The idea of the *popolo* as an instrument of justice is there, but also that of practical compromises to prevent civil war. Administrative offices should attract and accept talent and should recruit men who work hard—he thought this condition never prevailed at the courts of tyrants. These ideas of delegated and distributed power Bruni combines with certain assumptions, obvious for instance in Book XII: that hierarchy is normally maintained, that most of the time good family is the credential for leadership, and that fairly few people manage major foreign-policy decisions. Bruni's idea of equality before the law only limits the grossest exercise of unequal power in society. Bruni's commitment to military and commercial expansion for survival and strength shapes his ideas of good government.

NOTES

1. A list of his translations may be found in R. R. Bolgar, *The Classical Heritage.* London and New York, 1954, New York, 1964, 434–35.

2. Donald J. Wilcox, in *The Development of Florentine Humanist Historiography in the Fifteenth Century*, Cambridge, Mass., 1969, undertakes a full analysis of the organization and thematic coherence of Bruni's *History*.

3. Hans Baron, in *Leonardo Bruni Aretino: Humanistische-Philosophische Schriften*, Leipzig, 1928, was concerned to show the "civil" character of Bruni's humanism. He analyzed in depth Bruni's political writing and the situation to which it was a response in a number of later books and articles, perhaps most notably in:
"The Social Background of Political Liberty in the Early Italian Renaissance" *Comparative Studies in Society and History*, 2 1959–60), 440–51; *Humanistic and Political Literature in Florence and Venice at the Beginning of the Quattrocento, Studies in Criticism and Chronology*, Cambridge, 1955; *The Crisis of the Early Italian Renaissance, Civic Humanism and Republican Liberty in an Age of Classicism and Tyranny*, Princeton, 1955, 2 vols.; "Leonardo Bruni: 'Professional Rhetorician' or 'Civic Humanist'?" *Past and Present*, 36 (1967), 21–37; *From Petrarch to Leonardo Bruni, Studies in Humanistic and Political Literature*, Chicago, 1968.

4. "inest auctoritas magna propter elegantiam, et ingenuitas quaedam liberis hominibus digna," quoted by Eugenio Garin in *L'Umanesimo italiano*, Bari, 1952, 56–57.

5. The professional life of Bruni is fully documented in Lauro Martinez, *The Social World of the Florentine Humanists, 1390–1460*, Princeton, 1963, 117–23; 165–76, and a good bibliography is appended.

6. Georg Voigt draws a picture of Bruni's life and personality from contem-

porary accounts in *Die Wierderbelebung des Classischen Alterthums*, Berlin, 1880 and 1893, 2 vols, reprinted 1960; ɪ, 306–12; ɪɪ, 163–73.

7. E. Santini, *Leonardo Bruni Aretino e i suoi "Historiarum Florentini populi libri XII,"* Pisa, 1910.

8. See Map 3.

9. Marvin B. Becker, "Towards a Renaissance Historiography in Florence," in Anthony Molho and John A. Tedeschi, *Renaissance Studies in Honor of Hans Baron*, Florence, 1971, 141–72.

10. Nicolai Rubinstein has written much that is enlightening on this subject, using the archives of Florentine governmental deliberations; see particularly "The Beginnings of Political Thought in Florence," *Journal of the Warburg and Courtauld Institutes*, v (1942), 198–227, and "Florence and the Despots: Some Aspects of Florentine Diplomacy in the Fourteenth Century," *Transactions of the Royal Historical Society*, ser. v, 2, (1952), 21–45. He specifically analyzes Bruni's concept of Florentine liberty as shown in writings from before and after Cosimo's taking power in Florence, in "Florentine Constitutionalism and Medici Ascendancy in the Fifteenth Century" in N. Rubinstein, ed., *Florentine Studies*, London, 1968.

11. Cf. Ronald Witt, "The Rebirth of the Concept of Republican Liberty in Italy," *Renaissance Studies in Honor of Hans Baron*, op. cit., 173–200.

12. Cf. Nancy Struever, *The Language of History in the Renaissance*, Princeton, N.J., 1970, 111–25. "The practise of rhetoric is the practise of liberty." (125)

13. Wilcox, op. cit., 73–80 analyzes more carefully how and why Bruni proposed to accommodate factions and avoid creating dangerous exiles.

THE HISTORY OF FLORENCE

by Leonardo Bruni

PREFACE

It took me a long time and much inner searching before I decided to attempt a literary presentation of the deeds of the Florentine people. I wished to recount their struggles in civil and foreign wars and to tell of their great exploits in war and in peace. What appealed to me was the magnificent performance of this people, first in dealing with domestic foes, then in combatting their immediate neighbors, and finally in our own time as a great power fighting the tremendously powerful duke of Milan and the highly aggressive King Ladislas. They shook all Italy from the Alps to Apulia with the sound of Florentine arms, and even beyond Italy they caused kings and vast armies to cross the Alps from France and Germany. Add to this the conquest of Pisa. Considering the clash of character, the struggle for power, and the ultimate outcome, I think it fair to draw the parallel with Rome's defeat of Carthage. In the ultimate pacification and siege of Pisa, carried on as stubbornly by one side as by the other, deeds were done that deserve to be remembered, deeds no less impressive than those we read about and admire so much in antiquity. These actions seemed to me worthy of record and remembrance, and I thought that acquaintance with this story would serve both public and private ends. For if we think men of advanced age are wiser because they have seen more of life, how much wisdom can history give us if we read it correctly; for there the deeds and thoughts of many ages are visible and we can readily see what to imitate and what to avoid, and be inspired by the glory of great men to attempt like excellence. What held me back, however, was the labor involved in such an enterprise, and the gaps in our knowledge of certain times, and even the harsh sounding names that would hardly allow an elegant presentation, and many other problems. Having weighed all these ideas carefully and long, I came to feel mainly that any plan for writing was better than being idly silent.

In starting to write, therefore, I have been aware of my own limitations and of the weight of my task. But I hope that God will favor my enterprise and will help me to fulfill my good intentions. For if my abilities are not equal to the undertaking, He will support hard work and effort. Would that the men of earlier times, whatever their wisdom and erudition, had recorded the events of their day, instead of silently letting things go by. For, unless I am mistaken, the special duty of scholars has always been to celebrate the deeds of their own time. They should have labored to rescue those deeds from oblivion and from the power of fate; they should have sought to grace those actions with immortality. Yet I suppose that each man had his reasons for remaining silent. Some shrank back from all this heavy labor; some lacked the necessary ability; some neglected history because they preferred other forms of writing. It is not hard, with some effort, to write a little book or a letter. History, however, involves at the same time a long continuous narrative, causal explanation of each particular event, and appropriately placed judgments on certain issues. The great burden of the task may overwhelm the pen—it is a dangerous thing to promise something hard to carry out. Thus, while everyone pursued his personal comfort or considered his reputation, the public good was neglected and the memory of remarkable men and heroic actions was almost wholly lost.

I have decided, therefore, to write the known history of this city, not only for my own time but for earlier ages as far as they can be studied. The story will touch on the history of all Italy, for nothing important has been done in Italy for a long time without the participation of at least some Florentines. In explaining the various embassies sent out by this city, moreover, I shall have to discuss other nations. Before I come to the times that mainly concern me, however, I shall narrate what I think is the correct tradition concerning the city's founding and its origins. The facts will contradict some commonly held beliefs, and will shed light on what is to follow.

Book One

The founders of Florence were Romans sent by Lucius Sulla to Fiesole. To veterans who had given outstanding service, particularly in the civil war against Pompey, he granted part of the land of Fiesole as well as the town itself. Such a relocation of citizens and assignment of lands was called a *colony* by the Romans, because it meant the estates cultivated [*colere*] and inhabited by the new men were given to them as homes. Why new people were sent to this area, however, must be explained.

80 B.C.

Not many years before Sulla's dictatorship, there was a general rebellion among the peoples of Italy against the domination of the Romans. They had been allied with the Romans on many campaigns, had fought and labored by their side and shared the perils which attended their expansion, and yet, as they resentfully discovered, they had not shared in the rewards. Hence their indignation. After much conferring among themselves, they finally sent common representatives of the whole group to Rome to discuss the problem, demanding Roman citizenship and a share in the honors and offices of the empire for all Italians. The question came up during the tribunate of Marcus Drusus, and for some time the petitioners were left in suspense. Their demands were ultimately rejected, however, and then the peoples involved openly defected and declared war on their ungrateful allies. Because the war was made by former allies [*socii*] of Rome, it is known as the *Social* War. The Romans emerged victorious and severely punished the main rebellious provinces. They dealt most harshly with Picenum [the Marches] and Tuscany. The flourishing city of Asculum in Picenum was razed like an enemy town, and in Tuscany, Chiusi was likewise leveled. The people of Arezzo and Fiesole also suffered heavy blows above and beyond the war

91 B.C.

damage itself; many people's property was confiscated and many were forced to flee, so that these towns were left half-empty.

Such was the occasion, almost in fact the invitation, for Sulla's action as a dictator in granting his veterans these lands. When the veterans came to Fiesole, however, and divided the fields among themselves, many of them decided that amidst the security of the Roman empire, it was unnecessary to inhabit an inaccessible hilltop. So they came down into the valley and began to live along the banks of the Arno and Mugno. The new city located between these two rivers was at first called Fluentia. The name lasted for some time, it seems, until the city had grown and developed. Then, perhaps just through the ordinary process by which words are corrupted, or perhaps because of the flowering of the city, Fluentia became Florence.

Both Cicero and Sallust, who are great Latin writers, report the story of these colonizers. Cicero tells us, moreover, that the veterans, though excellent Roman citizens and strong men, showed no idea of moderation in spending when they found themselves suddenly and unexpectedly enriched by Sulla through civil war. They built grandly and created great households, great gatherings of people, and luxurious amenities, and soon they were buried in debt. To free them from this burden, Sulla himself would have had to return from the dead. What the father of Latin eloquence says of their buildings seems important to me, for it leads to the conclusion that the foundations of this city, from its very infancy, were magnificent. And even amidst the present splendor of Florence there still exist examples of ancient building that command our admiration. There is the aqueduct that brought water to the city from sources seven leagues away, and the great theaters placed outside the walls for popular sports and spectacles. These theaters are now located within the city limits and built over with residences. Even the temple we call the Baptistery was begun by classical builders and was consecrated by their pagan priests to Mars.

Out of nostalgia or loyalty to their old home, the colonizers seem to have consciously imitated Rome in their planning of the city and construction of buildings. They built themselves a capitol and a forum, one next to the other as in Rome, and they had baths for public convenience and an arena for watching athletic games. The temple of Mars was built in the same spirit of emulation, for this god, of course, was considered

31

the special patron of the Roman people. They were so eager to affirm their relation to Rome, in fact, that they copied lesser structures as well without thought to the expense. They brought water in by aqueduct, which was reasonable in Rome where all the local water was chalky, but superfluous in Florence, where perfectly pure water springs up in abundance. It seems likely, moreover, that their private houses matched their public buildings in magnificence, though there are no remains to make this clear. The ruins of the public buildings prove how ample those were.

Surrounded by such luxuries, the colonists lived, as Cicero tells us, without thought of the future and without saving any part of their wealth, until their money was gone. Meanwhile Sulla, their one hope, not only fell from power but passed out of this world. So, partly because of their poverty and partly because of their earlier experience of getting rich, they looked forward eagerly to some new disturbance. Soldiers and men used to civil war, they had no idea how to live in peacetime. Their thoughts ran ever to new dictatorships and new booty. And debt was an added incentive to draw the sword, for it is a spur that drives even 67 B.C. timid persons to dare make trouble. And at this very time, by chance, Cataline in Rome was fomenting a revolt. There was a vast conspiracy against the republic, involving many members of the upper classes—knights and even senators from the patrician families. Suspicion fell also on Gaius Caesar, the one who later became dictator, although at this time he had been deprived, for debts and suspicion of revolutionary leanings, of his very citizenship. Cataline had already made various efforts in Rome without much success. He now left some conspirators to carry on in the city and decided to go forth with the rest and start a war from the outside. His first choice was to take Praeneste by a night attack and to establish his headquarters there; but since that city was said to be well guarded, he changed his mind and opted for Fiesole. He came to this region from Rome and involved it in war.

The young city was critically imperiled by these events, but considering the happy outcome, I think it was a good beginning. This is because Lentulus and Cathegus and other leaders whom Cataline had left in Rome to organize a larger revolt were turned in by the Gaulish ambassadors they had contacted, were convicted in the senate, and died by torture. When Cataline heard this news, he gave up hope and tried to escape to Gaul, but he was surrounded by the Roman army and forced to try his fortune in battle, with the result that he and his followers were killed on a Tuscan field. The story is familiar, of course, but I wanted briefly to retell it because it happened here and affected the beginnings of this city.

The disturbance and the near proximity of war seems in fact to have done some harm to the city but also to have forced the people to learn a good lesson. From the trials of another, they learned to give up their favorite dream of new dictatorships and new booty. For the first time they realized that they must build on what they had, and that placing their hopes in revolution was both vain and dangerous; and all at once they changed, not only their ideas, but their way of life. What they believed and acted on, and the way they educated their children, changed. Now they feared debt, carefully watched and counted their possessions and cultivated thrift and frugal ways, were sober, limited their spending, and saw luxury and prodigality as the road to ruin. Having mended its ways, the city became prosperous, many people immigrated, attracted by the beauty and charm of the region, and new buildings arose. The population grew.

Only the nearness of Rome in her grandeur limited the growth of Florence. As great trees overshadow small plants that arise in their vicinity and keep them stunted, so the weight of Rome pressed on her surroundings and let no greater city arise in Italy. Other cities that had in fact been great were pressed down by the nearby power of Rome, ceased to grow, and even became smaller. How then might the city of Florence grow? She could not augment her borders by war under the rule of the empire, nor indeed wage war at all; nor could she increase the power of her administrators, since their jurisdiction was narrowly circumscribed by jealous Roman officials. As to commerce, in case it should seem that commerce could have added to the growth of the city, in those days it could not center anywhere but at Rome. That was the place where men gathered and where there were markets. Rome had ports, islands, rights of passage everywhere, privileges, official protection. Nowhere else was there so much privilege and power. If a man of solid worth was occasionally born elsewhere within the general region, he would see the difficulties that stood in his way at home and move invariably to Rome. Thus Rome drew to herself everything wonderful that was engendered in Italy and drained all other cities. The proof lies in any comparison of pre-Roman and Roman times. Before the Romans took over, many cities and peoples flourished magnificently in Italy, and under the Roman empire all of them declined. After the fall of Rome, on the other hand, the other cities immediately began to raise their heads and flourish. What her growth had taken away, her decline restored.

Since we shall be speaking at length about the cities of Tuscany, it seems appropriate to summarize the history of all Tuscany from its most ancient beginnings here. We shall observe what Tuscany was like both before and after the period of Roman domination, and in the latter period, what cities flourished, professing what sort of political principles, and exercising what sort of power. We shall thus arrive at our own times with a knowledge and understanding of Tuscany derived from the facts of history.

Before the Roman empire, the greatest wealth and power in Italy and the greatest fame in war and peace belonged to the Etruscans—such is the clear message of all the most ancient sources. The original home of this people was Maeonia, whence a vast multitude of Lydians, who were very famous warriors, sailed to Italy and settled in the region now called Tuscany. They expelled the Pelasgians and other earlier inhabitants, and called the region Tyrrhenia after their king, Tyrrhenus. Their greatness and power increased with their numbers until they had extended their borders from the western shore to the Apennines, and from the Tiber to the Macra. Later they received the Greek name, Etruscans, which referred either to their sacrifices or to their worship of the open sky. The region itself was soon called Etruria. According to ancient sources, the Etruscans consisted of twelve tribes. Originally, however, they all obeyed one king. Eventually, as royal power seemed burdensome to them, each tribe began to create a separate *Lucumo*, as they called the official who, with the help of a council, ruled them. One such *Lucumo* came to be supreme over the others, but in prestige only, not in actual power. Under this kind of chief, Etruria was ruled for a long time by the equal will and authority of all its twelve peoples; and internal concord, as usual, gave the nation wealth and power. The various cities the Etruscans founded within their borders became large and prosperous and they eventually held sway over lands far beyond their own borders.

The two seas that nearly encircle Italy bear witness to the power of the Etruscans, for both are named after them and no others. The lower sea was named after Tuscany or Tyrrhenia, the old name of the people, and according to certain Greek sources, this name applied to it from Sardinia to Sicily. The upper sea was called the Adriatic, and named after Adria, a famous port founded by the Etruscans on the Adriatic shore not far from the mouth of the Po, for they ruled that area too. (Livy V, 33) Once the Etruscans had crossed the Apennines, they conquered and occupied first of all every place on their side of the Po, and later the whole region on the other side up to the Alps, except for the farthest promontory held by the Venetians. Moving down the sweep of the shore, they took over most of the land and expelled the Umbrians, a people who were then numerous and powerful enough, as the old histories tell us, to lose over three hundred towns to the Etruscans. On the western side of the Apennines they took over all Italy down to the straits of Sicily. And wherever they went, they colonized. Historians preserve the memory of numerous towns which they founded, as well as of towns whose previous inhabitants they drove out and replaced with their own people. Some of those towns still exist, a continuing monument to their once great power. Among such famous ancient cities in the south, we may mention Capua. In the north, there is Mantua, which started as an Etruscan colony. It is known that the Etruscans who, as we have said, consisted of twelve tribes, sent colonies from each separate tribe across the Apennines and named cities after them. Adria was one such city, and gave her name to the Adriatic; Mantua was another, and is the only one still extant of the Etruscan plantations beyond the Po.

It seems that the power of this people goes back a very long way, that they were great, prosperous, and even imperial before the Trojan War. Hence Aeneas, having fled Troy after her defeat, turned to the Etruscan state for help against the Latins and Rutuli, so Virgil says. For Evander, when he was answering Aeneas' plea for help, began by telling him that he himself did not have enough power to resist the Latins and the Rutuli, and then directed him to the Etruscans:

> I plan for a vast people and well furnished armies
> To join you . . .

A little later he explains:

35

Not far from here, founded upon a rock,
Rises the seat of Agylla, where Lydia,
A nation famous for war, settled on the Etruscan hills.
This old and flourishing people, King Mezentius
Has yoked by cruel arms under his proud rule.

(Aen. VIII, 475–82)

If we may modify somewhat the poet's inventions, less corrupt and truer history tells us that it was Turnus, not Aeneas, who turned to Mezentius after suffering defeat and who asked for help from the wealthy Etruscans against an invading chief and his army. (Livy I, 2) Whichever view we accept, however, we must admit that the Etruscan nation flourished before the Trojan War. And it lasted intact at home 616 B.C. and abroad until the invasion of Italy by the Gauls, about six hundred years after the Trojan War and about one hundred and seventy years after the founding of Rome.

The Gauls had a multitude of infantry and cavalry, led by Bellovesus. They crossed the Alps and were joined by other multitudes migrating from Gaul and Germany. Together these peoples took from the Tuscans all that part of Italy which is still known as Cisalpine Gaul. (Livy V, 34) The last of the Gauls were the Senones, who occupied part of the Marches around the town of Sinigaglia. The wealth of the Tuscans was diminished by these and other Gauls, and they were forced after long wars to limit their domain to the western area protected by the Apennines. Meanwhile Roman power grew also and encroached on their borders from the other side. Thus the Etruscans were squeezed between two very vigorous peoples and were pressed on both borders. Still, for several centuries, the strength and authority of this people were not sapped from outside, and they remained independent and sovereign.

The Etruscans behaved very differently toward the Romans than they did toward the Gauls. Against those barbarians and savages, they waged implacable war. Against the Romans, they never fought with hatred and bitterness; in fact they were more often allies of Rome than adversaries. The efforts at imitation evident in Roman culture prove this, for no people imitates those whom they really loathe.

The Romans took from the Etruscans the magistrates' *praetexta* [outer garments with a purple border] and *phalera* [a metal disk worn on the

36

breast], their dyed togas and embroidered tunics, their chain and ring of office, the handsome golden chariots used in triumphs, the *fasces* [bundles of rods and an axe, carried before the highest magistrates and used for the punishment of criminals]—all the insignia of royalty and office. (Livy I, 8) The twelve attendants who prepared the way for Roman kings and consuls also derived from the Etruscans, who, since they were twelve tribes, sent one attendant to the king from each tribe. So the amount the Romans derived from the Etruscans was not insignificant. Lest anyone think we are simply flattering ourselves, moreover, we may note that this information comes from the oldest Greek and Roman sources. The Romans did not take from the Etruscans imperial insignia and other solemn ceremonial customs only, but also their letters and learning. Livy says that he has sources to show that Roman boys, before the time when they were given instruction by Greeks, used to receive their education from Etruscans. (Livy IX, 36) The Romans had taken so much of their religious ceremonial from the Etruscans that they admitted the most important parts still remained in the power of the authors themselves. As soon as a serious crisis arose in the republic, the Roman magistrates called on Etruscan priests and soothsayers to appease God by the proper rites. All knowledge of religious matters was referred to as Etruscan wisdom. It seems to me that the Roman willingness to borrow these things shows that they respected the Etruscans. Royal insignia, religious ceremonies, and literary studies are matters of weight and importance. Nor did the Romans admire Tuscany for the peaceful arts but despise her in war. The Etruscan attempts to besiege Rome and the sieges of Porsenna in particular are recorded, which are all the more impressive because by that time the Gauls had arrived in Italy. Nor will you find that anyone caused the Romans more trouble than the Etruscan enemy, or forced them to adopt dictators more often. The first war of Rome against Tuscany was started by Romulus, the founder of Rome, and from then on almost all the kings of Rome took up this same war again, only excepting Numa Pompilius and proud Tarquinius.

750 B.C.   The first war between the Etruscans and Romans, moreover, started around Fidenae, an Etruscan colony located across the Tiber, between the lands of Crustumerium and Rome. The Etruscans who had colonized Fidenae thought that the new city of Rome was growing im-

moderately and would become a threat. Gathering their own forces and those of their Etruscan neighbors in the region, they decided to war on the Romans before they gained their full strength, and they attacked her without provocation. The men of Fidenae took a lot of booty from Roman farms, and country people fleeing to Rome filled the city with fear and turmoil. Romulus called out his legions to avenge these injuries and quickly attacked first the bands returning to Fidenae and then the city itself. There was no time for help to come from Etruria. Romulus rode his men to the very gates of Fidenae, then feigned flight, which provoked the army to anger and indignation—such was the soldiers' ardor and their leader's excellence. When the army of Fidenae had been lured into the trap, they were forced to flee back to their city in a confused mass that contained both vanquished and victors. (Livy, I, 14) The town was thus taken and a garrison imposed by the king of the Romans. The people of Veii, the nearest Etruscan city to Fidenae, were troubled by the humiliation of their kinsmen, and now feared that they would have no more tranquillity at all with the Romans so near; so they sent out their young warriors to raid the Roman countryside and plunder the farms. Romulus now led his legions to fight and subdue this people. Such was the beginning of the first war between the Romans and the Etruscans. At it was rather lightly started, it was easily ended, with some relocation of people, some devastation of farms, but fights more like brawls than real battles. When hostilities ended, there was peace for a hundred years.

From this beginning, however, other wars arose later between the Etruscans and the Romans, either because the truce ran out or because the agreed on conditions were not being observed. The peace held, however, under Romulus and Numa Pompilius, and neither side broke it. After that, in the reign of Tullius Hostilius, war broke out again because of an uprising of the men of Fidenae, who rebelled against the Romans. (Livy I, 23, 24, 26) They had tried beforehand to draw into their counsels Metius Fufetius, a general of Alba, with whom they made a secret alliance. He had been forced to surrender formally to Rome after the battle of the three Horatios. Resenting this, he conferred secretly with the Etruscans. He was planning, since he had Alban legions attached to the Roman army under his command, to turn the standards around and attack the Romans once the battle had begun. Being a man of cowardly spirit, however, he kept neither his promise to his enemies nor to his own side. He neither fell upon the Etruscans along with the Romans, with whom he had joined forces, nor did he keep his promise to the Etruscans to attack the Romans. With a mind wavering between hope and fear, he kept his men out of the battle till he might see which side was winning, intending to decide his course then. In the two-pronged battle, the Roman fortune and the boldness of their very fierce king, Tullius, triumphed. He routed the enemy in a terrible battle and retook Fidenae. He killed Metius as well, and razed the city of Alba.

The next two kings of Rome, Ancus Marcius and Priscus Tarquinius, both continued the war with the Etruscans. This is perfectly clear in the case of Marcius, but we have different stories concerning the elder Tarquinius. Some say he fought for nine years, not only with Veii, but with almost all the Etruscan nation. Others tell the story of this king as though nothing at all had happened with the Etruscans. But if there is some doubt about Tarquinius, it is certain that Servius Tullius fought hard and long against the entire Etruscan people, with heavier preparation than any king before him. Certain authors tell us that his war with Tuscany lasted continuously for twenty years. (Livy I, 42) I find it possible to believe that the war was so long and so unrelenting, for in the forty-four years of Servius' reign, he is not known to have waged any other war. He gained such a reputation for his conduct of this war that, while he had ruled at first without popular sanction, later, on the strength of his victories, he did not refuse to submit his rule to the people's approval and to risk the name of king on the unpredictable votes of the multitude. We are not told that the Etruscans were conquered in this war, however, or that they lost even one of their cities. It seems simply that over a long period each side inflicted many injuries on the other, and that the ultimate result was a strengthening of Rome's position. These are the things that were done by Rome during the period of the monarchy in relation to the Etruscans.

When the monarchy ended and Tarquinius was driven out, he appealed as a suppliant to the Etruscans. He was counting on family loyalty, since he had sprung from them, and he gained two allies among them, Veii and Tarquinii. They sent a vast army to invade the Roman lands and fought against L. Iunius Brutus and Marcus Valerius, who was later known as Publicolae (for these were the consuls in those first years

566 B.C.

509 B.C.

39

of the republic). The battle was more unrestrained and cruel than any earlier one. Both sides cut down the right wing of the adversary with their swords. In the vast slaughter, it is believed that the Etruscans lost only one more man than the Romans. The greater loss, however, was the Romans', for Lucius Brutus, the leader of the movement to expel the kings, was killed in battle. The outcome was certainly such that both sides considered themselves defeated. The Roman consuls were bereaved by the death of one of their number and terrified by the enormous casualties among their men; they prepared to retreat at dawn; the Etruscans left the field before daylight.

Poresenna, king of Chiusi, with greater preparations renewed the war to restore Tarquinius. With this leader, the Etruscans beat the Roman army, surrounded and besieged Rome, and almost took the city. The only thing that saved Rome was the order of Horatius Cocles to destroy the Pons Sublicius, which was at that time the only bridge to span the Tiber. How great the danger was is apparent from the honors the Roman people granted him, not for any act of conquest, but simply for permitting the destruction of the bridge, thus giving his own people a moment of delay and a chance to defend themselves. They owed more gratitude for their safety, if I may say so, to the Tiber: when Roman valor could not protect Rome, the river saved the city. The Etruscans, since they were on the Janiculum and held all of Rome on the north side of the Tiber, besieged the southern side of the city for a long time. The besieged formed a plan to attack the person of the king, and since they had no hope of taking him by open warfare, resorted to cunning tricks to lure him away from his protectors. Hence the famous story of Mutius Scaevola, and his putting his own hand in the fire. (Livy, II, 12, 13)

But all these stratagems did not cause the Etruscan king to depart, and when he did go he insisted on taking hostages from Rome, not only men, but also women. Men of noblest birth were given, and high-born virgins. Among the latter was Valeria, daughter of Publicola the consul. There were many other maidens from patrician families. This was a triumph for the Etruscans unequaled by any other people. To no other tyrants or peoples had the Romans ever been forced to give hostages in order to gain peace. They themselves, indeed, when they conquered others, demanded almost nothing but hostages: for this to them meant, not only a guarantee of future peace, but an admission of defeat. The alliance thus created by Porsenna was further stabilized by benefits which accrued to both Etruscans and Romans. For the Etruscans were received with friendship and hospitality at Rome when they, after the alliance with the Romans, went on an expedition against Aritia under Arunte, the son of Porsenna, and returned after his death in battle. They were given houses in a beautiful section of Rome, which was known thereafter as the Tuscan part, and Porsenna after some years kindly gave back the hostages to the Romans. Tarquinius, who was still living in Tuscany, saw that he must seek help elsewhere and went to Manlius, his Tusculan son-in-law. (Livy II, 14, 15) Afterwards peace reigned between Rome and Etruria until Veii broke it.

483 B.C.   Veii was a city bordering on Roman territory, and, as often happens, friction arose through contact. After various small fights initiated by one side or the other, Veii finally started an open conflict with Rome. In the first battle of the war, the men of Veii overcame the Romans. The second battle, however, was perhaps the most horrible ever recorded. The Romans, after their first defeat, had made the soldiers swear that they would never return except as victors. The soldiers felt bound by this oath, and they fought with immense obstinacy. There were heavy losses on both sides. Killed in the battle were Cnaius Manlius, the consul, and Quintus Fabius, the brother of the other consul. The Roman camp was seized by the Etruscans, then the tide of the battle turned and the Romans recovered it. Nothing seems to have contributed more to the final victory of the Romans than the excessive zeal of the Etruscans in their storming of the camp. While they made that capture, their depleted front line was overwhelmed by the Romans. Hardly ever has fortune been so treacherous and so fickle as it was that day. Having been beaten, the Romans won. The victory was so bloody that, at the subsequent triumph, the consul stated that it was an occasion for weeping rather than rejoicing. And this battle caused Veii as much sorrow as Rome.

The Veii now got the help of all Etruria (for they had fought alone before), and avenged themselves in the siege of Veii at the Cremera River by slaughtering three hundred and six Fabians, all members of one clan, and their followers. They killed about five thousand men at one time, it is reported. The same forces then struck at the Roman

41

legions posted near Crema under the consul Lucius Menenius. Not only were army and consul forced to flee, but the whole camp was stripped bare. (Livy II, 42–52) The retreating army and stragglers were pursued and further cut down till they reached Rome. There the Etruscans again occupied the Janiculum Ridge, which is very close to the Capitoline Hill but on the other side of the Tiber. For some months they held it, as it were, besieging Rome. Then they crossed the Tiber and continued the fight both at the Collina gate and at various other places by the Tiber beneath the walls of Rome. As when Porsenna threatened Rome, it was a matter of life and death. Etruscan legions held the Janiculum and threatened to starve the rest of the city. Rome called out both consuls with their armies and the entire youth of Rome. They attacked the Janiculum in a two-pronged, fearful battle. Nor was the outcome favorable to the Romans. One of the two consuls was afterward arraigned for his military incompetence.

This one Etrurian city, to summarize a great many events, carried on the war against Rome for over three hundred and fifty years. Sometimes she had the help of other cities, sometimes she fought alone. Sometimes she was beaten in battle, sometimes she won. Her final overthrow, however, came when she had resumed the war on her own decision alone, and not by agreement among the Etruscan people. Thus, when Rome pressed her hard, she was refused help by the other Etruscan peoples. They were angry because she had not consulted them, and they were also, in some cases, fearful of the Gauls and anxious not to leave their own territories unprotected. Their answer when Veii asked them for help was given by a common council: "Resist the Romans yourselves, if you wish, but do not ask for allies to share the danger. When you hoped to win the war and take great booty, you did not ask us to join you." This allowed Rome to besiege Veii. Though abandoned by all allies, the city bore the siege a long time, having a lot of strength of her own. Only after ten summers and ten winters of siege was it taken, and then not by force but by the unexpected betrayal of secret passages.

The Romans took so much loot from this one city that it was as much as they had gained in all their previous wars together. Since the wealth of this city seemed too much for the army alone, the whole Roman people was called by a special edict to come and take part. This was done nowhere else. For Veii was a most opulent and impressive city, and its site too was so fine and had such possibilities that the victors considered many times moving as a people from Rome to Veii, the superior city.

Now the capture of Veii seemed to open the way for Rome to take over all Etruria. The Romans continued their attack on Falerii and Capena, cities which the war with nearby Veii had not left unscathed. They both surrendered without a very long struggle. The collapse, however, occurred for different reasons in the two cases. The Capenati were forced by exhaustion and the devastation of their fields to give up. The Falisci, on the other hand, were so impressed with the admirable virtue of the great Roman leader, Furius Camillus, that they surrendered to him of their own free will. Men who could not be bent by iron, or by siege, or by the devastation of their fields, were moved by the splendor of justice and honesty. Here is the remarkable story. The Roman camp was placed in a densely inhabited area near Falerii, and a certain Faliscan teacher, hoping for gain by his act of wicked treason, took some of the sons of the chief citizens who had been entrusted to him for their education, and led them to the enemy camp. He started them off on a supposed walk through a gate facing away from the enemy, then talked to them to distract them and brought them by various paths away from the city to a Roman outpost located between the Roman camp and the city. He was thus captured by his own will and brought to the commander. "General," he said, "today I have given you the Falisci, by giving you these children, whose parents are their chief citizens. No doubt you will remember to be grateful to me." When Camillus heard these words, he showed contempt for the crime of this immoral person. "Don't think, wretch," he said, "that you have come to criminals like yourself, who will not only tolerate your wickedness but reward it. My mind and that of the Roman people is quite different. We maintain the laws of war as of peace and fight our wars with armed enemies, not harmless children. Though we be the enemies of the Falisci, we do remember that we are bound together with them in human society. I shall conquer them with arms, with patience, and with virtue. These are Roman qualities. I shall not conquer them by crime." Stripping the man and tying his hands behind his back, he gave him to the students he had betrayed to be beaten and taken back to Falerii. The people of the city were greatly moved and, while they had burned till then with incredible hatred for the Romans and preferred ruin to peace with

43

them, now they gave themselves and their city into Roman hands. Such was the strength of their admiration for the good faith and justice of the Roman general. Thus was Falerii conquered.

Soon after this, the Romans attacked Tarquinii and Caere. The war spread to Volsinii, as fire spreads, and eventually it reached the central Etruscans, Clusium, Perusia, and Arretium. (These were the great and powerful cities of that time.) The war dragged on, and as the outcome remained doubtful and the threatened cities realized their great danger, they cursed their earlier unwillingness to help Veii, Falerii, and Capena, which had all appealed to them for protection. By negligence and laziness in their kinsmen's hour of need, they had allowed their people's strength to decline and that of the enemy to grow. Undoubtedly if all the Etruscans had waged war with a unified strategy, they might have defended themselves long and magnificently. The presence of the Gauls as a threat on their borders, or the discord among themselves, or fortune itself now favoring the Roman side, or a combination of all these things caused them not to go to war with a common plan. It was this that gave the Romans the power to succeed, for they used their own and their allies' armies to conquer, not the whole people at once, but each city in turn. The cities not directly involved acted as though the matter did not concern them and as though they themselves would not be next. They waited in idleness and lent themselves to each other's destruction. For the Romans could not have kept up the long siege of Veii if the other Etruscan cities had helped that one, indeed Veii would not have been besieged at all under those circumstances. As soon as even two of the other cities, not the greatest ones but only Capena and Falerii began to give some support, the Roman siege was almost broken. Yet the Etruscans, as long as the nation stood undamaged, were not blessed with this spirit of unity. When they had been divided and diminished, indeed, they took wiser counsel, but then it was of little use. So the Etruscans were beaten in a series of great battles. The most famous encounter took place at Sutrium, where 60,000 Etruscans were left on the field. Another occurred at Lake Vadimonis, where they were so decimated that they seemed to have been completely forgotten by fortune. Thus, they came to put their hopes in peace and no longer in arms.

283 B.C. About four hundred and seventy years after the founding of Rome by Romulus, who also saw the beginning of this war, all Etruria fell

into Roman hands. [See Maps 1 and 2.] These wars brought fame to many Roman leaders. The first king and the first consul, and all the kings and consuls after them, and the dictators, and the tribunes, all gave their best efforts to campaigns against the Etruscans, and so earned glory. Among the kings of Rome, some grant highest glory to the elder Tarquin, some to Servius Tullius. Among consuls, Marcus Valerius Publicola had the first triumph, but later there were many others, such as Marcus Fabius, Publius Servilius, Mamercus Aemilius, Aulus Cornelius Cossus, and others. The highest achievement was that of Marcus Furius Camillus, who defeated Veii and Falerii, but that of Fabius Maximus matched it, for he, toward the end of the war, pressed the Etruscans in more and greater battles than anyone else. And the Romans, after they had subdued the Etruscans by arms and the Etruscans had submitted to their power, called them by the honorable name of allies.

There was no more need to fear war, Etruria was safe from armed attack, but now she was besieged by debilitating leisure. It is a fact of human nature that, when the way lies open to greatness and honors, people readily take it; when that way is blocked, they become inert and do nothing. When the empire had fallen to Rome, the Etruscans could neither gain honors nor put their energies into major enterprises, and the Etruscan character quickly declined. They were far more shattered by inactivity than by the enemy's sword. Twice after their surrender 209 B.C. to the Romans, the Etruscans tried to rebel. The first attempt came in the days of Hannibal's invasion, under Aretine leadership. The second revolt was part of the Social War, when the Etruscans allied themselves with the Latins, the Marsi, and the Umbrians, and all were defeated by the Romans. The first rebellion was easily suppressed near its beginning, by the immediate frustration of Arretium's efforts to show some strength. The second rebellion was put down with heavy damage 94 B.C. to those concerned and with great cruelty. The Romans imposed especially heavy penalties on Clusium and Fesula. After this, however, the Roman empire appeared invincible and unquestionable, down to the time of Arcadius and Honorius. Etruria, therefore, was subjugated for about seven hundred years.

A.D. 401   At the time of Arcadius and Honorius, the Goths, under Radagasus and Alaricus, first ravaged Italy. Even before that the emperors had

45

been neglecting Italy, the wealth of the peninsula was largely exhausted, and her power was in severe decline. The Goths were followed by the Huns, these by the Vandals, these by the Heruli, and then the Goths invaded again, till not long after that, the Lombards gained control of Italy and established a number of different kingdoms there.

The decline of the Roman empire, however, ought, in my opinion, to be dated almost from the moment that Rome gave up her liberty to serve a series of emperors. Even though Augustus and Trajan may have been useful to Rome, and although other princes too may have merited praise, yet we should consider the excellent men killed in the civil wars of Caesar and by the fearful triumvirate of Augustus. If one considers the savagery of Tiberius after that, and after Tiberius, the fury of Caligula and the insanity of Claudius, and the crimes of Nero with his fierce delight in fire and sword, and adds Vitellius, Caracalla, Heliogabalos, Maximinus and other monsters like them, who horrified the whole world, one cannot deny that the Roman empire began to decline once the disastrous name of Caesar seized on the imagination of the city. For liberty gave way before the imperial name, and as liberty disappeared, so did virtue. Before the day of the Caesars, character was the route to honor, and positions such as consul, dictator, or other high public offices were open to men of magnanimous spirit, strength of character, and energy. But as soon as the republic was entrusted to one man, character and magnanimity became suspect in the eyes of the rulers. Only those were acceptable to the emperors who lacked the mental vigor to care about liberty. The imperial court thus opened its gates to the lazy rather than to the strong, to flatterers rather than to hard workers, and as administration fell to the worst of men, little by little the empire was brought to ruin. Can one deplore the rejection of excellence and not deplore still more the destruction of the whole state? How many luminaries of the republic were killed under Julius Caesar —of how many leaders was the city deprived? Under Augustus, whether from necessity or malice, what a host of proscriptions and of expropriations, what a work of destruction! So that when he finally stopped his killing and his cruelty, it seemed less like kindness than like fatigue. He chose as his son and his successor Tiberius, a man of disgusting character, who did not stop torturing and tormenting the citizens even while he took his meals. Caligula, the successor of Tiberius, killed just about everyone! What family in the city did not lose members at his hands? After Caligula there was Claudius' cruel folly, which destroyed the whole Roman nobility, not at his own wish, it is true, but at the whim of his wives and children. Nero was the next Caesar after him, and whom did he spare? He spared neither brother, nor wife, nor mother, nor teacher, nor the city itself. What a scourge of the citizens was his reign! He made such a slaughter of patricians, that it was said when he died the artisan class was beginning to fear a purge—the Roman nobility seemed to be gone, the rabble and the workers were all that was left for him to rage at and to ravage. It would take a long time to go into more detail, but the emperors were all of the same mind, fearing anyone in whom they could detect excellence, hating whomever they feared, and killing with the sword those they hated. As soon as hatred overcame fear, they also freely killed each other, and waged far greater war within the body of the state than on external enemies. A few examples may help to make this clear: Julius Caesar was assassinated, Tiberius, it is thought, was killed by Caligula, and Caligula is known to have been finished off by his guards. Claudius was poisoned with a mushroom by his wife Agrippina, and Nero died, not of a fever, but by the sword. Galba, Nero's successor, was killed by Otto. Vitellius laid Otto low, and Vitellius in his turn was run through by Roman swords. Domitian too was murdered, and others as well—but it would be excessive and unnecessary to name them all.

Vast internal damage and revolution, in short, preceded and made possible the withering and death of the empire. Roman power was internally drained away and, for lack of native citizens, her majesty eventually fell into foreign hands. Yet for a long time, the vastness of Roman power did endure through internal misfortunes. Though as badly afflicted as we have shown, Rome still remained safe from external enemies. The Emperor Constantine, however, enlarged the city of Byzantium and moved the capital to the east. The emperors thereafter began to view Italy and the western part of the empire almost as the abandoned part, to be neglected and left open to the invasions of tyrants and barbarians. They rolled into the empty territories like some flood and inundated them altogether. I shall describe them briefly here, since they were active in Etruria and even devastated the city of which we are writing.

Among the many barbarians who overran Italy after the capital was moved to Byzantium the first were the Goths, led by Radagasus and Alaricus. These people were the same whom the ancient writers call the Getae. This people was Scythian, and they first inhabited the part of Scythia which borders Lake Maestis [the Sea of Azov] and faces west. Attracted by the hope of more land, they settled on the longer shore of the Black Sea. Some writers in fact refer to this shore as the Gothic shore. Their original reputation, even while they lived in Asia and had not yet entered the neighboring regions of Europe, was formidable. Lucullus was the first Roman to wage war on them, and he defeated them in Moesia. Later Agrippa and other Roman leaders attacked them beyond the Danube. The multitude of them spread over various regions, however, and they could never be altogether subdued. Whenever the Romans ceased to press them, the overflow of their population used to enter Moesia and Thrace and other accessible provinces. Under Gallus and Volusianus, a pact was finally made with the Goths, but it was broken and forgotten soon after the death of these emperors, and until the time of Diocletian and Maximian, the Goths were more often en-emies of the Romans than allies. Under these emperors, however, the alliance was renewed, and the Goths greatly aided the Romans in the Parthian campaigns of Maximian. They also gave aid to Constantine when he was warring against Licinium, and supported other emperors of that period.

The long-standing alliance of the Goths with the Romans was even-tually strained by great internal difficulties that came upon the Goths. For the Huns, another Scythian people outstanding in arms and in cruelty, attacked those Goths called Ostrogoths, who still cultivated the far places of Scythia, and after a number of battles forced them into sub-jection. The Goths along the Danube were afraid that they too would be unable to resist the Huns, and turned to the Romans for help. They sent legates to Valens, the emperor, asking that, as friends and frequent allies, they might be allowed to escape the slaughter and slavery that threatened them from the Huns by crossing the Danube into the Roman empire. They spoke of their own imminent ruin, which would ulti-mately be harmful to the Romans also, and they promised to live in the domain of the emperor peacefully and to obey the laws he gave them. Valens saw some danger in such a host of barbarians, but he hoped they would protect that border of the empire from the power of the Huns, so he permitted the Goths with their wives and children freely to cross the Danube into Moesia. He put a certain Maximus with some regiments of guards in charge of the region, and told him to obtain whatever provisions would be needed by the newcomers. He also sent the Goths learned men to teach the Christian religion, which he himself professed. But the great influx of foreigners soon produced an intolerable shortage of goods, and the avarice of Maximus, who made a profit on commercial transactions, aggravated the shortage. The Goths in this situation began to complain and bewail their fate, and to blame the incompetence of Maximus (who did not permit enough supplies to come in) or his greed, because he was selling the provisions too dear. They would lose their slaves, then at last be forced to sell even their children and their wives; and when their families were gone, they would be led away themselves like sheep. They said they would rather serve the Huns, or die fighting them, than starve to death or be thus brought low by the greediest of men. Such were the complaints that began to be common among the Goths. Their princes, Phritigernus and Alatheus, were warriors and found idleness offensive. Both because of their own fierce nature and because of the popular anger, they hoped for a revolt. They led the Goths in an attack on the Romans and killed the governor as well as all the Roman soldiers they could catch. Fighting as a group, the Goths had overcome the Roman garrisons, and now they spread out to populate Moesia, Thrace, and the shores of Dacia. There was a great slaughter of the provincial people and many were seized as slaves. Forgetting the favor the emperor had bestowed on them, the Goths took over these provinces as their own and no longer recognized him as overlord.

Valens was in Antioch at this time; when he heard what had happened, he hurried to Thrace with an army to deal with the catastrophe. The battle that ensued, however, made a bad situation worse. The cavalry of Valens was beaten by the Goths, and the outnumbered foot-soldiers were surrounded and slaughtered. Valens himself fled with an arrow wound but, because of the pain, could not go far and had to be carried into a certain village house. The pursuing barbarians burned down the house with the emperor himself inside it.

The Goths devastated all Thrace and were finally stopped by bitter fighting only at the very gates of Constantinople. When Gratian, the nephew of Valens and the emperor of the west, heard this news, he was filled with sorrow and anxiety. He tried to think what he should do to save the state, and it seemed best, as Nerva had done in appointing Trajan, to make a powerful general his co-emperor. He chose Theodosius, a remarkable Spaniard. Theodosius was made emperor as the last hope of the empire, the man who would quell the Gothic uprising. He took the purple from Gratian at Sirmium and immediately marched into Thrace, where he beat the Goths with great energy and success. He won numerous battles and retook all Thrace. But as he was pursuing the last of their troops, he fell ill. Gratian, who was afraid that Theodosius might not recover, made peace with the Goths at that moment. And when Theodosius did recover from his illness, he accepted the decision without protest in order to maintain his colleague's honor. As he had beaten the Goths in war when they were his enemies, so now he kept their friendship by his good faith and kindness, and he frequently found their services useful to the state.

Gratian died at Lugdum [Lyon] in Gaul, and his brother Valentinian, somewhat later, at Vienna, and when Theodosius himself died at Milan, A.D. 395 he left the empire to be ruled by his sons, Arcadius and Honorius. During their reign, part of the Gothic host became land hungry again, and under Alaric, a man of great energy who had declared himself their leader, they invaded Italy via Pannonia [Hungary] and Firmium [Friuli?] into Italy. Another mass of Goths entered the same region under Radagasus. So the record shows that two Gothic leaders and their armies invaded Italy in one year, during the consulate of Stilico and Aurelian. Their fate, however, was very different. Radagasus crossed the Alpine peaks with an enormous following and devastated Tuscany with barbaric fury. Rome was already trembling at his proximity when he was met and defeated by Stilico, the brilliant general of the Emperor Honorius. Having driven the enemy into the mountains of Fiesole, near Florence, he starved them of all supplies and wiped them out so well that not one of two hundred thousand Goths escaped. (So many, they say, were with Radagasus.) The majority were killed, the rest captured and sold. Radagasus himself with his closest companions was captured while shamefully trying to flee when his cause was lost. Stilico brought him back in chains, and, after displaying him in military triumph, executed him. This defeat of the Gauls is said to have occurred on October 23rd, and it said that, because the great victory had saved the city from the utmost terror of the barbarians, the day became a holiday in Florence and the name was inscribed in the Florentine temple. Our own diligent research has established that this victory over the Goths took place in the reign of Arcadius and Honorius, in the consulship of Stilico and Antemio, ten years after the death of Theodosius, in the four hundred and ninth year of Christian salvation. We cannot be sure of the day, or of the inscription. Radagasus, and the Goths who followed him, certainly did end their career in Etruria.

Alaricus brought another group of Goths into Italy and set up camp near Ravenna. He then sent ambassadors to Honorius to ask for places where his people could settle. He promised that, if Honorius so desired, he would go into the regions of Gaul held by the threatening power of the Vandals and the Alani, where he would call on the loyalty and friendship of the subjects of the Roman empire. This alliance was made with the barbarians. Then, as they were marching on Gaul and had arrived at the city of Pollentia at the foot of the Alps, expecting no hostilities, the Goths were suddenly attacked by certain of Honorius' generals, despite all promises. At first the attackers slaughtered a multitude of Goths. The soldiers were sure that on that day they could wipe out the whole host of the barbarians since, contrary to military discipline, in overconfidence of peace, they had not chosen a fortified place nor protected themselves with ditches, but had simply encamped with their horses and baggage in the midst of a field. And thus great slaughter was done at first, and the blood of the barbarians flowed all over the ground wherever the attackers penetrated. But the host was greater than could be killed in one attack. Frightened but numerous they huddled around their king. In their astonishment they were divided as to what to do, and religion, it is said, held them back for a time. For, to complete a tale of crime, the generals of Honorius had chosen Easter Sunday for the attack, to be sure to catch the enemy off guard. The Goths, considering the day inauspicious, at first withdrew and willingly ceded to the enemy. After a while, however, when they saw the attackers come on unrelentingly and ferociously cut down their own people, they became mad with anger and indignation and struck back in blind rage. These men, who had been filled with the hope of victory by the great slaughter at the beginning, were easily overcome when the righteous force started cutting them down. Having been defeated, the Goths became victors—fortune had turned. They flattened the scattered forces of Honorius' men with incredible carnage. They filled the place with corpses and gore. And from this place, filled with wrath and elated with victory, they took out their just fury on our people. They forgot about the march on Gaul and ceased to observe the agreement concerning areas of settlement. They rolled over all Italy with frightful force, attacked all places indiscriminately and devastated far and wide with fire and sword.

Against this fury of barbarians the emperor pitted Stilico, with a new army. He stopped their wild attacks. Relying on his expert knowledge of warfare, he sometimes surrounded them, sometimes came up to them from behind, sometimes hit them straight on, and he would have overcome them completely if he had really wished to. But he had long aspired to become emperor himself, and he actually wanted to maintain the terror in Italy. For this reason he neither let the Goths win nor lose, he covertly supported them while openly he refused them the means either of war or of peace, and when they wanted to leave Italy he kept them there. When all this was revealed at court, Honorius ordered the death of Stilico and his son Eucherius, for whom he was wickedly trying to gain the throne. The just wrath of the prince and his righteous vengeance for such treason led very soon to worse troubles. For, when Stilico, the greatest Roman general, was removed and the Romans' courage was dulled by his death, the Goths rushed freely over Italy and

A.D. 410 furiously invaded that city which had conquered the world (it is a shameful thing to have to report), defiling everything except the sacred places, which the barbarians did respect, with slaughter and bloodshed. The city was seized and some parts of it were burned. Then after a few days the barbarians departed with priceless booty and a great crowd of captives. Among their prisoners was Placidia Galla, the daughter of Theodosius and sister of Arcadius and Honorius. She was taken from the splendors of the imperial palace to the rough camp of the Goths (so strangely does chance mix all things together), and fortune constrained her to follow the all-powerful lord of the barbarians. When they had left Rome, the Goths orgied in wreaking similar destruction on Campania, Lucania, and Bruttia [provinces around Rome]. Having gone down the length of Italy, they tried to cross to Sicily but wind and shipwreck blocked the way and saved Sicily. They were discussing whether to rebuild their ships or to journey back whence they had come, and amidst the discussions and delays, Alaric died at Cosentia [Cosena, in Calabria]. The Goths buried their king where no vengeance could be taken on his body, diverting the river Basentus [Busento] with the help of many soldiers and prisoners, putting him under the channel with a lot of rich spoils and all the royal treasure, then redirecting the river back into its original bed. They then took all their Italian captives and, whether for the glory of the chieftain's burial or to prevent their giving away the whereabouts of the grave, killed them down to the last man. Ataulf, a relative of Alaric, now became king, and they went again to Rome and took away whatever booty was left to take. Having settled in Etruria and afflicted other regions near it, they finally went into Gaul like some storm bringing evil weather. Rome, however, was thus sacked by the Goths one thousand one hundred and sixty-four years after its founding and eight hundred years after it had been taken by the Gauls. Placidia Galla, moreover, whose seizure and abduction we have described, was taken in marriage by Athaulf. After his death, for he was murdered at Barcelona by his own people, she was married to Constantine, a remarkable man, by whom she had Valentinianus, the next emperor after Honorius.

After this came the invasion of Attila, king of the Huns, who spread unprecedented terror through Italy. We have said that the Huns were a Scythian people. At first they settled on the shores of Lake Maestis, then they moved to Pannonia. When they had grown more powerful and extended their rule over many other peoples in all directions, the throne came to two brothers, Attila and Bleda. Attila, however, killed Bleda by trickery and ruled alone. He was the most powerful king ever seen. For enormous and powerful nations obeyed him. He had a fierce nature that put terror into people and he seemed to have been born to be the terror of the world. Having devastated Macedonia, Moesia [Bulgaria], Thrace and Illyria [Yugoslavia], he marched through Germany into Gaul. He combined cunning with violence. For while he was attacking both Romans and Goths, he did not want them to combine their forces. So he wrote to the Romans that he was marching against the Goths, ancient enemies and, as it were, escaped slaves of his people, whom he wished to seek out and subdue wherever they were. He asked the Romans to join him in the fight and and gain vengeance on their enemies, or else to remain neutral. To the Goths, meanwhile, he said that he was moving his troops against the Romans—they should either remain passive or join him. When these things came out, the Romans and Goths decided to form an alliance. Theodoric, king of the Goths, and Aetius Patritius, who was sent to Gaul by the younger Valentinian, joined together and united their armies against Attila. The news irritated Attila extremely, and he proceeded to devastate everything—he razed every town he could take in Gaul, burning the churches, and submitting every last thing to fire and sword. Then the greatest and most terrible battle occurred, in which over one hundred and sixty thousand men are said to have died. In that battle Theodoric, king of the Goths, was killed by the Huns. Attila himself with a vast number of his people fled from the slaughter to their camps. The Goths were prevented by the death of their king from besieging the camp. Thus the decision of Mars seemed balanced equally, for one side lost its king, the other admitted inferiority in battle by letting themselves be shut into their camp. Attila, therefore, not long after this, went back to Pannonia and then, when he had restored the strength of his army, decided to invade Italy rather than Gaul. Therefore, he took great hosts of Huns and other peoples and besieged Aquileia, which was on the Italian border. Attila remained occupied for a long time with this siege, for all of three years were consumed before the city fell. They say that the barbarians had begun to be seized with boredom and to despair of ever taking the city, and they were thinking that the enterprise should be abandoned, when Attila, while riding around the city on a tour of inspection, noticed some storks taking their young off the high towers. Delighted, he said to those who were with him: "Look, fellow soldiers, this is a portent, the birds remove their children and abandon the city they know will be destroyed. Now act with me: attack the walls and we shall gain the victory. This day brings the end of your labors and ample plunder." Excited by his urging, the barbarians seized their weapons and attacked the walls with more vigor than usual. Nor was faith in the omen unimportant. The city which they had besieged for so long, they suddenly took in a short battle. Attila killed the citizens and razed Aquileia to the ground. Then he moved the army on, and filled Vicenza, Verona, Milan, and Pavia with equal terror, killing the townsmen and plundering the houses. The rest of Italy was sapped with fear and expected the terrible conqueror with terrified trembling, but Pope Leo the Great (in those days popes ruled with humility and holiness, not with the intolerable arrogance of today) took upon himself for the sake of all, to go to Attila, and when he reached him in his camp on the Mincio River, the gentle leader softened the victor's savage ferocity by his prayers and persuaded him to leave Italy and return to his own dominions. After this, Attila threatened several times to return and strike the Roman empire again, but his death fortunately intervened. For after he had enjoyed a banquet with indulgence and enthusiasm, while he slept blood flowed from his nostrils and blocked up his respiratory system, killing him instantly.

After the savagery of the Huns, the Vandals' fury burst on Italy. This people had come from the most northern shores of the ocean, had traveled through many lands, and had settled with the permission of the Roman rulers in Pannonia. At the request of Stilico they had gone back from Pannonia across the Rhine almost two years before Rome was sacked by the Goths. They remained some years in Gaul, then crossed into Spain, and then into Africa, to settle around Hippo. Not much later, they occupied Carthage and many other African cities and settled there. Honorius' successor, Valentinian, made an alliance with them, but he was soon killed at Rome by members of his household, and when his successor, Maximus, forced his widow, Eudoxia, to marry him, Eudoxia called on the Vandals for help. Genseric, their king, led them in a naval expedition to Italy, and they entered Rome itself just forty-three years after the Goths had sacked it. No cruelty was missing from their devastation of the city. Citizens were taken captive, the city was looted, the churches too, which the Goths had left intact, were torn apart by the Vandals. Then Genseric led them back to Africa, loaded with spoils and carrying a willing or captive Eudoxia along.

The fourth invader, after the Goths, the Huns, and the Vandals, was Odoacer. He came into Italy at the head of a vast army of Toralingi and Heruli, defeated the patrician Orestes and his army at Pavia, and overthrew Augustulum, the Roman emperor who had succeeded Maioranus and Antemius. Thus he took over not only Italy but Rome itself. Against him, after he had occupied Italy for thirteen years, Zeno, the eastern emperor at Constantinople, sent Theodoric, king of the Goths

[Ostrogths], a man of very high standing in the eastern empire who was to liberate Italy. Theodoric came of those Goths who had remained in their own part of the world and been for some time subjugated by the Huns. He entered Italy with a powerful army and first defeated Odoacer not far from Aquileia, on the Sontius River [near modern Trieste]. He battled him again and more critically near Verona, and finally besieged him at Ravenna, forced him to surrender, and killed him. He took over Rome and Italy, very quickly receiving the willing submission of all the people. His auspicious beginnings led, however, to unfortunate consequences, for, after his victory, the multitude of Goths spread out everywhere and took over the cities that had trusted him as if he had conquered them. The peoples of Italy did not find they had been liberated, but that they had received a new master. And when he died at Ravenna after doing much harm to Italy, he was succeeded by his grandson, Attalaricus, son of his daughter, Amalasunta, who ruled with the boy. When Attalaricus died, Theodasus followed, then Vitiges, then Hildebatus, then Eraricus, and finally Totila, the cruelest of all, became king. All these Gothic kings ruled Italy. But Justinian, emperor of the east (successor to Justin, who had followed Anastius, who succeeded Zeno) sent Belisarius with an army to Italy to fight Theodasus—and the following story was behind it.

Amalasunta, the daughter of Theodoric, having lost her son, Attalaricus, took Theodasus, her cousin, as co-ruler. He was ungrateful and wanted to rule alone, so after a short time, he killed the queen on an island of Lake Vulsinius where the royal palace and treasure were. But this action infuriated the Goths so that they came near revolting. And Justinian, informed of the situation, sent Belisarius to liberate Italy. When he had brought his troops into Italy he first laid siege to Naples, since the Goths held very firmly to this region. He took the place and caused a great massacre of Neapolitans and Goths who had shut themselves into the town from the beginning of the siege.

In the army Theodasus sent against Belisarius there was a military mutiny. It happened in Campania and was provoked by his murder of the queen. The leader, Witiges, a man of extraordinary nobility and ancient, formerly royal, blood, made himself king. Witiges, then, made king by the army, turned his army back to Etruria and Flaminia and, to stabilize his rule, killed Theodasus. He entered Ravenna, took the throne there, and made Amalasunta's daughter, another grandchild of Theodoric, his wife and co-ruler. While the Goths were thus engaged, Belisarius took advantage of the discord to move his army near Rome and to be welcomed by the populace of that city. The fortunes of war after this varied. Witiges had calmed the internal conflicts of the Goths and was able sometimes to beat Belisarius, whom he besieged for a long 537–38 time in Rome, afflicting with such famine the people and the army within that the defense was bitterly hard. But the fortitude of Belisarius overcame all the difficulties and he finally got provisions, attacked the Goths on the march, and had a series of successful battles with them in Etruria and Flaminia. The forces of the Goths were exhausted in the A.D. 552 end, and Witiges, with his wife, was captured at Ravenna and carried off to Constantinople.

All Italy seemed to be liberated, and so it was, but lack of time prevented Belisarius from consolidating his victory. While he had defeated the mass of his enemies with great courage, he scorned in the same spirit of high magnanimity to destroy the rest; and the seeds he left soon brought new fires and disasters on Italy. For the Goths who remained in different regions of Italy and in the north beyond the Po stayed out of the war, and when they knew Belisarius was gone, they got together and organized themselves, electing as king, first Hildebaldus, then Eraricus, and when both of these were killed within two years by traitors, Totila was chosen. He restored the army of the Goths and appeared with vast forces before the Etruscan cities which had declared their independence from the Goths, thanks to the victory of Belisarius. Totila ravaged them with more than the usual barbarian fury. Using both force and cunning, he further subjugated all Italy, which had recently been celebrating its liberation by Belisarius, and imposed a harsher servitude than ever. After a long siege he entered Rome and tore the city apart; he even razed part of the walls, he killed the citizens or sold them, and he devastated the city so completely that, according A.D. 546 to some authors, it lay for more than forty days without a single inhabitant. After more than ten years of his rule of terror, Narses, the eunuch whom Justinian sent with an army, defeated and killed Totila and A.D. 552 destroyed the whole Gothic army by massacre. Such was the tale of Totila, whose savagery earned him the title, scourge of God. He was of the Gothic race though born and educated in Italy—we want to mention here that many authors, misled by confused traditions, have described him otherwise.

Freed at last from the rule of the Goths, Italy was soon overwhelmed by the fury of the Lombards. This people came from the northernmost reaches of Germany, on the edge of the ocean. They left their country led by two chiefs, Ibor and Aionis, seeking new lands for settlement. They defeated the Vandals, the Herules, and the Gepidae in war, as well as other people they encountered. Having changed their homeland so frequently, they settled for a while in Pannonia. From there they were called into Italy at the invitation of Narses. For when Justinian was dead, his successor, Justin, recalled Narses from the administration of Italy with little grace, and Narses, offended, is said to have called the barbarians together, either because he wanted to see them win or just as revenge for the imperial ingratitude. They say Justin's wife, Sophia Augusta, recalled Narses in a humiliating way because he was a eunuch, and that he replied that he was preparing a loom for her that she would not be able to finish weaving in a lifetime. Thus filled with hatred and fear, he insisted that Alboin, the king of the Lombards, should come, always saying that he should leave the poor backcountry of Pannonia for the wealth of Italy. Alboin was persuaded by these pleas, and he got the Lombards and their wives and children ready. To be quite sure he could hold on to Italy, he got two thousand Saxons to join him as well as other barbarian people, moved by the same hope of A.D. 568 finding better homes. So he came with a vast host of men, women, children, and horses along the Adriatic shore, which is an easy path into Italy, and the whole multitude invaded. They spread from there in all directions and settled everywhere. Venice and the cities of the north had been afflicted by the Gothic devastations and recently further weakened by the plague. Thus Alboin was able to make them all submit by threats and by force, almost without discussion. He took Verona, Vicenza, Milan and other cities of the region. Pavia, it is true, required three years of siege but then it surrendered to the Lombards. Thus by the time Alboin died, three and a half years after he had entered Italy, almost all Italy down to Ravenna and Tuscany, except for a few well-fortified castles, was in the power of the Lombards. And there is no doubt that the king, had he lived a few more years, would have subjugated the whole country. But he died in the midst of his victories, at

Verona, killed by a trick of his wife's. The cause of his death is reported as follows.

Before the arrival of the Lombards in Italy a great war erupted between Alboin and Cunemundus, the king of the Gepidae. Both sides brought their troops into battle, and the king of the Gepidae was killed by Alboin in hand-to-hand combat. The Gepidae were laid low and their fortunes reversed, and their king's daughter, Rosamunda, a virgin of great beauty, was taken away by Alboin among the captives; captivated by her beauty he soon took her to wife. Alboin, as was the German way of flaunting a warrior's powers, had had a bowl made of the skull of the enemy he had slain, plated with silver and gold, and he made use of this bowl on solemn occasions when Rosamunda was not present. He used this bowl at a great feast in Verona, but on this occasion the queen was present, and he saw that she was feeling troubled. Being full of drink and of his recent successes, he ordered the queen to come over and drink with her father. The queen's proud heart was anguished, but her manner was affable as she obeyed the king's order. Soon, as if driven by furies to avenge her father, she took two soldiers into her confidence, men she knew were both hostile to the king and entirely enslaved by love for her. She let them into the bedroom while the king slept, and they killed him for her. Then she got into a boat and fled on the Athesis River [Adige] to Ravenna. The Lombards buried Alboin with royal splendor and elected Dephone [more correctly, Clephona], a man of high nobility, their king. He was far inferior to Alboin in virtue and far crueler. And when he died within two years, the Lombards went for almost ten years without a king. Their leaders, scattered across the various cities of Italy, waged war so diligently that there was no need, it seemed, for royal authority. These leaders spread Lombard power from place to place till they had subjugated Italy down to Brindisi and Tarentum, except for the city of Rome which, it appears, never came under their rule.

After ten years they decided to elect a king, and they had a succession of kings down to Desiderius, who was the last Lombard king. As the Goths had first made a capital at Ravenna, the Lombards established their kingdom at Pavia and through their chiefs governed Tuscany, Flaminia, Umbria, Samnia, and other regions of Italy. It is clear that the Lombard people dominated Italy for more than two hundred and four years and had many kings during that time. Eventually, because they were inflicting serious damage on the Roman people and the popes, Charles the king of the Franks, who was later for his deeds known as the Great, was called into Italy by the prayers of Pope Adrian. He fought several fortunate battles with Desiderius, the Lombard king, and finally forced him to surrender at Pavia after a siege. Taking him with his wife and children to France, destroying the other Lombard leaders, he finally lifted this heavy Lombard yoke from the necks of the Italians. For this and other merits, he was given many privileges by Adrian who had called him, and he was called Augustus by Leo, Adrian's successor, who crowned him with the imperial name and office. So the division of the Roman empire which still exists today was started, with some claiming the name of Roman emperor in Greece and some in Gaul and Germany. For a clearer picture of this office, it will not be amiss to say a few words.

The Roman empire was founded and shaped by the Roman people. The later kings never attained such wide domains as to merit the name of empire. The reality and the name of empire emerged under the consuls and dictators and military tribunes, the magistrates of a free people. The empire was created by the armed conquest of almost all Africa and a great part of Asia to beyond the mountains of Armenia and the Caucasus. The conquest of Europe included Spain, Gaul, Greece, Macedonia, Thrace, and other regions, and the Rhine and the Danube became the borders of the empire. The seas, with their islands and their shores, all obeyed Rome, from the Black Sea to Britain. All this was done in four hundred and sixty-five years, by the free people of a single city. Unconquered by external foes, these people were oppressed at last by internal discord and civil war. From that time, they began to have emperors, and the word *imperator*, which had meant arms and forts, came to mean devastating civil wars within the walls. The word still referred to legitimate power, but the actuality was true domination. Surrounded by armed troops, the citizens were subjected by fear. External power, since Germany and certain provinces were added to the empire by the emperors, was somewhat extended, but the strength of the empire at home was diminished by an almost continual reign of terror. While they reigned alone at first, Nerva, the twelfth emperor after Augustus, began the practice of taking a co-ruler: thereafter two emperors ruled as colleagues. Until the time of Constantine, however, the division of functions did not alter the primary authority of the city of Rome. After Constantine moved the capital to Byzantium, it became amply clear that the two emperors were appointed to rule two domains: one, Italy and Rome, the other, the east. The highest power was soon felt to be the power of Constantinople, as those who ruled there often gave to their co-ruler the task of governing Rome and Italy. Once the empires were divided in practice, moreover, they came to be called the eastern and western empires. When the barbarians took over Italy, the western empire ceased to be. After Augustulus was, as we have shown, overthrown by Odoacer, no one—unless it was some tyrant— renewed the name of emperor in Italy and the west until Charlemagne, to whom, as we have said, Pope Leo gave the title.

As is clear from all this, between Augustulus and Charlemagne the empire ceased to exist for almost three hundred years. Odoacer, the king of the Toralingi, ruled Rome and Italy for thirteen years after dethron ing Augustulus. The Goths, who defeated Odoacer under Theodoric, ruled this region for almost sixty years. Narses took it away for a short time. Then the Lombards held Italy for two hundred and four years. After defeating and pursuing the Lombards for almost twenty-five years, Charlemagne, crowned emperor of Rome, restored the forgotten name and dignity of the empire. While it is true that before that time, there were two emperors who governed, one depended on the other and they were associated in the rule of a single empire. After Charles there was no association at all, and nothing remained in common between the eastern and western empires—they were divided in spirit, divided even in their emblems. Before Charlemagne, the emperors had added a golden eagle to the red banner of the ancient Roman people. The successors of Charlemagne, however, displayed a black eagle on a golden banner, a symbol never used by the Roman people. The process by which the position of emperor was passed on was also new, and some thought that the old series of emperors and the old system of succession should be maintained while others, though without legal basis, approved the new model of election by the pope as an expedient procedure. And it seems clear to us from the evidence that the Roman people at the pope's behest or the pope himself without any orders from the Roman people created the emperor. It is known that this task be- longed [in antiquity] to no authority higher than the Roman people

61

itself. In the earlier period, the papal position itself depended greatly on the emperor, and no one ruled [the church] unless, after election by the senate, the clergy, and the people of Rome, he was approved by the imperial authority. We leave these questions, however, to the judgment of those considered more learned in church law.

Charlemagne himself, whatever the means of his election, certainly suited both divine and human plans. He was truly worthy of the high position of emperor. He deserved his name for greatness not only for his deeds but for the many virtues that were in him. He was most strong and most merciful, gave high justice and showed equally firm self-control, and besides his great glory in war, he was zealous for literature and learning. He came three times to Italy with his armed host. The A.D. 773–74 first time he subdued Desiderius, king of the Lombards, near Pavia. The second time he marched against Araisus, the duke of Benevento, and went as far as Capua. The third time he restored to Rome Pope Leo A.D. 800 who had been unjustly expelled by the Romans. That was the time he gained the imperial title and position. In addition to all this, Charlemagne waged war most successfully to overcome the Huns, the Saxons, the Acquitainians, and others, fighting himself and employing his sons and generals.

His successors, who found they possessed the part of Italy which had been the Lombard kingdom, called themselves kings of Italy. Among them were Pipin, the son of Charlemagne, and Bernard and Lothair, his grandsons, and Louis, the son of Lothair. Lothair and Louis were not only kings of Italy, but also Roman emperors. But these and other successors of Charlemagne governed the Roman empire first from Gaul and later from Germany, until the time of Arnulf, the king of Germany, who was the seventh successor and heir of Charles and the last emperor of his line.

After that the empire was far away in Germany, and few of the emperors lived in Italy permanently, though many visited as they were supposed to do and brought armies. Little by little, the Italian cities began to want liberty and to acknowledge the empire's authority nominally rather than in practice. The city of Rome and the name of Rome received respect for their ancient power rather than for their present awesomeness. . . . Meanwhile those Italian cities that had survived the various floods of barbarians began to grow and flourish and to regain their original independence. In Tuscany, however, many cities and large and important towns had perished between the time of the first Roman wars and this new era: Caere, Tarquinii, Populonium, and Luna, which had once been great centers along the western sea coast and in the Mediterranean region; Veii, which, as we have said, had withstood a ten-year siege from Rome; likewise Rusellae and Capena and Falerii. Clusium and Faesulae were barely alive. Florence, some say, was razed by Attila the Hun, others say by Totila, and they report that it was (after a long period) restored by Charlemagne. It seems clear to us, however, that Attila the Hun was never in Tuscany at all, and that he never crossed to this side of the river Mincius, which flows from Lake Garda to Padua. Totila, king of the Goths, did, as we have shown, fall fiercely on the Tuscan cities after Belisarius had briefly liberated them from the Goths. I am convinced, therefore, that a confusion of names has led some authors to take Totila for Attila. I think it likely that desire for vengeance burned in the heart of Totila and made him want to destroy this city to prevent any new defection, for it was here that somewhat earlier the thousands of Goths under Radagasus had been killed. Because of this painful memory angering him, he would have wished to destroy Florence, a city that stood like a monument to the defeat of his people in Etruria. If so, Florence lay in ruins for two hundred years, from Totila to Charlemagne; but it would be very surprising indeed, if while the city lay empty for so long, there were still plenty of people around it. For we cannot think that Charlemagne brought new inhabitants in from Rome, since that city had been recently involved in trouble and so much afflicted by earlier devastations as well that it needed to gain new inhabitants and could not possibly send them forth. About that time, in fact, it is recorded that, for lack of Romans to inhabit Ostia, colonists were brought there from Sardinia. I think, therefore, that Totila had indeed done great harm to Florence and killed many citizens and torn down the walls, but I don't believe that he destroyed the city altogether nor that it was entirely without inhabitants for all that time. I see still standing the rich and large temple of Mars and other buildings from before the period of Totila, and when I consider these unharmed remains I cannot believe that the whole city was destroyed nor that it was totally uninhabited for so long. More likely, I think, the walls were restored by Charlemagne and he recalled the nobility, which, when the

63

fortifications of the city were destroyed, had fortified capacious castles on their estates. I think, therefore, that the city was put back together as a city after being in a sense dismembered. Rather than refounded, in my opinion, it was essentially restored.

I have mentioned the Tuscan cities that perished. The main ones which reëmerged after being long swamped by calamity were Pisa, Florence, Perugia, and Siena. The Pisans found they could dominate the sea coast with their fleet because theirs was the only Tuscan maritime center that remained after Tarquinia, Luna, and Populonium disappeared. The Florentines prospered by cultivating their land. The Perugians gained great power because of their fertile land and their strategic location. Siena stood high for the splendor of her urban amenities and her excellent old families, and she attracted the resources freed by the destruction of her near neighbors, Rusellae and Populonium. Arezzo was next door, and almost surpassed all other cities by the quality of her soil and the size of her territory, but she lay between Florence and Perugia and was held down by the power of these two sturdy neighbors. Cortona, for instance, was for a long time not an independent city but a dependency of Arezzo; she only recently reacquired her ancient autonomy. Next after these cities came Lucca, Volterra, Pistoia, Orvieto, Viterbo; for Sutrium and Nepete and all of Tuscany in the vicinity of Rome had been badly hit, first by the good fortune of Rome and then by her sufferings. These are the cities worth noting of those which survived the long period of storm and danger. But Perugia was the oldest power among them. It was named after one of the Etruscan tribes and was, even before the Roman empire, the first, second, or third of the capital cities of Etruria. Neither Chiusi nor Arezzo, which were also ancient capitals, ever stood so high. Pisa was not a great power in ancient times and seems not to have had much standing in the eyes of the ancients. All her strength has developed since the time of Charlemagne, but far more nobly at sea than on land. Her oldest origins are not native but Greek. As long as the Etruscans flourished by sea and land, Pisa enjoyed no greatness. When our maritime cities were ruined, however, she was able to dominate. It is clear that Siena is a newer city, for old authors say that the Florentine and Aretine lands ran right up to her walls. Later she grew and flourished, with splendor and magnificence to rival any. Arezzo and Chiusi and Volterra are the oldest. We have said that they belonged to Tyrrhenia, which flourished in Italy even before the Trojan War. Cortona, according to certain writers, was founded by the Pelasgians even before the arrival of the Tyrrhenians, but it was soon captured by them, and they expelled the Pelasgians. Viterbo was an offshoot of Arezzo's, according to the ancient traditions of both towns.

There were alliances among these towns, and Florence, Perugia, and Lucca were mutually very friendly. This was so, I think, because the territories of Pistoia and Arezzo separated them, and there could be none of the border disputes which commonly bring trouble. Siena and Pisa, divided by the territory of Volterra, also enjoyed mutual peace and friendship. But these alliances shifted frequently because of the ambitions of certain groups and the fears of others. For people are quick to embrace arguments that suit their wishes. During the first period after the barbarians had stopped, our cities prospered in peace, I believe, but as soon as they had begun to grow big, with no fear of external enemies, they started to act envious and competitive.

The many disputes between the popes and the emperors brought plentiful tinder to our local quarrels and fights. For the empire which began with Charlemagne and was founded mainly for the protection of the Roman church, once it was, as we have explained, transferred to Germany, fell into the hands of successors whose purpose in life seemed to be the persecution and overthrow of the popes. Where help had been looked for, there was the bitterest harm. The cause of the fighting was essentially that the church tried to hold on to certain powers of jurisdiction while the empire tried to usurp them on the basis of its ancient prerogatives. Against the emperors, the popes used decretals and powers of censure, which at that time were their only arms, and urged cities and princes to refuse obedience to the empire. Threatening heavy punishments if people obeyed the papal decrees, the emperors made themselves feared by the use of arms. The dispute remained unsettled, and people shifted from one side to the other.

Over this great issue there was so much violent dispute in Italy that finally not only cities but peoples living within the same walls were divided into parties. Two parties appeared in Tuscany: one favored the pope and was opposed to the emperors, the other was devoted to the imperial name. But the side which, as we said, opposed the emperors was essentially composed of those who were concerned about the liberty of peoples: they considered it degrading for Germans and barbarians to rule over Italians under the pretext of the Roman name. The other faction consisted of men devoted to the imperial name and forgetful of the liberty and glory of their ancestors—men who preferred to serve foreigners rather than be ruled by their own people. The struggle of these factions caused a vast amount of harm. For public affairs involved more greed and rivalry than good and honest government, and in private life there was more and more hatred and enmity. Thus the disease took hold of private and public life at the same time—first it was nourished by dispute, then it worsened and became deadly hatred, finally it burst out in arms and slaughter and the devastation of cities.

This fever reached its height in Tuscany during the time of Frederic II. His grandfather, whose name was also Frederic, had expelled the pope and persecuted many places friendly to the papal party; after a long siege he had laid low Milan and had done much harm to Parma and Piacenza, while setting up four false counter-popes. Frederic II's father, Henry, had been no less a foe of the church. It was Frederic II, however, who brought the full impact of civil war to Tuscany. On his father's side, he was of Swabian [German] origin, but on his mother's he was Sicilian. He rose to rule jointly with his mother Constance in Sicily and received much support in this position from the pope. As soon as he was called to be emperor, however, after his rival, Otto, was removed, he, like his father and grandfather, warred with great destructiveness against the papal throne. He kept up the battle for thirty-three years (as long as he ruled) and persecuted three popes in succession: Honorius, Gregory, and Innocent. When he was finally deposed by the Council of Lyon from both imperial and royal positions, he did not, like his ancestor, renounce his faults, humiliate himself before the pope, and return to the fold. Instead he showed contempt for the council and its decretals. He not only tried to strengthen all the dominions he still held but even did what he could to occupy neighboring regions. Since he ruled in Sicily and Apulia, as we have said, through his mother's line, and wished also to extend his power, he put pressure on every one of the cities of Tuscany, hoping to empty them of enemies and make them into firm allies. He not only tried to do this for the moment but to guarantee the future. For he had plenty of sons, and since the human mind is all too self-flattering and credulous, he thought he could arrange a firm basis of power for them in Italy. He thought all he needed was to get rid of opposition in Tuscany and to make sure his friends and followers totally controlled those cities. For this purpose he invaded Tuscany with an army, demanded aid from the cities for himself and his sons, warned some and attacked others outright, trying to make them all expel all members of the opposing faction. Nor was it difficult to persuade them, for their heads were hot enough and there were lively enmities among the citizens already. The result was a great number of internal battles, citizens slaughtered and houses burned and other accompaniments of civil war. The same things were recorded in almost every city. The exiles, moreover, did not go quietly away; rather they occupied certain outposts belonging to their cities and from these spread war, slaughter, and rapine through the countryside. Frederic himself, the real author of the evils, would then, on the request of the cities or of his own will, mount sieges against the rebellious places which he claimed had risen to trouble the empire and injure his majesty. If some of his friends were unable to expel the opposing faction from their town, he would declare the whole town his enemy and fall on it with fire and sword. The dispute of factions which had long led to increasing civil disturbance and contempt of the rights of citizens in Tuscan towns, now, through Frederic's fury, issued in slaughter and bloodshed, expulsion of citizens, and uttter devastation. He introduced great cruelty into the violent struggle. When certain men of the other faction were captured and sent to him in Apulia, for instance, whether to satisfy his own anger or to please his followers, he first mutilated them by the loss of eyes and limbs and then killed them with various tortures. The vengeance for such actions was not long delayed, for both he and his sons got their lesson from the faction he had persecuted in Tuscany when it gained strength to overthrow his family and, to its glory, was able to make the guilty pay with their lives.

The following speech attributed by Bruni to Giano della Bella shows with unusual clarity what he believed was essential to the liberty of a civic constitution. The essence of liberty is the rule of law, the inability of a faction—be they the noble, the rich, or the poor—to attack violently other citizens and change their lives without regard for judges and legal punishments.

Book Four

Speech of Giano della Bella *

1292 One who tried to stop the disorder and decline of the [Florentine] Republic was Giano della Bella, a man who showed great courage and wisdom during that stormy time. He was descended from well-known men, but was himself of middling station and very popular. This leader spoke separately with many people about the power of the nobility and the excessive passivity that was destroying the people, for they kept letting individuals suffer injustice without recognizing that they were all as a group being subjected to shameful servitude. *He said it was stupid to think one would not be personally hit, when after the first people were oppressed, the force would strike others too, spreading like fire. Resistance was necessary now, and the evil must not be allowed to grow. For though the disease had been allowed to develop, it was not yet so established that it could not be healed. But if they paid little attention and everyone looked to others to start, matters would reach the point where they would seek a cure in vain.* By saying these things over and over he fired up men's minds and stiffened their resolution to take the Republic in hand. The popular classes arose and supported the effort, going forth to take the matter to the government. When the people were thus gathered at last, and different opinions were being voiced by different persons, Giano della Bella arose and spoke most fully, addressing the crowd in the following manner:

"I have always been of the same mind, good citizens of wise judgment, and the more I think about the Republic, the more I am convinced that we must either check the pride of the powerful families or lose our liberty altogether. Things have reached the point, I think, where *your tolerance and your liberty are no longer compatible.* I think too

* Extract from L. Bruni, *History of Florence*, Book 4.

69

that no one of sound judgment can be in doubt which of the two is to be preferred. Though I well know how dangerous it is to talk of this, I am not afraid. *A good citizen, I think, ignores his own comfort when his country needs his advice, and he does not cut down his public statements to suit his private convenience.* Therefore I shall speak my mind freely. It seems to me that the liberty of the people consists in two things: the laws and the judges. When the power of these two things prevails in the city over the power of any individual citizen, then liberty is preserved. But when some people scorn the laws and the judges with impunity, then it is fair to say that liberty is gone. For in what sense are you free in relation to people who, with no fear of judgment, can do to you and yours whatever violence they please? Therefore think what your condition is, and consider the crimes of the nobility: tell me, any one of you, whether you think the city is free or whether it has been for some time in subjection. The answer will be easier for those who have a neighbor in the city or in the nearby country who is one of this circle of powerful men. For what do we possess, that they don't want to take? And what have they wanted to take that they have not promptly tried to take, and what don't they feel perfectly justified in taking, whether by legal or illegal ways? Our very bodies, if we will only admit it, are no longer free: remember the citizens who have been beaten, chased out of their homes, the numerous examples of arson, rape, wounding, and killing in these last years. The doers of these evil deeds are so well-known and publicly recognized that obviously they either don't care to conceal their crimes or they are unable to; they stay visible; we see men who deserve prison and torture strutting around the city with a crowd of armed retainers, terrifying us and the officials. Would anyone tell me that this is liberty? *What is the difference from tyrants who kill, expropriate, take whatever they want, and fear no judges?* And if one man destroys liberty in other states, what shall we think of ours where a great number do it all at once? We have certainly been for some time subjected, believe me, and under the empty name of liberty, we suffer shameful servitude. You may object, however, and say: no one doubts that what you say is true, but what is the cure—don't give us nothing but complaints. To this I say that we can shake this servitude from our backs with no great difficulty. For if the destruction of laws and judges is the cause of our loss of liberty, let us expel those criminals and our

70

liberty will be restored. If you wish to be free, therefore, (*which you should wish as much as you wish to live*) reinstate those two things to primary authority, and protect them with all your strength and zeal. You have many laws against violence, killing, theft, assault, and other crimes. These laws must be renewed against the powerful, I say, and *new measures must be taken for, as everyone knows, the perversity of men has increased from day to day.* First of all, I think, the punishments for crime must be increased when the powerful commit them. *Surely if you want to tie up both a powerful man and a puny one, you don't use the same kind of bonds. You tie the lion with chains, but the weak with ropes and thongs.* Punishments are the bonds of law, and likewise must be greater for great and powerful men. The ones we have don't hold them now. It seems we must stipulate also that family and household are to be included in punishments. *We should consider clan and kinsmen as complicit in the crime, for their support enables the criminal to proceed.* Two things usually prevent our judges from doing their job: difficulty in proving the case and lack of power to bring the criminals to justice. For they frighten witnesses from testifying against the powerful men, and this fear destroys the whole judgment in one stroke; and even if proofs are given, the executive is afraid to act. If you do not change these things, you will have no republic. *What are the best of laws if the judgments are made void?* So you must first of all, I think, take care of the problem of witnesses; in the case of powerful men general public knowledge must be sufficient evidence of guilt. Thus when a crime has been committed, and neighbors for some distance say that a certain powerful man committed it, the judge need not find other proofs, which will fade away because of men's fear of the powerful one; but public knowledge, as we have said, will suffice to convict. As to the second problem, putting the judges' decision into action, please pay attention—I think it is a greater matter than people realize, depending less on the officials than on the will and vigor of the public. For if the people really wants as it should to keep its power in the Republic, the decisions of the judges against the powerful persons will readily be carried out. But if the people is full of respect for others and considers them superior to itself, this will chill both the judges and the officials. All this was foreseen long ago when the Gonfaloniere di Giustizia was created, but I marvel at the diminution of his reputation and power. *It is stupid to be surprised, however, when the people itself is negligent and cold, that the people's vicars are overcome and are not brave.* And still at that time so much was omitted that the constitution was only begun rather than perfected. So the authority of the Gonfaloniere di Giustizia needs to be very much strengthened. He should, above all, I think, have at his command, not a thousand armed men as heretofore, but four thousand, to be recruited in turn from the whole people. I also think, the Gonfaloniere should reside in the same building as the priors, so that he will personally hear the complaints of the citizens and provide for the needs of the Republic. The Gonfaloniere will not remain at home whether because he is slow to hear or because, as we know has happened, he is privately persuaded to slow down his work. A third provision which was not made at that time seems to me necessary—that none of the powerful, even if they become members of a guild, can be raised to become priors, and thus put into a position to help criminals and to impede justice. *Their existing power is sufficiently burdensome to us, without adding the armor of public authority.* In this way if you resuscitate the laws, restore punishments, empower the judges to deal with powerful men, you will force them to cease from tyranny. And if they go on unrestrained, you will have to exterminate them with iron and fire as you would incurably sick limbs, putting aside that excessive and extreme patience of yours which is leading you with eyes and ears open into slavery. I have said what I think are the measures needed by the Republic and are necessary for our liberty. If they were difficult and expensive and involved a lot of labor, I would tell you that they had to be carried out anyway because of their great usefulness. As they are easy, however, and lie in your hands, who is so fallen that he would rather serve in pain and humiliation than be equal to others in right and honor? Our ancestors were not willing to serve even the Roman emperors, though the title of the nation and the dignity of the people made servitude less dishonorable. Are you willing to go on serving the vilest of men? Our ancestors bore death and wounds and loss of goods and carried on almost infinite struggles for the sake of dignity and power. You, out of fear and laziness, have submitted to tyrants who ought to be your subjects. It seems that a people, that is a vast multitude of strong men, who have conquered by their military art all their neighbors and have smashed a thousand enemy battalions, would be ashamed to fear this or that family at home and patiently to let their pride make us slaves. I shall stop now, so that my momentum does not carry me too far. For I feel too much reverence to chide the people, yet when I remember your degenerate passivity I cannot be silent and calm. I only ask you to think of your own liberty and your welfare."

Book Twelve

In the midst of anxiety about wars that were going on and wars that threatened to come,* a new and previously unheard of movement sprang up all over Italy. People in every town suddenly started wearing white and, after performing certain religious rites, walking in solemn procession to other nearby towns. They looked like long rows of white-washed soldiers, praying aloud for peace and love as they went. It was an amazing and almost incredible sight. The pilgrimage took about ten days, and the pilgrims lived mostly on bread and water. For a time one saw no other form of dress in the towns. The pilgrims were able to enter foreign places freely, even though the cities involved might only recently have made peace. No one seemed to want to try any tricks on the pilgrims, and no one harmed a visitor. For about two months enemy towns were in a state of tacit truce, while people went to foreign cities and other people visited their own. Everywhere amazing hospitality prevailed, everywhere they found a kind welcome. But how it all began is unknown. It certainly spread through northern Italy starting at the Alps. The first people to come to Florence were the Luccans. Such ardent religious feeling flared up at the sight of them that the very people who had been most scornful when they had heard of it became the first to change their apparel and, seized by divine inspiration it seemed, to wander forth in like manner. The Florentine people divided itself into fourths. Two of these parts went to Arezzo in a vast crowd of men, women and children, and the other parts went to other places. Wherever the army of the whitened ones went, the inhabitants would follow their example and move on. Thus from northern Italy the pil-

* Bruni has been describing the expanding warlike power of Milan in the late fourteenth century. See Map 3.

grimage spread to Tuscany, from Tuscany to Umbria, from Umbria to the Sabine and Picene regions and the Marches. Carrying on from there, the movement reached the farthest coasts of Italy, and it appeared among every people.

While religion thus occupied people's minds, no one worried about the threat of war. But after the ardor of the whitened ones had died down, people went back to their previous fears. It seemed a dangerous situation to have Pisa, Siena, and Perugia already in the power of Milan, and the Uberti castles closing off the Tuscan region on the other side. Uguccione, moreover, lord of Cortona, appeared to have abandoned his Florentine alliance and also to have attached himself to Milan. The sign of this was his making some new and intolerable claims on Florence: refusing to allow the transport of crops by the people of Montepulci through his territory; and closing by means of barriers the water passages through the marshes known as the Chiane, so that no transport could occur without his permission. Lucca, the neighbor of Pisa, seemed, spontaneously or for fear, more inclined than ever to ally with Milan. She refused to renew her alliance with Florence. That was the situation at the onset of the year 1400, though no action was taken at the beginning of that year to deal with anything but the doubts concerning Uguccione of Cortona.

Montanina, a fortress located on the farthest border of the Aretine region and close to Cortona, belonged to certain noble friends of Uguccione who were considered likely to do anything he wanted. Its location meant that it could do us a lot of harm if an attack began from there. If it were on our side, on the other hand, it could threaten Cortona. Certain Aretines, therefore, were commissioned to take Montanina by a trick. People appearing to be a party of hunters called to those inside the fort, who came out to talk fearing nothing; thereupon the fort was suddenly invaded, the party gave a smoke signal, and there was a rush of more numerous attackers. Thus Montanina was taken away from its garrison, and fear of attack from that side subsided.

Next they wanted to remove the barriers and obstacles that had been placed in the Chiane. They sent Fabiano Bostoli to Fojano to do this job, and at the same time had Niccolo Albergotti bring cavalry to the spot in case Uguccione should come out to give any trouble. If so, Albergotti was to attack and kill him without hesitation. Uguccione in

75

fact did not venture forth to stop the action and did not even dare leave Cortona. So the obstacles were removed without enemy resistance and the fortress built by Uguccione beside the marshes was burned.

At the same time about four hundred of Galeazzo's horsemen entered the region of Casentino, where the towns were embroiled in quarrels and where, as we have shown earlier, there were plenty of pretexts for war. War was also kindled between the Bolognese and Astorre, the lord of Faenza, concerning the castle of Salerolo which had been recently seized. Galeazzo was thought to be the hidden author of this conflict, for Alberigo, a dedicated ally of Galeazzo, had formed an alliance with the Bolognese against Astorre of Faena, and by combining forces, he was able to make a serious attack on him.

From the beginning of the year there were some terrifying signs of plague. It flared up terribly in the summer, with heavy losses among both men and women of all ages. The only remedy known was flight. Many citizens, therefore, migrated to Bologna. Even in the half-empty houses of the city, however, more than 30,000 people died.

In the same year there were many other new developments in Tuscany. In Lucca, Paulo Guinisi seized control, and Uguccione of Cortona, of whom there were doubts, departed this life. Count Roberto di Poppi, an ally who had openly defected from Florence, also died. All these events had their consequences. Cortona fell into the hands of Francesco of Casale, a relative of Uguccione, who was certainly a more desirable and more peaceful ruler. Roberto di Poppi, regretting in his last hours that he had broken with Florence, recommended his son to the Florentines and appointed a number of our citizens to advise him. The youthful ruler, therefore, was back in favor and was well received and kindly treated by the Florentines. Many things were done in Casentino for his preservation and the safety of his castles. Paolo Guinisi, after he had taken over the government of Lucca, wanted to be thought neutral. He was known, nonetheless, to learn towards Milan, for Galeazzo had immediately sent him congratulations on his coup, and promised him great things. When the Florentines tried to renew the Luccan alliance, he refused the offer while making conciliatory speeches.

In the same year there was a major conspiracy against the Republic which, though soon revealed, brought about considerable upheaval in the city. For a large number of Florentines had gone to Bologna because of the plague, and had found there all kinds of people, including some hostile to the current government. Soon there were talks and arrangements starting, and the number of those interested grew into a multitude. Their plan was to invade the Republic, to oust the present regime, and to take over. They had already chosen priors and other officials whom they planned to install immediately, some from their own number, some from the sort of men who don't belong to either party. All was planned and the time for action was at hand when Samminiato de' Ricci, one of the conspirators, in trying to win over Salvestro Adimari, told him the whole thing and named the conspirators. When Salvestro had heard it all, he was in doubt and unsure what to do; he left Samminiato and went to Bartolomeo Valori, to whom he told the whole business; Valori immediately reported it to the government. Thus the conspiracy was revealed. Some as a result were executed, while many others, being absent, were condemned to exile.

Toward the end of that year, Giovanni Bentivoglio of Bologna, a man of great distinction and popular favor in that city, took over its government. When the news reached Florence, orators were sent at once to congratulate him in the name of the Republic. In order to make a finer impression, the orators who were sent were from the [Committee of] Ten, hence men of considerable position in the government—this was an unprecedented gesture. When they arrived in Bologna these orators greeted and congratulated Bentivoglio with many joyful words, and they offered all the support of Florence for the maintenance of his power and position. Galeazzo of Milan sent his own ambassadors to do the same thing, for both sides were anxious to gain the new lord's alliance. It seemed much might be done through alliance with him, because of the greatness of his power and the strategic location of his domain—things which both sides tried eagerly to gain.

While this was the situation, a new hope dawned and new intrigues began. The background was as follows: the Emperor Charles, whose visit to Italy we have described earlier, left two heirs, Vincislas and Sigismund. Vincislas was the older and had been named Caesar before the death of his father. Charles considered him the successor to the imperial throne, and well before his own death, passed onto him the crown of Bohemia. When Charles died, Vincislas had long been crown prince, therefore, but he had in no way at all shown himself worthy of it. He neither visited Italy nor took up any of the responsibilities attaching to the imperial crown. He was renowned for two qualities only: total dedication to the pursuit of pleasure and a knack for accumulating money. Everything else he neglected, to live a lazy and dissolute life. Since this was his record and since the name and authority of the Roman emperor were being diminished by this claim to the succession, the imperial electors held a meeting and agreed, with the assent of other leading nobles, to remove him and to make Robert, the duke of Bavaria, a man of great promise and high standing, the new emperor.

Thus chosen, Robert sent orators to Italy to seek the acceptance and favor of the Apostolic See. Controversy had lingered and still existed, for not all the nobility and people in Germany rejected Vincislas, but some still considered him emperor. Robert had been newly elected, however, and his reputation was very good. He was expected to do great things, and the Florentines began to pay attention to him. Surrounded on all sides by territories and cities dominated in actions and policy by the duke of Milan, they were in fear of his great power and of the vast number of his troops. They were driven to look for forces that might come from a distance. They paid great honor to the imperial orators at Rome and then sent ambassadors to Germany, urging that he come himself to Italy and offering him Florentine help and money. He listened willingly to the Florentine ambassadors, with his mind mainly on the money and full of hopes of what he could do with it.

The following year upheavals ensued in Bologna that were greater than ever. Bentivoglio had continued the war against Astorre of Faenza which the Bolognese had begun earlier. He had used in this war the help of both Florence and Milan, and later of Count Alberigo, who had long maintained a bitter feud with Astorre. Astorre, on the other hand, had allies of his own, especially Carlo Malatesta, a powerful captain and famous warrior, and so peace was finally made between Bologna and Astorre. This peace infuriated Alberigo, for though he was an ally of Bologna, peace was made against his will. Calling this action treachery and fraud, he turned his anger and indignation against Bentivoglio. He began favoring the Bolognese exiles, gave them aid, and urged them to start a new war on the lord of Bologna. Alberigo had a cavalry of about twelve hundred men. A combination of this cavalry and the exiles invaded Bolognese territory, and various towns soon began to defect, till the whole territory was filled with upheaval and with fear. The lord himself had been inclined by his own feelings and by the clash of factions towards Florence, but the power of Milan had threatened, and he had chosen, therefore, to be neutral. He had not been willing to renew the Florentine alliance. Pressed now by war and terror, however, he was driven to ask the Florentines for assistance in the form of an army. The Florentines, in order to commit him more to their side, responded by sending not only the army he asked for but also Bernardone, their commander-in-chief. War in the Bolognese territory was now completely overt, with the other side receiving overt help from Galeazzo.

In Tuscany there was no open war; but the power of Milan was expanding from day to day at such a rate that it seemed he must do something finally. More and more in this situation the Florentines put their hope in the arrival of the newly elected Emperor Robert, hoping his passage would more or less end the power of Milan. For there was great hatred between them, and Robert had written publicly to cities and kings that Galeazzo had tried to kill him with poison. Finally the Florentines, relying on these hopes, agreed to give Robert a large grant of money for coming into Italy. They promised 200,000 ducats, of which they agreed to hand over a portion before he set out, and the rest after he arrived in Italy and marched into the lands of Galeazzo. While embassies and messages were frequently exchanged, he began to prepare his journey and the Florentines to arrange for the funds. To pay the enormous sum, Giovanni Bicci, a wise and honest man of the highest credit among merchants, was sent to Venice. He showed perfect loyalty and diligence in the way he handled everything.

The word spread throughout Italy that on the Rhine a great army was being mobilized and would soon cross the Alps with the emperor. Everywhere people were tense and expectant. There were equally serious preparations going on in Milan. Knights were gathered, money was collected, cities and towns were provisioned, and guards were assigned to block land and water routes of access. While people's minds were turned toward the new prince's arrival, at Pistoia a civil war broke out. Not only within the city but also in the countryside of Pistoia there were two bitterly hostile factions. Ricciardo Cancellieri, a Pistoian knight and leader of the opposition, was suspected of fomenting revolution. His enemies grew violent and his friends protected him, until at last, partly for fear of his adversaries in the city, and partly to take advantage of the support he had, he occupied a castle in the Apennines called Sambuca. And he defeated all those who attacked it. Soon forces joined him, not only from Pistoia but also from the territory of Bologna and Modena. For these are near neighbors, and the factions had friends and followers there. People in Pistoia itself were so divided and had such conflicting wishes that there was great danger to the city. A large force of infantry and cavalry, therefore, was put on guard around the city. Garrisons were placed around Sambuca, moreover, that hindered the movements of those within. Ricciardo, however, had such tactical foresight, and his followers were so bold in his service, that he defeated his besiegers again and again and put them to flight. The holders of Sambuca harassed and raided the villages of the region by day and by night. And all this greatly enhanced the renown of Ricciardo.

The Emperor Robert's arrival was several times expected and several times delayed. He finally arrived at Trent late in the fall. When he arrived there, he wanted at once to fulfill the conditions which would bring him money, so he invaded the area of Brixen. That city belonged to Galeazzo of Milan, and the agreement with the Florentines was that they would give him money when he entered on Milanese territory. The town of Trent and Brixen are near neighbors and their territories mingle around Lago di Garda. To meet the new emperor in this region, Galeazzo sent a number of captains with large armies against him. Indeed Galeazzo had built the very best army of Italians. When the Italian knights encountered the German and the skirmishing began, it was amazing how superior the Italians seemed to be. For the Germans had light and simple reins that were suitable for speed and distance but useless for turning the horse in a small space or maneuvering in battle. The Italians held their horses close and had them trained to shift quickly and turn in a crowded space. These bridles allowed the Italians to hurt the enemy and then return quickly to their own ranks, also to shift course in mid-charge. The Italian knight, moreover, had arms that protected him well and so he feared no danger, while the German was poorly armed. Many of them had only chest coverings and cuirasses with javelins strapped on. But you cannot press a lance if you are lightly armed, and they had to put their faith in throwing javelins rather than in thrusting home a lance. Soon, therefore, the Italians began looking upon them with scorn and disdain, and a small number of Italian horsemen dared to attack even a large group of Germans. Finally assaulting the emperor's camp in full force, they put such pressure on the Germans that they were terrified. With heavy losses they were forced to yield and retreat with their banners; the emperor, seeing his people demoralized and fearful, returned to Trent. Because things seemed to be going badly, moreover, one leader accused another. The bishop of Cologne and Leopold, the duke of Austria, departed, taking home most of the army. The emperor remained in Trent, alone and disgraced, and he hardly knew what he should do. To return across the Alps after launching an unsuccessful campaign would bring shame and loss of reputation, but to stay in Italy with such puny forces seemed pointless. At this point Francesco da Carrara and other leaders who were around him, as well as the Florentine representatives, urged him to move on to Padua, where, they said, he would be able to save his reputation, for there were still great possibilities in Italy. Though he really wanted to go back across the Alps, he was moved by shame and hope and decided to follow their advice. He left Trent, stopped in Treviso, and journeyed from there to Padua.

There a new Florentine embassy arrived to see him, consisting of four Florentine knights of some of the greatest noble families: Rinardo Gianfigliazzi, Maso degli Albizzi, Filippo Corsini, and Tommaso Sacchetti. They brought six hundred well-trained Italian knights, led by Sforza and Baldasar of Modena. Welcomed by the emperor, the ambassadors talked about ways of mending matters, but they discovered that he was not very bold or confident of himself. For it was his opinion, he said, that neither he nor the Florentines had the forces to overthrow Milan. They would absolutely have to win the alliance and aid of the pope and the Venetians. And then he demanded so much money that it was clear he intended to throw no resources of his own into the affair; everything was to be done with Florentine money.

When the ambassadors saw this, they decided to send back Maso degli Albizzi and Andrea Vettori (who was among the earlier Florentine ambassadors to the emperor) to Florence to report what they had seen and heard. The situation could not be easily enough communicated in writing. When they returned, therefore, and described it all to the council of citizens, everyone was greatly disturbed. For to do what the em-

81

peror demanded seemed almost impossible, but if the emperor went home, the enemy would remain as real a threat as ever and with swollen reputation and pride in his victory, it seemed he would stop at nothing. After discussion in the council, therefore, they decided that all measures should be taken to keep the emperor in Italy. Through the ambassadors who were still in Padua, they promised him, if he would stay in Italy and try as best he could to wage war during the winter, a great reinforcement of Italian forces and a great sum of money besides. In spring, however, he must enter on the enemy's lands and make war on him. He must promise also not to make peace or truce or any kind of agreement with the enemy without the agreement and consent of Florence. Meanwhile, they assured him, their representatives would make every effort to get the pope and the Venetians to ally with him, which would not be too hard, they said, if the war was going well.

The ambassadors said all this to the emperor, and lengthy negotiations followed. It did not seem quite honorable to oblige himself to fulfill these conditions, and they were also somewhat difficult to fulfill. Controversy arose concerning the money promised him for coming south, of which he claimed the second part was due now. The sum promised was ninety thousand florins, which, he said, ought to be handed over to him before anything more was expected. After that perhaps there should be discussion of further arrangements. The Florentines said they had promised money on condition, and that the emperor had not fulfilled that condition. They did not owe money to him, and furthermore, they had already spent twenty-five thousand of this sum on assisting him. After almost a month of this kind of quarreling, payment was definitely refused him, and the emperor, insulted, decided to leave. He sent his forces ahead to Treviso by land, and went off himself to Venice, both to see that marvelous city and to win support there if he could. He was received with great magnificence, and everything was done which they usually do for princely visitors. The next day he began to speak of his situation, and bitterly to attack the Florentines. He claimed that they had begged and pushed him into coming too hastily and at the wrong time to Italy, and now they were refusing to honor their promises. Thus cheated and disappointed, he was being forced to return to Germany and to suffer damage to his reputation.

There were two Florentine ambassadors in Venice at the time, Filippo

Corsini and Rinaldo Gianfigliazzi, wise and well-conducted men who were there because they meant to deal with just this. In reply to his statements, they said it was like bitter death to them, to have to contradict the things the prince had said, but in truth their listeners should excuse them, first because they had not spoken freely but only when forced to, and second because they were speaking only in self-defense, not to accuse others. The disagreement and quarreling had all turned on the question of payment. They admitted that a promise had been given but said one must understand what had been the basis of the promise, for on this hung the judgment of right and wrong in the case. Before he even left home, the emperor had required and received more than half the money they had promised him, for the preparation and equipping of his army, and that had all been given him on faith. About this the emperor could and should not in any way blame them. The remainder of the sum was promised on a condition, that he enter with a powerful army on the hostile territory of Galeazzo. Of these two conditions (be it said with all courtesy) neither had been fulfilled. For he could not be said to have come when he had not stood his ground, nor to have come with a powerful army when he immediately had to withdraw for fear of the enemy. The agreement had been meant in a serious way, not in the caviling spirit in which the emperor was now interpreting it. The Florentine people had not promised a vast sum so that he would make momentary contact with the enemy and then withdraw, but so that he would stand fast and cause destruction to the enemy. We don't see what anyone can say against the Florentine people. The people themselves can justly complain, if they wish, of having spent as much money as they have for false hopes.

When the Venetians had heard it all, they seemed to approve the case of the city; but for the common good, they urged agreement, and since this was not forthcoming, the emperor departed. When he had covered a day's navigation and was stopping in Ciavoli, the Venetians had by great effort finally got the Florentine ambassadors to make the transfer of funds to them, and could send some eminent persons to the emperor to bring him back. Having received the money and called back his forces, he stayed another few days in Venice and then returned to Padua in better spirits; there he spent the rest of the winter, occasionally giving signs of being about to go to Rome, then not going after all. In the end, since neither the pope nor Venice would definitely give him help and support, while the Florentines demanded things that seemed hard to carry out, he decided to put off the whole enterprise to another time. He left Padua in the month of April and in large laps made the journey beyond the Alps.

During the same period ambassadors from Milan described in Venice their quarrel with Florence and made their accusations. The Venetians, however, when they had heard these arguments, called certain Florentine ambassadors who were in Venice on another mission, so that they might hear all that the Milanese said and, if they wished, respond. To let the reader judge the case, I shall put down here what were the accusations of our adversaries and what were our replies. The Milanese ambassadors to Venice, therefore, when they were given audience, gave the following kind of speech against the Florentines:

"We speak to you, oh Venetians, who have been designers and mediators of truces and treaties, in complaint against those who, violating both faith and law, have destroyed our peace and truce. *For if you designed and mediated our current peace, it seems you are to some extent responsible for it.* If nothing more, you ought at least in this quarrel to hear both sides. We say that these men are chiefly to blame for their failure to keep their promises and disregard for their legal commitments and contracts. To break promises and violate faith is always disgraceful, but it is still more abominable when it brings on war and upheaval despite formal peace treaties. *For if faithfulness to oaths and the sacredness of law break down, what remains to tie men together? How can one still put trust in another? Anyone who violates faith and disregards promises in time of peace dissolves the social bonds of mankind.* You, oh Venetians, know what agreements to truce and peace were recently made, and with what solemn oaths these arrangements were sealed, but how Florence kept those oaths you have seen for yourselves just now.

"In time of peace, while no one expected them to do anything, their ambassadors went to Germany and incited Robert, who claims to be the Roman emperor, to come into Italy and fight Galeazzo of Milan, with whom they had solemnly sworn to remain at peace. They agreed to pay a great sum of money, and expressly contracted to hand this payment over only when he had invaded the land of one with whom they had just made peace, invaded his land and brought about his destruction.

84

No one can deny that this is what their ambassadors tried to arrange, and everyone ought to wonder at such cunning and deceit. These are the same Florentines who have been sending messages and publishing documents, not only all over Italy but also in France, claiming that they, desiring only peace and tranquillity, have been attacked. Their actions now show clearly that they desire not peace but war, not tranquillity but disturbance and the downfall of others. Such is the result of spiritual restlessness and too much wealth. This city, against all the precedents set by our ancestors, has thus tried to get French and German troops to invade Italy—foreign and barbarous peoples, a clear threat to the honor of our Italian name. They have invited those whom nature herself excludes from Italy, to come and lay their yoke on us. Such is their blindness that they do not see the French and German invasion as the common downfall of all Italians, sure to lay a yoke on Florence as well as on others. The Romans gained praise and glory because, when the Cimbrians and Teutons were preparing to invade Italy, they undertook a great military campaign and annihilated them. By many costly battles they broke the French and liberated the Italians. These new Romans, however, as they like to call themselves, try even with bribes to invite the same barbarous and cruel invaders, such is their people's restlessness, and perverse ambition, and despicable lack of concern for their country and their race. *We all know what to call the man who opens the gates of his country to the enemy.* They have earned the hatred of all Italians, surely, by bribing foreigners to trample on Italian soil.

"Galeazzo, they say, helps their Tuscan enemies. We reply that Pisa and Siena would not need anyone's help if they were not cruelly vexed by Florence. Because of the threat to themselves that does exist, they flock to Galeazzo for protection. It is no disgrace to him if he defends these old friends of his father against the depredations of Florence. It is surely abundantly clear that Galeazzo did not seek Tuscan entanglements for himself, but that he was called in, begged to come in by those who had been robbed of most of their possessions, found themselves exhausted, and yet were unwilling to submit to further damage and humiliation. Not Galeazzo's willingness to help, but their arrogance toward their neighbors, is to be deplored. But to conclude briefly, there are three reasons, oh Venetians, why we were sent to you here: first to complain of a violation of the sworn peace, second, to demand punishment of the violators in accordance with the terms of the contract, and third, to tell you not to be amazed if we resist by war those who broke the peace. The first of these points is a matter of honor, the second of justice, and the third of necessity." With this, the Milanese ambassadors ended their speech.

The Florentine ambassadors heard it all and discussed it for a little while, then made up their minds how to reply to the specific points of the accusation. Then they spoke in the following manner for the honor of the city:

"We consider it our gain, oh Venetians, that our enemies desired to give a speech like this. Had they been silent, perhaps the truth would have remained hidden, but now the provocation of their words will bring it to light. With your encouragement and help, we made peace with Galeazzo of Milan, and signed a treaty, thinking he would cease from desiring to hurt and entrap us. Convinced of this, we not only put down our arms, but put all thought of war out of our minds. He, however, like one incapable of striving towards anything but wars and upheaval, acted with hostility even in peace. We won't mention his condottieri and their men who, just after peace was signed, devastated the land of our allies, the Luccans, sacked Volterra, extorted booty and captives from San Gimigniano and Collegiani, and afterward brought prisoners and booty from all this to Siena, which was in his power. He did all these things against the oath and contract of Milan, violating the integrity and good faith of his promises. We won't discuss these actions, as I say, but just pass over them. But it does seem important that during the same peace, he sent into Tuscany a greater army than before and occupied our next door neighbor, Pisa, garrisoning all the towns and castles of that city and subjecting them to his own power. He also added Siena to his dominions, an ancient town very near us. And did he not make Perugia and Assisi effectively his subjects? Did he in doing these things preserve the peace and respect the sacredness of oaths? *It is not only by knocking down walls and mounting a direct assault that one starts a war, this should be recognized, but also by building and setting up siege machinery, even if it is not drawn right up to the wall.* It was not right for Galeazzo to plan war when peace had been made, nor, after he had put down his arms, to retain an armed spirit. He surrounded us with a multitude of towns and cities to fear, he prepared something

86

very like a siege around us, something as well constructed as siege machinery—was this not a breach of the peace? Did he not invade Tuscany against his word and violate the peace treaty? This is undeniable. The things our adversaries have said, therefore, about breakers of truces and of treaties, and about defectors from faith and promises, we say even more strongly, showing that it was he who violated the peace, he who broke promises, he who defected from faith, and he who despised the oaths he had given. We stand against this breach of faith of his part, and we say we were driven by necessity. Can anyone be so under the spell of these people and so unable to think for himself as not to see that, when the duke had put troops in Tuscany and taken Pisa, had subjected the Sienese government to his own, had made Perugia and Assisi subject cities, had by strenuous efforts gained Lucca, and was trying to do the same to Cortona, he had done all this in order again, despite the recent peace treaty, to make war on Florence? These things, therefore, he did against his faith and legal oath, violating his promises and the peace. If we made public in Italy and elsewhere that we wanted peace and tranquillity and that he was aggressing against us with his attacks, we spoke no more than the truth. *Even after making peace and swearing to it, he could not limit himself but prepared all things for our destruction; what can we suppose he would have done without oaths and peace treaties?* When he says that we are incapable of peaceful behavior, we say let him be silent and let others judge who themselves are capable of peace. He who has not let his immediate family live in security, nor his kin, nor his neighbors, nor his allies, nor nearby peoples, who subjected Verona and Padua by fraud, who now plans wholly to subjugate Tuscany, and whose greed is never satiated, is wholly unfit to say these things of us. We want peace if only we are allowed to have it. What his ambassadors say concerning the French and Germans entering Italy at our invitation makes us ask who is responsible for this; isn't it he and his restlessness and violence that are bringing them in? He is not satisfied with northern Italy but, with incredible ambition he seeks Tuscany and Rome also for himself. His greed and ambition have gone so far that he makes himself the ultimate promise of a kingdom of Italy. His words are all deceit, his deeds are all meant to trap others, he has no honor left, for his is stained and rotten. If our word does not convince you, ask the lords of Verona and Padua, whom he expelled by fraud. Ask the Pisans and Sienese, whom he wanted to rule by tyranny and succeeded in subjecting by fraud. For what he did to his own relatives is too shameful to mention. If we try to defend ourselves against so much greed and perfidy, and if some upheavals arise in Italy as a result and some foreign peoples enter, whose fault is it? Is it his who moves and attacks, or ours, who are driven by necessity to seek help from anyone we can find? The Roman emperor coming into Italy, however, ought not to seem a foreigner. The others who came in were not six hundred thousand strong, like the Cimbri and Teutons, nor were they such a force and such a multitude that Italy needed to fear them. In closing, we demand the vindication which they demand, for the violation of peace and of truce. We declare that the duke of Milan owes us some recompense for his violations and his disregard of sworn pacts. We plead with you and all powers for recognition of our rights. For as they say, *no one should be amazed if he attacks us, since everybody has grown used to seeing him make war with and without excuse.* Having faith in God and justice, we resist his violence." Thus spoke the ambassadors in reply.

The Venetians showed their approval of what the Florentine ambassadors had said, so that these would feel they had sufficiently defended the honor of the city; at the same time, as a neutral power, the Venetians tried to placate the tempers of both sides with grave and prudent words.

The following year, which was 1402, great battles were fought around Bologna. Even before the emperor's complete withdrawal, Galeazzo, elated by the way things were going for him, sent part of his forces into Bolognese territory, to overthrow if possible the new lord of that city. When the emperor had left, he sent more troops into Bolognese territory. The generals in charge of these forces were the lord of Mantua, recently come into the grace and friendship of Milan, and Pandolfo Malatesta and Ottobuono of Parma, as well as other captains. The arrival of these forces immediately put the city in great peril, for there were enough powerful exiles to make the castles and towns of the area rise up, and the citizens inside the city were not all happy about the government of the lord of Bologna either. The Florentines responded to the danger by sending the captain Bernardone with a large number of troops. They added more troops in time, as they learned of reinforcements sent to the enemy. Large forces were sent to the aid of Bologna by the lord of Padua and other allies, and the lord of Padua sent two of his sons along. All the forces of the Florentine people and of their allies, and all the forces of the enemy, were finally gathered around Bologna. Both sides made encampments around the city, but the enemy's were farther from the city and ours were closer, lying halfway between the enemy's lines and the city. The general-in-chief of the Florentine armies was Bernardone, and the armies of the enemy were commanded by Duke Alberigo.

With the armies thus arrayed for some time, the enemy, who was more numerous and stronger, finally initiated an attack on the encampment of the Florentines and their allies. Our camp was near Casaleccio, four miles outside Bologna. The defense of this spot seemed vital, because water from the Reno flows to Bologna through there; if the enemy could divert this stream the city would be in serious trouble. The enemy left camp, therefore, and mounted a sudden attack on ours. Our men met them with bitter fighting and resisted vigorously, and Bernardone was there to encourage and guide them. But the attack of the enemy was so forceful that our men retreated from the bridge over the river, and they occupied it. Then suddenly, not only over the bridge but also by other ways, they crossed the river and attacked our people; it was not a matter of feats of arms anymore but of slaughter or flight everywhere. Bernardone was captured and the other leaders were almost all taken too, except those who fled into the city of Bologna. The two sons of the lord of Padua boldly laid waste around them, but finally surrendered to the lord of Mantua. The camps were all taken by the enemy with enormous booty.

This calamity soon led to greater ruin. The Bolognese citizens of the opposition rose in insurrection, and men of various factions now dared to raise their heads against their master. There were battles throughout the city during the night. Bentivoglio fought with amazing skill and won universal praise for it. Friends and enemies alike admitted that he was the first and best of fighters. With the whole city in arms, however, and victorious enemies holding all the territory outside, the party of the opposition was able to seize one of the gates and let in the exiles and part of the enemy force. With such a multitude of enemies swarming around, Bentivoglio was captured and soon killed. Two Florentine ambassadors were in the city, Niccolò da Uzzano and Bardo Rittafè. Bardo was wounded and died soon after. Niccolò was taken prisoner and carried to Pavia, where he suffered wretchedly in prison.

Bologna after the return of the exiles received a civil government. A formal republic and formal liberty were restored. This indeed was what Galeazzo had promised the exiles. The pleasure only lasted two or three days, however. Then certain persons sent by the duke with a military force ran through the city shouting the name of Galeazzo, usurped the authority of the city's officials, and proclaimed the entire lordship of Milan. The people and the exiles were disappointed, but they had to bend their necks to the yoke of servitude.

When the Florentines heard that the army had been defeated and Bernardone taken prisoner, they were terribly frightened and anxious. When they learned that Bologna too had fallen, they were even more terrified, expecting the enemy from hour to hour. Without the general and the army, they seemed to despair completely. Had the enemy approached promptly to follow up his victory, the city could not have withstood him. The enemy, however, whether because of weariness or internal discord, let the time for action pass in useless settling down. When many days had passed and the enemy with his army had not appeared, the city gathered its spirits a little and began to rise up and repair its strength. They sent some troops against the partisans of the Ubaldini, who had rebelled after the enemy's success, and against Ricciardo of Pistoia and his followers who, upon hearing of the defeat, had captured many places. The troops the Florentines sent put a stop to such outbreaks.

Those who discussed possible means of defense against the great danger that threatened thought of two hopes; one, that Pope Boniface would go to war, the other that Venice would. There was some basis for these hopes, for the pope definitely was not pleased to see the cities of Perugia and Bologna both captured. The Venetians long before had begun to show displeasure at the growth of Milanese power. Florence tried with the utmost zeal to make an alliance with both cities. Yet both stood still and seemed horrified at the idea of actually going to war. The Venetians definitely wanted a somewhat unfair treaty of alliance, by which war would be made more at the expense of Florence than of Venice, and yet Venice would have the right of complete discretion in the matter of making peace, which they could do at any time without the consent of Florence. These conditions seemed too hard and beneath the dignity of the Florentine people.

Amidst all this came the hope of peace. The enemy seemed to want to make peace after taking Bologna, and sent representatives to Venice to propose rather reasonable conditions. The Florentines suspected deception and fraud, and finally decided to agree to the peace and to the Venetian alliance at the same time, thinking that if the peace began at the same time as the alliance, the peace would be more durable and the conditions demanded by the Venetians less important. They instructed their representatives to sign, with the addition of a few corrections, peace with the enemy and an alliance with Venice.

While the city was just doing this, word came through that Galeazzo was dead. The death was first announced by Paolo Guinisi, lord of Lucca, but it was not considered a certainty. Later it was repeated as a certainty, but a deep secret. At once letters were sent to the representatives in Venice not to agree to the peace nor to the alliance. The Venetians learned of the duke's death only from the Florentine embassy, having heard nothing before. There had been signs, however, such as some forces sent towards Tuscany through Piacenza and Lunigiana being suddenly recalled. The leaders of the army, who were still before Bologna, had received orders not to move from that spot. It now proved that Galeazzo had become ill soon after Bologna was taken. He had died somewhat later of the same illness, at the Milanese castle of Marignano. These facts had been kept secret at first. Eventually they had to be made public, and there was a magnificent funeral. It also came out that Galeazzo, while he lay ill, had passionately desired peace with Florence. Hence the attempt to send a mission to Venice and to make a new peace. He realized that his sons were still young and were being left in the midst of great danger. So he was in a hurry to make peace before he would leave the world. This would have been accomplished, too, if he had lived just a little longer. His sudden death brought such a reversal of things that those who before had hardly any hope left for their own safety were now filled with high confidence, while those who had just considered themselves victorious lost all hope of being able to resist.

CHRONOLOGICAL GUIDE

Ancient History
as described in Leonardo Bruni,
History of Florence, Book I

B.C.	750	First war between Etruscans and Romans.
	666	Rome captures Fidenae and Alba, Etruscan cities.
	616	First invasion of Italy by the Gauls.
	509	Tarquin, exiled king of Rome, gains Etruscan allies against Rome.
	483	Another war of Etruscans and Romans.
	394	Veii, and important Etruscan city, falls to Rome.
	283	All Etruria falls to Rome.
	209	First Etruscan rebellion.
	94	Second Etruscan rebellion.
	80	Sulla, Roman general and dictator, founds Florence.
	67	Cataline builds up conspiracy against Rome.
	63	Florence joins Cataline in war on Rome and is defeated.
	60–44	Julius Caesar most powerful leader in Rome.
	49–44	Julius Caesars dictatorship.
	27	Octavianus Caesar gains power. Rules as first emperor to A.D. 14.
A.D.	14–37	Reign of Tiberius
	37–41	Caligula
	41–54	Claudius
	54–68	Nero
	68–69	Galba
	69	Otto, Vitellius, Vespasian in succession.
	69–79	Vespasian
	79–81	Titus
	81–96	Domitian
	284–305	Diocletian and Maximian—first pact with Goths.
	306–337	Constantine the Great
	372	Huns route Visigoths from steppes ("Scythia") into empire.
	378	Valens, emperor at Constantinople, killed by Goths at Adrianople.

379–395	Theodosius. His general, Stilicho, fights Goths in Western Empire.
401–423	Arcadius and Honorius. Visigoths invade Italy.
401	Stilicho defeats Radagaisus at Florence.
406	Stilicho executed by government.
406	Vandals invade France, Spain, and Italy—settle in northern Africa.
410	Visigoths, led by Alaric, sack Rome.
445–453	Huns, led by Attila, invade Italy.
489–535	More Ostrogoths, led by Theodoric, take over Italy.
535–554	Justinian sends troops from eastern empire to retake city.
546	Totila, leader of Ostrogoths, takes northern Italy and Rome.
552	Totila defeated by Justinian's general, Narses.
568	Lombards, led by Albuin, take over northern Italy.
774	Charlemagne conquers Benevento and Spoleto, takes over Lombard kingdom.
800	Charlemagne crowned emperor of the western Roman empire.
1052–1115	Countess Maltida of Tuscany. Florence develops guild government.
1152–1190	Frederick I wages six wars against the pope in northern Italy.
1176	Florence comes to control dioceses of Florence and Fiesole.
1190–1197	Henry VI wars against pope in Italy, gains control of Sicily.
1211–1250	Frederick II, ruler of Sicily and emperor, wars against pope.
1228–1229	Papal soldiers ravage Apulia; Frederick's soldiers retake it and devastate it again.

Medieval and Renaissance Florence:

Internal:

1252	Florence coins florin which becomes standard gold coin for Europe.
1260	Ghibelline regime imposed on Florence by Siena, using Florentine exiles.

1266	Ghibellines finally overthrown.
1282	Law forbids nobles from joining government unless they belong to guilds.
1292	Giano della Bella leads commoners in struggle against nobles.
1293	Law excludes nobles from guilds unless they practice trade or profession. They maintain power, however, through the Guelf party organization, in which they, along with some commercial leaders, play a major part.
1343	Bankruptcies of major banks. Unemployment; famine.
1348	The Black Death, and epidemic of bubonic plague, sweeps both Asia and Europe. Florentine population and economy suddenly reduced, perhaps by ⅓ or even ½.
1370	**Leonardo Bruni born.**
1378	Revolt of the Ciompi, or poor textile workers. A minority of these obtain guild organizations of their own. The minor guilds, representing all the poorer crafts, gain power within Florentine government. Guelf party ousted as an unofficial government, never to regain that role.
1380	**Poggio Bracciolini born.**
1382	Popular revolt under Giorgio di Scala, a member of the nobility, defeated. Government revised, the two poorest guilds dissolved, and power restored to the commercial oligarchy.
1404	**L. B. Alberti born.**
1426	**A. Rinuccini born.**
1427	First income tax.
1444	**Leonardo Bruni dies.**
1452	**G. Savonarola born.**
1454	**A. Poliziano born.**
1459	**Poggio Bracciolini dies.**
1434–1464	Cosimo de' Medici unofficial head of Florentine government.
1464–1469	Piero de' Medici, unofficial ruler.
1469–1492	Lorenzo de' Medici, unofficial ruler.
1478	Pazzi conspiracy.
1492–1494	Piero de' Medici, unofficial ruler.

1494	**A. Poliziano dies.**
1492–1498	Savonarola powerful influence on Florentine Republic. He is put under papal excommunication, jailed by Florentine enemies, executed as a heretic.
1498	**G. Savonarola dies.**

External:

1260	Battle of Montaperti—Siena defeats Florence.
1375–1378	War with Rome.
1384	Arezzo becomes Florentine territory.
1386–1388	Gian Galeazzo Visconti incorporates Verona, Vicenza, and Padua in his Milanese state.
1395–1401	Contest over position of emperor (as well as unresolved schism in papacy). Robert of Bavaria is claimant to position of emperor.
1399	Pisa and Siena join Milanese in a federation headed by Visconti.
1400	Assisi and Perugia join Milanese.
1401	Robert of Bavaria, called to help Florence fight expansionism of Milan, is defeated by Milanese forces.
1402	Bolona falls to Milanese. Florence apparently saved at last moment by death of Gian Galeazzo and subsequent dissolution of his domain.
1405–1406	Florence wars with Pisa, incorporates that city into Florentine state.
1454	Peace of Lodi—a settlement among major states of Italy. Porcari conspiracy in Rome against Pope Nicholas V.
1478–1480	Florence at war with Rome and Naples.
1494	French invasion. Pisa taken from Florence by French troops, which then march on to Naples.

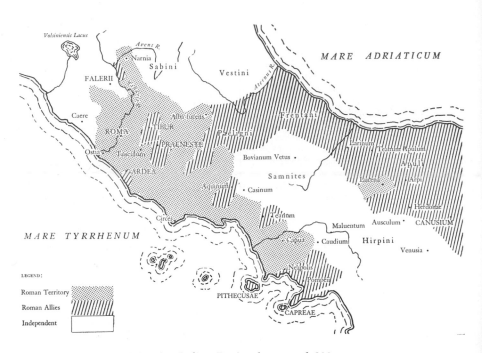

Map 1. Italian Peninsula around 300 B.C.

Map 2. Italian Peninsula around 264 B.C.

Map 3.   Major northern Italian powers, 1390–1433

*Overlap (shaded) of Venetian and Visconti
realms at points of greatest expansion.*

FLORENTINE EXPANSION

Pistoia	1329
Arezzo	1337, 1384
Pisa	1406
Piombino	1406
Cortona	1411
Anghiari	1440

VISCONTI EXPANSION*

Novara 1331	Parma 1346
Bergamo 1332	Tortona 1347
Pavia 1332	Genoa 1353–6
Cremona 1334	Verona 1387
Piacenza 1336	Vicenza 1387
Brescia 1337	Padua 1388
Cortenuova 1337	Pisa 1398
Bobbio 1342	Lucca 1399
Asti 1342, 1382	Siena 1399

*Visconti control of Milan dates to 1311.
Title of "Duke" obtained in 1395.*

Visconti Realm 1390 ― ― ― ― ― ―

Venetian Realm 1428 ――――――

Florentine Realm 1433 ―・―・―・―

Papal States (Traditional) ・・・・・・・・・・

Holy Roman Empire (Traditional) ― ―― ・・・―

Leon Battista Alberti

Leon Battista Alberti 1404–1472

Leon Battista Alberti was the illegitimate but cherished son of a Florentine merchant in exile.[1] He was born in Bologna and raised, after his mother's early death, in Venice and Padua. In 1421, when his father died, Battista became truly poor, and his student years at the University of Bologna were hard. The cheating of certain relatives had brought this poverty on him, and the lack of concern from his family made it harder. He wrote numerous Lucian-like allegorical dialogues on the fickleness of fortune and the courage of ragged virtue. Feeling particular pride in the Alberti name and disappointment in the lack of a strong, legitimate and loyal family, he wrote a book of four long dialogues, *On the Family*. Alberti served as a papal secretary at the court of Pope Eugene IV, where he could share with several fellow secretaries and with some cardinals his enthusiasm for both Greek and Latin literature. Shortly after some new manuscripts of Plautus were uncovered by Poggio Bracciolini's researches, Alberti wrote a Plautian play which—though an unclassical moral allegory under a thin veneer of classical language—was widely circulated as a genuine classical work.

He "returned" to Florence, his family home, when Cosimo's rise to power in 1434 ended the exile of the Albertis. He was then a poet and man of letters, and he soon became a friend of Cosimo's son, Piero, with whose help he organized a contest of Italian poetry. The poetry was meant to show that one could write on the model of Latin poetry, yet write in Italian. Alberti was remarkable in his generation of humanists for his desire to make classical learning enrich, not eclipse, the Italian language. He also took a great in-

terest in mathematics, art, architecture, and the crafts. Unlike most humanists, he became a close friend of the great Florentine artists of his day. The
fruit of this interest was twofold. He wrote the first broad theoretical works
on the arts: *On Painting, On Sculpture,* and *On Architecture*; and he himself
became a painter and architect. While his paintings have been lost, and only
one great medallion self-portrait testifies to his skill in the representational
arts, he made a number of lasting famous contributions to architecture. In
Florence, under the patronage especially of the rich merchant, Giovanni
Rucellai, he designed a palazzo, a chapel, and the facade of Santa Maria
Novella. He also enjoyed the patronage of some of northern Italy's minor
dictators—Sigismondo Malatesta, Lodovico Gonzaga, and Lionello d'Este
—so that church buildings designed by him may be admired still in Mantua
and Rimini, and he dedicated writings to the dukes of Urbino and Ferrara.

The writings of Alberti's middle and later years show a repugnance for
politics, a Stoic belief that the strong individual does not pin his hopes on
anything so largely out of his control: such is the message of *Theogenio* and
of *Ichiarchia*.[2] In a casual piece of wit which is recorded in his short *Vita* (an
early autobiography, I believe), he expresses succinctly his disappointment
in Medici Florence:

"When a stranger was inquiring after the place where he would find justice
administered, 'Good friend,' said he [Alberti], 'I don't really know.' Some
of his fellow citizens were listening and said, 'Do you really not know where
the Palace of Justice is?' 'I just didn't remember,' he replied, 'that justice
herself lived there.' "[3]

Alberti's early work, *De Felicitate*,[4] or *Happiness*, is a dialogue of newly
captured slaves. As far as I know it is by centuries the first work of fiction in
which an author imaginatively identifies with slaves. The purpose is not
apparently to show the inhumanity of man and commerce, though these are
inevitably implied, but, by exhibiting the utter degradation that fortune can
bring, to set forth what ordinary mortals, neither vicious men nor Stoics,
generally ask of life. Stoicism, by implication again, is the only possible consolation here, but to ordinary mortals it is too difficult. As the dialogue shows,
they want to be free. The dialogue also shows why freedom is precious. It is
not a question of being able to make choices and take risks. It is a matter of
having one's roots firmly planted in a dignified and autonomous community
—the family and around it, the village or town.

Alberti's *De Porcaria Conjuratione*,[5] or *The Conspiracy of Stefano Porcari*,
was written just after the event and, of course, from the point of view of
the victor—for Leon Battista Alberti was a not ungrateful employee of the
papacy against which Porcari conspired. Nevertheless, and in contrast to

Poliziano's account of the Pazzi conspiracy, Alberti's account shows objectivity and historical imagination. He enters with sympathy into the political dynamics and the psychological background of the revolt.

The motives of Stefano Porcari, according to Alberti, were love of glory and a sense of injustice done to his personal ancestors (he was a Roman aristocrat) as well as to the age-old community of the Romans. Again the thing that makes life worth living is freedom, not in the sense of a rich personal career—this Porcari throws away—but in the sense of community dignity and autonomy. Roman dignity and autonomy, of course, appear to Porcari and his friends to be destroyed by the powerful presence of the pope and his horde of legally protected, economically privileged clerics. Inspired by the classical stories of Rome, Porcari treads in the footsteps of Cola di Rienzi in the fourteenth century and Arnold of Brescia in the thirteenth, both of whom led somewhat more successful rebellions.

The tool of Stefano Porcari is rhetoric, and Alberti's interest in telling the story lies largely in capturing the rhetoric. He does not just make up historical speeches to explain positions, as Bruni does in his *History*, but he makes up speeches that suggest the magnetism and glitter of oratory. Humanism and rhetoric, studies Alberti dearly loved, did not seem harmless to him. In his own writings he struggled for moral depth and consistency, combining the sophist's and philosopher's concerns. He seems to have realized, as the *Conspiracy of Stefano Porcari* shows, that politics is the realm of the sophist. And his disgust with politics was largely a disgust with the level of political debate and with the evil motives that direct politics and have evil effects. As he says in *De Republica*: "The good can rarely win in a republic, for the crowd is 'hostile to reason and full of corrupt judgment.' "[6] And . . . "the people is a broken trumpet and no one can make good music on it."[7] What is more, other animals rarely do harm to members of their own species, but man does so abundantly. Men, in fact, are more often hurt by other men than by anything else.[8]

In the Porcari story, Alberti illustrates these pessimistic ideas by a concrete example. Yet he also suggests, it seems to me, that there was something noble about even Porcari's lack of gratitude to the kind pope, Nicolas V, and about his cunning deceptions and outrageous will to disturb the peace. If so, Alberti was to a degree a relativist.

NOTES

1. All the biographical facts here given are documented by Girolamo Mancini, *Vita di Leon Battista Alberti*, Firenze, 1911. Reprinted, (Bardi) Rome, 1971. A

bibliography may be found in Joan Gadol, *Leon Battista Alberti, Universal Man of the Early Renaissance*, (University of Chicago Press) Chicago, 1969, 245–57.

2. Both *Theogenio*, or *De Republica*, and *Ichiarchia*, are printed in Anicio Bonucci, ed. Leon Battista Alberti, *Opere Volgari*, iii, Firenze, 1843–49.

3. *Vita anonyma*, ed. L. Mehus, in *Rerum italicarum scriptores*, vol. xxv, Milan, 1751. Cf. Renée Watkins, "The Authorship of the *Vita anonyma* of Leon Battista Alberti," *Renaissance Studies*, iv (1957), 101–12.

4. Ed. G. Mancini, *Opera inedita et pauca separatim impressa*, Firenze, 1890.

5. Ed. L. Mehus, *Rerum italicarum scriptores*, vol. xxv, Milan, 1751.

6. Leon Battista Alberti, *Opere Volgari*, iii, Firenze, 1843–49, 192–93.

7. Ibid., 193.

8. Ibid., 215.

HAPPINESS

by Leon Battista Alberti

In the days of our fathers, some Italian merchants bought a number of slaves from the Scythians [Moguls] who had captured them in Asia, for Themirius [Timur Beg or Tamerlane] their king had ravaged the province like a hurricane with his one thousand two hundred armed men. The merchants took the slaves they had bought to Italy by ship. When they arrived at Tarento, the famous Italian port, and found themselves and their possessions safe, they wished to call it a holiday and thank the gods for the favorable winds and the good navigation that had brought them home. The sailors therefore took out the slaves, and brought them to an ancient temple which stood by the shore. There during the sacrifice they placed what they deemed a sufficient number of armed men at the doors of the temple to prevent any bold slave from attempting flight or inciting a riot. And after the ceremony they offered the slaves an ample feast with much wine. Encouraging them to be of good cheer and hope for the best, the merchants said to them:

"Listen, men, remember first of all that it was not we who brought adversity upon you but the power of fortune. We ourselves were not the ones who imposed slavery on you, but we rescued you from those who did and we are bringing you to kinder masters. Take the lot that fate awards you and be of strong and untroubled spirit. Remember that Italians are well known, among other virtues, for their mercy. Our religious heritage demands a sense of responsibility, and our ancient self-restraint has trained us to be humane and forbearing as masters.

Therefore be full of hope, anticipating from us what you would expect from any truly religious people. At this feast, meanwhile, you can lessen your grief and sweeten your bitterness with wine. Forget your sad longings on this day of feasting. Butler, pass the strong wine. You who are seated here drink till you are drunk, drink and then sing."

A meal was provided then to those who were lying around, and they ate it eagerly without many words. Then, however, the newly enslaved began to think of home, parents, family and spouse. First an amazing silence fell upon them. Then sighs and tears began. Finally there were laments like the following.

For the oldest among the slaves began to speak: "What misery, what wretchedness is ours! At our age we should be living our brief remaining years in the homes of our ancestors, and enjoying our rest. Instead we are here to be bullied by foreigners. Pitiful lot, to have fallen from domestic prosperity to total poverty. Oh, precious grandchildren whose wealth and work were already lightening the burdens of age for us. Oh poor abandoned family whom we governed and protected with our cautions and advice. What a bitter turn of fortune at our age to fall from commanding others to servitude. For this were we spared through the dangers of war and wounds!"

Thus spoke the old. When these things had been attentively heard, the next in age and in order of seating spoke: "We think you fathers the happiest of us, for the common fate of all of us is servitude, but you in this great misery have the best lot, for you will soon be set free by a death that does not come untimely. You are old, you have achieved honors, your children and grandchildren have grown up; as citizens of your country you have proved your value in war and in peace. You may well comfort your afflicted souls with the thought of your worthy past. But we who are at the age to earn merit through deeds of arms and council, to rise to honor and authority, to begin to enjoy the pleasures of our children and to take our share of happiness; oh misery, to be enslaved at just the prime of life. We have lost everything, both what we had obtained for ourselves and what we had hoped to pass on to posterity. All lost by one stroke of fortune and nothing left but the fact that we may die. If for this reason we do indeed seek a quick and bitter death, however, shall we not die in slavery and in despair of liberty?"

When they had sorrowfully continued with comparisons to show that the old were more fortunate than those of lesser age in the present situation, the adolescent slaves spoke in their turn, lamenting their ill fortune:

"If you who are older are unhappy, we are the most unhappy of the unhappy, we alone are the ones whose loved spouses, whose Venuses and Cupids, whose delights are torn out of our arms. To us this time was promised for our pleasures, for wedding celebrations, games to watch, poems to be recited. Oh, what misery, instead of wives and spouses we shall have salt sacks and jars of metal to fill. We shall herd sheep instead of attending weddings. We shall have blows and beatings instead of games, and instead of poems we shall have contests like this of bitter lamentation and weeping. Farewell beloved, farewell arms, horses and all well-loved things, farewell zither and farewell dear studies now lost to us. We shall serve and we shall live. Oh unhappy companions like ourselves in misfortune. Oh, those are most unhappy by far whom catastrophe tears away from the sweetest union of companions. Weep, shore, weep, and cry with us, oh seas, and moan our misfortune and condole with us, oh winds!"

As the young slaves continued unendingly to complain, the mothers who were kissing their small children and weeping spoke up also. "We can hardly say what our misery is," they said, "What your sorrows are and what our complaints against fortune, for sorrow closes our throats against the words rising from our hearts. These small children almost kill us with the weight of misery, for we see them in their innocence made most unhappy of all. For if servitude is sorrow, they have been born to perpetual sorrow. Oh pitiful children, parental care and the concern of your other relatives can do nothing at all for you in the present catastrophe. Let us die."

While the mothers expressed their harsh sorrow and sweetly pressed their babes to their own breasts and faces, the old and nearly all those of other ages answered them with one voice: "Only the children and babes are happy in this terrible situation, for they take what they are about to suffer without any resentment. They have no memory of lost joys to make them grieve, and any change of fortune can only bring some betterment for them."

The merchants listened to these lamentations and felt sorry. They finally imposed silence on the sufferers, and ordered plenty of wine to be poured so that the violent anxieties might be washed away with alcohol and sadness and anguish be buried in sleep. And the wiser among the merchants said to their companions, "Do you see from the various laments of these people how all that human reason judges of happiness and unhappiness merely accords with common opinion?"

The Conspiracy of Stefano Porcari

by Leon Battista Alberti

Rumors of what has been happening here have surely reached you, but I imagine that you might like to hear more from a friend. Such extraordinary actions, when reported from unreliable sources, seem hardly credible because of the inhuman wickedness involved. I shall try like a friend to satisfy you even beyond your hopes. It seems true that one who gathered the story while there was danger, and put things together as they happened, knows more about what was really done than one who has only heard the tale told. It was such a hideous crime that from the very beginnings of human history till today nothing more horribly destructive, shameless, and totally cruel has been plotted by anyone, however lawless. During the days marked by Pope Eugene's funeral, Stefano Porcari, a Roman knight—had he only been as reasonable as he was intellectually gifted and fluent of speech—began to harangue his fellow citizens at meetings and to try as hard as he could to stir up trouble. He urged them as powerfully as possible to take up arms and avenge their ancient republic, their honor and their liberty. I should not like to say what might soon have happened, for the crowds were getting more and more excited, but a foresighted and statesmanlike lawyer, Lelius Valejo, intervened to stop him.

Pope Nicolas, who had just taken over from Pope Eugene, was warned by his usual advisers that the city would never be peaceful if he did not get rid of this man who was ready to start a revolt. The pope, however, who was just initiating his pontificate, was much inclined to show mercy and try to reconcile all sorts of people to himself by acts of benevolence and tolerance. He wanted, therefore, to win over this otherwise honorable and certainly very Roman citizen, hoping he would give up his criminal desires for the prospect of honorable peace. He sent him as vice-governor to the Hernican region of Latium, raising him to the office with an elaborate ceremony. When Porcari returned from this mission, however, it was easy to see that nothing had calmed his old rebellious spirit and that he was as violent and swollen with ambition as ever. On a day of customary public games, brawls broke out among some of the young men and Porcari himself was there—urging his followers to fight and inciting people with his facial expressions, his gestures, his hands and his words. He was stirring up mad hatred in the crowd and urging them to armed rebellion. Nicolas realized he had to deal seriously with this man's bold and revolutionary zeal. As a man of piety and mercy, however, he did not wish to hurt the man he had just appointed to an office, even on account of recent acts. He decided not to wipe out Porcari's boldness with one stroke but only to make him yield a little ground. He sent him to Bologna, therefore, hoping to placate both the rebel and his followers by alleviating the poverty of the former and by showing the latter that their absent leader was well treated. He wrote the Bolognese officials to be sure that Porcari lacked for nothing to maintain himself in comfort, and for the rest, to keep an eye on him.

Porcari was an impatient spirit, and what he had earlier tried to do by means of public gatherings, he now decided to continue in the isolation of his new situation. He was set to apply his fortune and his generosity of mind in order somehow, even if by total destruction, to regain liberty. He decided to persevere in his course with amazing tenacity, whether because it made him personally happier or because he hoped for glory from posterity if he took enormous risks for a high and possibly unattainable ideal.

For accomplices he took men he thought useful. First of all he sent to Rome a young nephew of his, excited and eager to fight. This nephew pretended to be on a military mission while gathering for his own purposes both arms and a band of brigands like himself. He also went about carrying away as many people as he could with mighty hopes for what could be done. When everything was ready, on a day that had been set earlier, Porcari himself secretly left Bologna and arrived in Rome at the fourth hour of the night, taking up his quarters in a place that was not his own home. There he called together those he knew were favorable to his designs. At the house, which was packed with people, he gave a seemingly impromptu speech, which he had prepared carefully for days. He gave it with such confidence and won such approval from his audience that everyone said nothing more was needed to get action than just to set the time.

He began by lamenting that great city's loss of her ancient glory and by cursing the evils of the present. If anyone still had some of the ancient spirit and valor, he could not show it without danger to his life. He was not sorry to be doing what he was doing, for he considered himself responsible to his country and his fellow citizens. As they could see, his whole concern was for their honor. Nor did he doubt that all those present, who, as he recalled, were strong men, had also dreamed and desired actions worthy of their strength. They had lacked only his opportunities or been led by the obstacles to think about private rather than public concerns. And he was sure that, if he were well understood, and they appeared to be understanding him, none of those present and none of those outside who had heard about his lofty plans would consider themselves Romans, or even men, if they did not truly share his feelings. He affirmed that he was trying to achieve this unity and that it was essential—for he himself would inevitably be informed upon soon. The essential thing was for them to be ready, not just to know what needed doing (with his reasoning to guide them and with the pressure of existing evils, anyone could know that) but to be ready to act, ready to do what was needed, what would serve, what would win undying honor and glory.

Then he paused a moment, silently expressing by his posture and by sighs the grief on his face. Extending his arm and gazing at those around him he asked whether, among so many excellent and deserving citizens, there was one to whom the present state of his own affairs or of his country was even tolerable. Was there anyone who could look at their shared degradation without weeping? Poverty, servitude, insults, injuries and such could happen to people and be tolerated because they were habitual and because of the idea that, even though one was suffering, one was in one's own country. But a new sort of cruelty had now been found by those who liked to call themselves the most pious of men: now they would not let a citizen live—innocent citizens were being exiled, banished, or killed. All Italy was full of Roman exiles, while the city was emptied of all but barbarians, and if anyone admitted to loving his country, it was viewed as a crime. He inveighed bitterly then against the ruling group, with all sorts of angry words and accusations. He aroused the envy and indignation of his audience against the many corrupt and selfish people who, while they demanded reverence as if they were gods, were obviously crazed with too much power. Citizens, meanwhile, who deserved a better fate, were surviving on the sufferance of such as these.

Yet the intolerable situation could not be blamed on anyone but themselves, for having so long accepted the evil and lacked heart to resist. It was time now to remember what they could do if they pulled themselves together: all the things it would mean not to be servile, not to be a subject people. Since they had everything necessary, there was nothing left but to carry out the enterprise. He had brought three hundred soldiers in arms into the city, and a strong force of four hundred exiles was also waiting; there would be many ready fighters eager to join in, and help forthcoming from elsewhere. As to those to be attacked, they had less troops than the number of the present assembly. The gods would favor the uprising, the people would be grateful to those who participated, the world would admire their courage, and posterity would never forget them. The enemy was hateful to both gods and men, quarrelsome among themselves, unarmed, lazy, sunk in luxury, and incautious.

There was nothing needed to pluck the fruits of victory but to go through the necessary struggle, to fight vigorously, to follow out the good plans that had already been made, and to show the patience they had shown heretofore. All the plans were now complete, and even if their enemies resisted, they would be beaten. Those who had waited in patience would arise now and give these nonworkers what they deserved. All that now separated the rebels from victory was one day. In one day they would be rewarded. Let them rejoice, let them get ready to seize the wealth. A million gold coins would be taken on the following night.

He was moved, however, by love of his country rather than by wealth. He cared more for the honor and happiness of the citizens than for any personal advantage. He would later express some ideas on how to use their victory, when they had made themselves the masters of all the people. For now he urged them to serve their country, the common cause, and the plans now well under way, with courage and unity. Thus Porcari.

What was going on became known to the pope through an informer. It appeared clear that Porcari was secretly planning on the very next night. He had realized that if riots were called for at night, many would join in who would not move in the daytime, feeling that darkness might cover their crime. The next day, therefore, armed men were sent to take over Porcari's house. Some of the conspirators were captured. Only Porcari's nephew, sword in hand, managed to cut a path through the midst of the enemy and escape. At the time of the raid, Porcari was not found hiding there. They found him that evening, however, in a cupboard of his sister's. They decided to get more information out of him by applying the torture of hanging. What he had been zealously planning was revealed.

On Epiphany, when the pope and the cardinals and the governor and the lesser priests customarily appear in the cathedral to perform the rites, a certain conspirator would set fire to the straw and hay in the papal stables, which neighbor the church, in the hope that guards would leave the church to go and deal with the emergency. Then Porcari was to appear. The dormitories and cellar where he had planned to hide that night, with the help of the sacristan, were next to the cathedral, and he would have some armed men with him. He would be loosely draped in a distinctive purple and gold mantle and appear to be accompanied by just a few attendants. He assumed that the officiating priests would let him go through as though he were just attending mass, not knowing anything about his return and its reasons. Armed men and swords would not be visible. Only on a sign would those who had been hidden come out and rush to the spot. They would break through the altar rails and seize the pope, not without killing those around him whom they most hated. Then, as they had planned, they would take him to the fortress, along with the brother of the captain of the fort. By threatening these prisoners, they would make the captain hand over the fort. Once it was occupied, Porcari was sure that he would have popular support.

111

While these things were being done at the cathedral and the fortress, other conspirators would pretend to be officials taking some criminals to the prison on the Capitoline, where the prison was within the fortress precincts. They would thus be able to enter the fort itself and occupy it without a fight. The final step would be looting and slaughter all over the city. Porcari had decreed that the whole papal crowd should be exterminated. He said he wished to act so that within the city walls, there would be no more need to fear the chief—his teeth would truly have been drawn. Certain people, to make the action more acceptable, did not wish to pollute the temple itself but to seize the pope on his way to mass, as he entered the cathedral doors. The chains had already been bought with which he was to be shackled. They were calculating the loot as follows: from the pontifical quarters and private treasure, two hundred thousand. From the college, two hundred more. From the merchants and those who held public office, two hundred, and from the salt stores and private possessions of citizens considered public enemies, another hundred thousand.

Dying, Porcari said, "You won by three hours of daylight. Victory awaited us with the coming of night."

Such were the dangers. At present we are like people driven by stormy seas toward unsafe cliffs, looking with fear and sickening indignation now at the sea and now at the cliffs. As they say, the troubled mind is always restless, so we strike now on this side and now on the other, all of us wearing the same expressions and uttering the same remarks when we meet, all torn by mental agitation. We are grateful, we are grieved, we are frightened when we look back. There are certain differences among us in what we say and think. It should have been thus, let me resolve thus, it was about to turn out thus, this is what will happen now. . . . When anyone begins reasoning with himself or trying to convince others, he will use not only true or plausible arguments, but all sorts of merely possible or even impossible circumstances. No one, it seems, can speak of anything else. All of us together are very much troubled by our common misfortune, and I am sometimes moved even to tears, pitying the noble and distinguished men from other nations— French, Spanish, and German—when they talk more or less like this:

"Oh miserable fate—did we not leave our home, our relatives, our comforts and all the things we held dear? Do we serve the pope in order to be the prey of wicked thieves? To be sacrificed to cruelty and to the mad fury of violent men? Look at these venerable Camillos and Coruncanos who when they see anyone who is not one of themselves start speechifying about barbarians and foreign tourists. Look at this civilized folk with their famous philosophy of life, this people chosen by Heaven to rule the world and to govern on high principles!

"What can be done against such savage enemies? What can we do amidst upheaval and immorality? What can we do in the midst of desperate poverty, with shortages of just about everything? All Latium was pacified, and the last thing we were all expecting was surely that some Roman should hit on the idea of improving his lot through revolution. The fields were to be cultivated, the city to be made golden by the coming jubilee, the dignity of the citizens to be enhanced; such were the things anyone might have expected from the present pope. No expropriations, no new taxes, the highest degree of justice, great concern with the embellishment of the city. What is wrong with too much prosperity? Men not only go crazy in abundance, they are transformed into dangerous maniacs. Dear gods, our innocent guests! They bring gold from the ends of the earth (from the Ultima Thule, so to speak) and carry to this spot the rewards of all men's labor and lives; they lay out public funds, pour out wealth—and all for shiftless and lazy men like the majority of the Romans to live in admirable and splendid comfort. No harm had been done to them, they had not been insulted at all, only they found it hard to have foreigners around who showed more culture than they themselves possessed. In an hour's time, however, they were ready to seize the property of thousands, to kill and altogether ruin thousands. They were ready to profane the temple with slaughter, to make the altar hideous with blood, to undertake the utter subversion of the college, the priesthood and religion! They had decided to seize the pope himself, whose foot the greatest kings are glad to kiss, and tear him from the sacrifice, pull him along, throw him in chains, and kill him! Surely we should get out of here and fly beyond Sarmatia. Let us leave this cruel place and all its greedy clans." Thus some do speak.

"We who have lived here all our lives disagree. We are touched by the fame of the city, and we live in it with love for the citizens. We look at the matter, not like those whose minds are quite overwhelmed, but

113

rationally, and we see it as our duty to admonish everyone not to hate the whole city because of the evil done by a few. There are a good many honest and responsible men here, worthy of ancient Rome. And none but the very worst fail to value tranquillity and peace. Among the cities of Italy, this one is not among those least known for an interest in worthy studies. There are only a few thoughtless people, who must pay the price of their stupidity. For the rest the pain and danger of upheaval is even greater than for us. The dignity and veneration associated with this city enhances us who inhabit it. There is nothing to show that living at the Curia would have more advantages elsewhere than at Rome, where everything is available that is needed for religion, for daily life, and for pleasure. We have besides a most skillful prince full of wisdom and sagacity, and we have the perspicacity of the cardinals, thanks to whose counsel we can expect to be safe. We shall be safe also because of the continued prayers of all men, and can continue to trust ourselves to the care of the gods."

Though the older men all speak and think this way, things do look different to different people. Some, wanting to appear cautious, say one must keep on reconsidering this matter. They know that popular uprisings are easier to excite than fully to quell, and that people are never unready for change, provided there is someone they can follow. Of those who laid the foundations for this criminal plot, only six have been punished and are gone. The others, who, if they exist, have survived, are said to be numerous and varied, and not to have given up the ambition that first moved them. People say that it becomes the chief's duty to guard his threatened life, yet also that it offends his majesty to have to take such precautions.

People also say that men are rarely found who want to take the lead in such criminal plots, but that there are many who want to be second in rank to the leaders who throw themselves into danger. When the real leaders are removed, those who were second are made leaders. When I hear these pople speak, I am neither unmoved nor totally convinced by what they say. Even further reasoning does not decide me. I do see clearly what the Italian situation is. I understand that some can conclude that everything is now out of hand. I remember the time of Eugene. I have heard about the troubles of Boniface and have read of the difficulties of many popes. I am not unaware that, as they say, the first pig does the grunting, and this prince will lead them all if he goes away. From another angle, I find the pope's majesty obviously solid. Never since antiquity has a pope who hated arms really had to fight a war. I think this one is zealous for peace, and more than amenable in dealing with princes. Hence I am not much afraid of external aggression. I also think the plague of internal evils will die down. My understanding of the matter, however, and my conclusions, are far from settled. I only know that I am waiting in suspense to see what the further developments in this situation will teach me.

Vale

Poggio Bracciolini

Poggio Bracciolini 1380–1459

In one part of *De Nobilitate*,[1] Poggio tries to characterize the actual nobilities of his time. He does not—like Bruni, or like Machiavelli after Bruni —focus only on the *rich* as a force in politics, or on the leaders of organized *factions*. Instead he starts with the word "noble' as commonly used and arrives thereby at what we would call "hereditary *ruling classes*." He sketches a picture of the nobility as it appears in Florence, Naples, Milan, Venice, Rome, and northern Europe, and adds some words on the nonhereditary ruling groups of the Turkish empire. Chasing the word "noble," he stumbles on a rich variety of observations stored up in his own well-traveled head. He shows a rudimentary but lively interest in social analysis and unusual novelistic gifts. Poggio delights in his own sharp wit, freely experiments with rhetorical styles, and shows a certain complacency without conceit which allows him to laugh at himself. These are the marks of his charm and readability.

Poggio was known for his beautiful handwriting and thorough knowledge of Latin, and thanks to these talents he had a lucrative career as a scribe in the papal service. From humble beginnings he rose to fame and wealth through the assistance he gave to Italian collectors of classical manuscripts, men like Niccolò Niccoli, the Medici brothers of Florence, and Cardinal Orsini in Rome. The personal efforts and diplomatic connections of Poggio brought to light works previously unknown to western students, works that had apparently been gathering dust in monastery and cathedral libraries. Among these works were Lucretius' *De Rerum Natura*, some of the orations

118

of Cicero, Ammianus Marcellinus' history, parts of the writings of Tacitus, and eight comedies by Plautus. These works greatly enriched the thinking of the humanists. Poggio's own vivid letters to his Florentine friends won him a certain reputation as a writer.

He was over forty when he began to write more lengthy and systematic pieces. Then his treatises and polemics gained him wider fame, although his enemies, especially the famous humanists, Valla and Filelfo, tried to show that he wrote inexcusably imperfect Latin. Meanwhile he spent more and more time in Florence, bought a villa, and, in 1434, at the age of fifty-four, gave up his church position to marry a wealthy young lady of eighteen. In 1453 Poggio even had the honor of becoming chancellor of the city.[2]

His major treatises, against monastic parasitism, and concerning avarice, obviously dealt with questions interesting to the urban capitalist reading public. So did his well-known compilation of racy stories, most of which are jokes about churchmen and adultery. The *De Nobilitate*, written in 1440, discusses a major bourgeois preoccupation: the possibility of status not founded on heredity.

We are inclined to think that status was more consistently hereditary in feudal than in commercial society—that the late medieval city, being commercial, not only allowed former serfs to become free but poor men to become rich. We imagine that in the surrounding feudal society there was a little flux around the hereditary core of nobility and in commercial society, more mobility. Poggio apparently, looking at both structures with fifteenth-century eyes, did not think so. What struck him was that ascent through impressive achievement and climbing by means of ruthlessness and time-serving were possible, though exceptional, in both. He was conscious, too, that in both, most people thought of status as hereditary and wanted to bequeath it.

In criticism of this social picture, however, he called upon another general belief important in his time and dear especially to Florentine humanism: belief in self-control and self-betterment. Through his main speaker he states the view of human nature most compatible with this belief: first, nobility is acquired by achievement rather than by inheritance or bestowal; second, even the citizen with no important official position and no great wealth may, through the way he leads his own private secular life, benefit the community and earn "nobility." Even the opposing speaker stresses personal character, though he defends hereditary wealth and public office as providing essential platforms for achievement. In commercial society more than in feudal society, I believe, it was possible to possess wealth and/or to be well known for one's ideas without having any political—administrative, military, or judicial—work to do. This fact made it possible for Poggio to reopen the clas-

119

sical defense of private versus public life. Not only did he defend the self-made man, but he also suggested an idea of citizenship that was highly individual-istic. An élite exists but it is neither hereditary nor institutional.

The discussion takes place at Poggio's own home. One speaker is Lorenzo de' Medici, the brother of Cosimo, unofficial ruler of Florence, and Lorenzo vigorously defends those who, on the basis of hereditary wealth, hold public office and make a magnificent display of their treasures. The other speaker is Niccolò Niccoli, himself a rich Florentine who was unusually reluctant to hold public office. He needles Lorenzo about fame and wealth as masks for sloth and vice. By their mutual tolerance and their gentle joking about each other and Poggio, they suggest that intellectual life is and ought to be quite free and open: "All are free to judge for themselves," Niccolò concludes his final speech. It is striking, especially when we consider the furious polemicism of Poggio and his circle, how peaceful and willing to compromise he makes the speakers in this dialogue. Competition seems to be tempered here by an ideal of social harmony.

NOTES

1. Poggio Bracciolini, *Opera Omnia*, Basel, 1538; reprinted with an introduction by Ricardo Fubini, Turin, Italy, 1964, vol. i. The present translation is based on this text with some emendations from the edition of 1513 (Strassburg, Prelo J. Schot).

2. For Poggio's life, see William Shepherd, *The Life of Poggio Bracciolini*, Liver-pool, 1837; Ernst Walser, *Poggius Florentinus Leben und Werke*, Leipzig, 1914. A bibliography of scholarship on Poggio to 1964 is included in the republished *Opera*.

ON NOBILITY

by Poggio Bracciolini

[Translated with David Marsh]

I AM SURE, most excellent Father,[1] that some people, without openly reproaching me for this effort, because it would be too unfair to
blame a man for using his time so honorably, will nonetheless complain
that I took up a task beyond my capacities to perform adequately. I myself, perhaps, would have to agree and confess that the subject requires
greater talent and eloquence than mine. I would add, however, that I
entered the contest, as it were, more to practice my skill than to show
it off. Others may enter later with more success, having greater powers
of expression.

Sometimes I am amazed to think that *nobility*, a term so widely used
and so differently understood, not only by laymen but also by great
scholars, has not been fully discussed by any Roman or even Greek.
There were only some brief remarks from various authors and a single
book from each of two, Aristotle and Metrodorus.[2] Seeing the gap in
our Latin tradition and considering that the Greek treatises are missing,
I felt it would not be unreasonable for me to set down something that
might serve as the basis for discussion. More learned men, stimulated by
our attempt, will be able later to produce more polished treatments. The
first to write on any subject generally appears duller and ruder. In no
field are the first discoveries so completely and firmly established that
succeeding generations have nothing to add and correct. Even philosophy, the fount of wisdom, and even what are known as the liberal arts,

have required time to develop. For men have arrived at the heights of learning only step by step, and the pioneers have always had to provide incentive for others, who went on to look for greater perfection. My little book, I think, will probably arouse the interest of someone else and lead him to work hard to make up for my omissions and mistakes. Those who are learned and eloquent enough, I earnestly entreat to make the attempt for the general benefit of mankind. For such labors performed by various individuals will vastly increase the splendor and glory of the Latin language, and I will be generally thanked because my clumsy efforts led others to write and to win fame.

I do ask my readers' indulgence if I have not shown enough erudition and stylistic elegance to suit the subject matter or to satisfy them. I have preferred to write in my own rude and unlearned way rather than not to write at all, when I had the time, and when the question was one which few people seem to be able to work out correctly.

To you, Gerardo, I dedicate this little book, to a man whose virtue and learning will bear comparison with those of our greatest forebears. It is a sort of testimonial of my love for you, and it will go forth protected by your great name. Not a little favor and prestige will come to my work through your greatness, for people will think that anything dedicated to you must be of flawless quality. Please accept this little book, then, on the subject of true nobility.

This subject is one I have often heard discussed, and, in particular, not long ago by some highly eloquent men who are also my close friends. For one day, when I had retired to the country from the city for a change of air, there joined me at my invitation, Niccolò Niccoli and Lorenzo de' Medici, my closest and most learned friends. I had lured them to my villa mainly to show them some sculptures I had brought there. When they were in the garden, which I had eagerly ornamented with a few imported marbles, Lorenzo looked around and smiled at my treasures, with the remark:

"Our host, having read that illustrious men of old used to ornament their homes, villas, gardens, arcades, and gymnasiums with statues, paintings, and busts of their ancestors to glorify their own name and their lineage, wanted to render his own place noble, and himself, too, but having no images of his own ancestors, he acquired these meager

122

and broken pieces of sculpture and hoped that the novelty of his collection would perpetuate his fame among his own descendants."

"If nobility is what he wants," said Niccolò, "he will have to dig elsewhere for the stuff of it, not in broken images and pieces of marble —not very important things for a wise man to have—but in the soul. The only stuff that I believe can raise a man to noble eminence is wisdom and virtue."

"Partly," said Lorenzo, "I agree that these qualities contribute greatly toward giving a man nobility—for virtue is something that has been judged divine and worth all men's striving—but we know in fact that nobility does come from paintings, sculptures, elegance, wealth, and ample possessions, as well as from public offices and positions of authority, even when those so distinguished are not noted for their virtue. Even men of outstanding intellect have, as we know from our reading, wanted such ornaments. Even the most learned among the ancients spent time and energy on the acquisition of sculptures and paintings. Cicero for one, and Varro, and Aristotle, as well as other Greeks and Romans known for their versatile knowledge and for lives that were meant to show forth virtue. They adorned their libraries and gardens with art in order to ennoble those places and to show their own good taste and well-spent efforts. For they believed that the images of men who had excelled in the pursuit of glory and wisdom, if placed before the eyes, would help ennoble and stir up the soul."

"Well," said Niccolò, "if sculptures and paintings confer nobility, then sculptors and painters must be more noble than other men, since their homes are full of works of art. Even moneylenders, no matter how wicked and abominable, would be noble just by being rich and holding public office. What a disgraceful thing, however, to say that a man could rise to nobility by crimes and thefts and base profiteering."

Then Lorenzo: "If you think about the meaning of the word, we should call noble not only sculptors and painters, since their art brings them fame, but also the wealthy—no matter how they amassed their property—and we should call noble men famous for great crimes. Both a great literary man and a famous robber we should call noble, one marked out by his learning and wisdom, the other by his notoriety. Writing to his brother about seeking the consulship, Cicero says of his opponents, Antonius and Catiline, that "They are in no way as distinguished for their birth as noted (*nobiles*) for their vices."[3] For the ancients called a man noble (*nobilis*) if he was known (*notus*) in some special way, be he notorious or admired, as long as he was frequently spoken of. Our own Cicero says that Pythagoras was of outstanding wisdom and renown (*nobilitas*)[4] and calls him, in another passage, 'a renowned (nobilis) philosopher, by whom not only Greece and Italy, but even the whole uncivilized world was influenced.'[5] In *For Archias*, likewise, he speaks of philosophers 'who wish to be praised and widely known even when they proclaim their scorn for praise and renown (nobilitas).'[6] And Livy writes in one place, 'This battle nearly equaled in renown (nobilitas), the disaster of Allia.'[7] And elsewhere, '. . . since they had previously made this subject widely known (*nobilitare*) in their savage speeches.'[8] These passages clearly show that a thing was called noble when it was widely mentioned and discussed.

"Our own concern, however, is not with the renown that goes with vice and encourages men to do wicked things, but with the fame that does not scorn virtue and is mixed with it. If you deny that such renown comes from the things we just mentioned, you run against the general opinion and universal sentiment of men. For everyone agrees that a person is noble and can be called noble if he comes from an old family and if his wealthy ancestors held public office and enjoyed high honor. If you respect our own customs, then, and our traditional ideas, and if you consider the general opinion authoritative (for in such matters, it has the most authority), you will have to accept my description of nobility."

"Who do you think should decide this issue?" Niccolò asked, "the wise or the masses? If you choose to be guided by the beliefs and habits of people in general, however, you will find that there is no basis at all for nobility, for these popular beliefs and customs differ widely and contradict each other. No fixed standard can be derived from them, as far as I can see. The word, 'nobility,' to be sure, is generally agreed on, but the meaning is much disputed. And I often think that one who adopts a noble title is the last to merit such a distinction. If nobility is really something, standing, as it must, on a definite rational basis, it ought to be one and the same thing for all people. The masses, however, when they call someone noble are thinking of everything but virtue and

124

reason, and the significance of the term fluctuates to suit the beliefs and habits of different classes—beliefs and habits that are contradictory. The term seems to derive, not from a certain understood model, but from unreflecting behavior. I am forced to doubt, on this account, that the common everyday word, 'nobility,' is more than an empty name.

"If it means anything at all, it must originate in either vice or virtue. But it is foolish to think that nobility arises from vice. And if it arises from virtue, it must be always one and the same, not vary with local custom. Nobility must be a fixed reality. But among us nobility is not much like this, it varies and goes from this extreme to that, seemingly without any firm basis."

"What you mean by this diversity," Lorenzo said, "is not quite clear to me. I wish you would explain it. I should also like to know what view that other people hold you are willing to accept."

"No," said Niccolò, "the debate is hardly suited to this time and place, and perhaps (looking at me), it will not please our host."

"On the contrary, Niccolò," I said, "It will be my delight to see you help us resolve this problem. It would be pleasant to know the answer and well worthwhile. I am not so foolish or silly myself as to hope to acquire nobility with these hastily assembled fragments of sculpture. One ascends to nobility by quite another route, I think. I have looked for these things and purchased them just for the joy of it, and to make the garden more beautiful. Lorenzo, our friend, enjoys teasing me: he thinks that if he can make me despise these objects, he will be able to make off with most of them. While we are on the subject, however, please do discuss the subject as Lorenzo has asked you to. I am not surprised, myself, that the nations agree so little, when even philosophers argue enough to leave me in doubt as to the right opinion."

Then Niccolò: "I scarcely think it has escaped you how manifold and varied is the practical meaning of nobility, for what seems to some the height of nobility, others regard as common. Let me begin with the Italians, who are the model for all nations, showing the others what humanity, virtue, and the general art and science of living really are.

"What could be more different than the opinions of the Neapolitans, the Venetians, and the Romans? The Neapolitans have a more visible nobility than the others, and they seem to equate this word with sloth and idleness, for their nobles spend their lives cherishing an empty kind

125

of leisure, sitting and yawning on their estates. They think it a crime for a nobleman to pay any attention to farming or supervising his estate. All their days are spent in their courtyards or on their horses. As long as they come of an ancient line, no matter how dishonest and silly they are, they think themselves noble. They abhor commerce as vile and shameful, and are so swollen with vanity that no matter how poor and wretched one of them happens to be, he would rather die of hunger than give his daughter in marriage to even the wealthiest merchant. And they prefer theft and robbery to honest work. I know a Neapolitan of knightly rank, a man distinguished for his birth and wealth, who, as befits the head of a household, used to gather together the wines made on his various estates and offer them for sale. For this he was vilified as a merchant; and commerce has so base and foul a name among these sluggish and idle folk, that even with a large dowry he could scarcely marry off his daughter.

"The Venetians run to the opposite extreme from this folly. Their nobles all engage in commerce, even those called knights. They are just a sort of faction set above the rest of the population and consisting of those who hold public office or those whom they call of 'senatorial rank.' To this rank and to eligibility for office, they are qualified by birth. Some are so puffed up by the public esteem for their high title that they despise any commoner they meet, even though they and their parents may be silly, stupid, foolish and poor while the commoner is learned and wise. I would rather be the ass of Apuleius[9] myself, that be such a creature or the son of one, less reasonable and capable of foresight than a humble ass. These Venetians, however, devote their attention chiefly to commerce and do not think it improper for a noble. Unlike any other people, moreover, they frequently elevate to the nobility someone who was without rank. Anyone granted citizenship in Venice for some outstanding service to the Republic, even if the service was a crime, becomes a registered noble. How foolish beyond measure, to call a commoner noble because he has earned citizenship by some service, or to believe that what wise men regard as the reward of virtue and honorable deeds can be bestowed for the performance of evil.

"Among the Romans, those who are viewed as noble despise commerce, consider it base and vile. They think it honorable and proper to a noble, however, to devote himself to agriculture, to tend flocks and

126

herds, or to make a living by breeding of cattle. The pursuit of this kind of wealth can even open the way to nobility among them, if a man from a newer family attempts it. Theirs, then, is a rustic kind of nobility, but honest, and it certainly differs from the Neapolitan one.

"We Florentines seem to have the right idea of nobility, for we consider noble men of ancient lineage and those whose ancestors have held public offices. Some nobles engage in commerce; others, delighting in their titles, engage in no business but amuse themselves with hunting and hawking.

"Among the Genoese, as among the Venetians, the nobles are devoted to trade, like the commoners, especially to maritime trade, and are distinguished only by birth. Elsewhere some nobles live in scattered mountain fortresses, making other men's journeys dangerous as Cacus[10] did, and such are the nobles of Lombardy. It is not very different in the Veneto, where the so-called nobles live on the produce of their estates and on their family inheritance, desiring no occupation but hunting and hawking. They believe that birth alone bestows nobility and that lack of occupation is necessary to maintain it.

"What shall I say of other nations? They are much like us. The Germans consider those noble whose inherited property gives them enough to live on, and who rule over fortresses and small towns far from the cities—and often they engage in highway robbery. The more humane among them attach themselves to the courts of princes and grow used to a more civilized life, yet they remain somewhat rude and harsh in manner.

"There is but one standard of nobility in France, for to the French it is unacceptable for a nobleman to live in the city, and they all flee to their estates. Those who do live in the cities are considered boorish and inferior. They disdain merchants as a lower species, while they, the nobles, languish on their estates without a care for the future. Their number is always increasing, since nobility can be acquired by wealth or by public service. The sons of merchants or of other middlemen leave the city for the country, buy an estate and live on its produce; they thus become seminoble and confer nobility on their descendants. Others put off the purchase of an estate and serve princes instead, which also leads to the honor of noble rank. Among the French, then, the country and the woods do more to win a man nobility than the cities and the fruitful

127

use of leisure or of business. People we would call rustic, they esteem as noble.

"The British, now known as the English, imitate the French, and likewise consider it a disgrace for a noble to live in the city. They inhabit large estates, separated by woods and pastures. They judge a man by his property, and they tend to their farms, sell wool and cattle, and willingly work at rural tasks. I have seen a former tradesman who bought expensive estates and moved his family there, whereupon his sons became noble and he himself was generally received in the houses of nobles. Many commoners have been elevated to the nobility for outstanding service in war, receiving their title along with other gifts from the prince.

"The Spanish have two kinds of nobles, those of ancient origin and of great wealth who live in towns, and those who live in the country on great estates, enjoying a more elegant style of life than their neighbors. Most of them hold knightly rank.

"Among the Greeks those who serve the emperor in his palace—however low their birth—gain the status of noble by virtue of their familiarity with the ruler and service to him. Our rulers, likewise, the pope, the emperor, kings, and princes make men noble by patents and letters without regard to virtue. Hence the absurdity that nobility may be gained by habitual allegiance or by sealed letters of patent.

"The heathen peoples have different customs concerning nobility. Egyptians and Syrians have no nobility but that which is granted to soldiers, and these alone stand above the rest of the people, whom they rule and whom they regard as slaves. Yet it is a fact that these soldiers are all purchased slaves themselves, who are later given command of the cavalry and put in charge of provinces. They may be so elevated by fortune's favor that the most powerful, with the support of his armed forces, can sometimes take over the kingdom. The Turks and Tartars also base their nobility on arms, for the leaders of armies are enriched with estates and considered noble, even when they joined the army as slaves. (A great number did, since boys are bought by the government for the army.) In these countries it is enough to excel in arms to be considered noble.

"What a vast variety, then, of human customs. What diversity among these, to say nothing of other nations. Are we not forced to admit that, since nobility is revered on such disparate grounds, there is no sure definition in all this to guide us? Yet if nobility is really something specific, there must be some definite basis for it, some stable and solid foundation on which it can be built."

To this Lorenzo: "Nobility may seem manifold because of national differences, but I think all the nobilities you have just described are real and true nobilities and rightly esteemed such. Different states also have different laws, which vary according to the needs and desires of governments, for different laws seem helpful to some and harmful to others. Men do, nonetheless, respect the power and authority of laws, and do not consider them invalid because they are not universal. I think that those different Italians, French, Germans, British, and heathen are noble, if they are considered noble by their countrymen.

"I would not call city-people more noble than country folk, nor businessmen who act worthily in the conduct of their government more noble than idle gentlemen sitting at leisure in their courtyards and well satisfied with that life. We ought to respect custom which, since it instills habits, exercises supreme power over human conduct. While custom varies, moreover, as you can see in the diversity of nations, yet all agree on certain marks of nobility: superior wealth, honorable occupation, freedom from employment, military glory, private magnificence, or sheer prestige—in any case some kind of outstanding excellence."

"You are greatly mistaken," said Niccolò, "for the only custom we should either approve or adopt is the one which accords with reason; any other may be considered an abuse of the idea. Laws are based on the desires and needs of the governed, and since these are not the same among nations and individuals, laws too must necessarily vary according to the variety of human concerns. Yet all laws have the same origin, inasmuch as their ultimate source is the sense of fairness and justice, so that they seem to urge and recommend what is honorable and useful for each nation. But the kinds of nobility which I just described, contradictory and various as they are, differ so much that they do not clearly share an ultimate source or basic idea grounded in reason. They seem to arise from mere opinion by arbitrary choice and without rational justification. I do not acknowledge, therefore, that anyone can be called noble on this basis. What is noble about a man who languishes in idleness, pursues no honorable purposes, possesses no virtue, no wisdom, and no learning, but has only ancestors and a long family history? I rate

129

people like that as cheap cattle. Nor shall I ever admit that a citizen, or anyone else, merits the name of noble if he is dishonest, unprincipled, contemptible, vicious, or totally undistinguished; I shall recognize in him nothing but a man who leans on the character and honorable position of his ancestors.

"I also fail to see what sort of nobility can come from trade, or how activities which philosophers have considered vile and base can lead to it. Cicero says that commerce is not so very contemptible if it makes really large profits, but otherwise he sees it as a low and common kind of employment.[11] If something is at all contemptible, surely it has no touch of nobility, and such employment serves no noble purpose. Workmen and artisans are all without nobility, for their work does not require virtue—for this reason, we look down on this whole class of men.

"Nor will nobility be the result of riches, whether we acquire them ourselves or inherit them, for we know how wealth is gained. It is not usually by virtue, for virtue advises us to abstain from doing things for money; and inherited wealth, the result of someone else's work, should win no praise for us. Saint Jerome has a golden maxim: a rich man is either a wicked man or the heir of a wicked man.[12] (Don't think, Lorenzo, that I aim this remark at you, for your good and humane father[13] was blessed with a prudent and diligent character and with the favor of fortune.) Riches cannot, it is clear, make us noble. Nor can public office, status, honors, or power. All these can fall to destructive, criminal, useless, dissolute, mad, and delirious men; and such men certainly remain wholly undeserving of the name of noble, for noble is a term that has nothing in common with vice or crime.

"Nor can I believe that an ancient family, a long list of ancestors, can confer nobility on people, when the ancestors were bold, criminally minded, steeped in dissipation. The descendants of such ancestors will, in fact, seem less noble because of the crimes of their parents. And if your parents were honorable and you come from a long line of meritorious ancestors, but you yourself are lazy, sluggish, unattractive and empty of virtue—there's nothing noble about that. Besides, if a long line of ancestors could confer nobility, everyone would be equally noble, for everyone's origin goes equally far back and no one but has ancestors that could be traced back a thousand years.

"Some people think they can preserve inherited nobility, as they see

130

it, by hawking and hunting. They say they are noble because they worry about no business matters and because they have a famous name and a coat of arms. But the zeal of the idle for pursuing birds and beasts has no more odor of nobility about it than the lairs of the wild animals themselves. Clearly there is more grace in a certain kind of ancient and virtuous style of farming than in mad and frenzied chasing through groves and thickets, an activity that makes men seem like wild beasts. A noble person need not despise such things as recreation, but he will shun them when they become dissipation. Many people actually give all their attention and spend their whole lives on activities that show, not their nobility, but a sort of suppressed madness in them.

"Our countrymen attach honorable status to military service and view it as a sort of training for nobility or way of showing nobility, but again I fail to see what grace or adornment it confers on a man. Some of our officials and other citizens wear a gold pin in token of knighthood, although perhaps they don't even have a horse and know nothing of warfare. Their lives are unrelated to their splendid dress. Artificial elegance like this kind of empty display can no more ennoble them than it could make them brave on the battlefield. They may be businessmen in fact, but they are nearer to the position of the obscure footsoldier than to the splendor of the nobility they claim. Some boast of the knightly status of their grandfathers and greatgrandfathers and vaunt their own nobility by reference to their descent, but they seem to me just ignorant. Among the ancients, the equestrian order never even had the full status of nobility, and I am greatly surprised that we should think so differently. The Romans did not count knights as noble, for knights generally worked as tax farmers, fulfilling the base function of collecting revenues. Patrician families alone were called noble, along with the families of those who had celebrated triumphs or held the position of consuls and senators. The equestrian order was viewed as part of the commonality. Many knights, however, did by magnificent achievements in peace or war win nobility for their line. Marius and Cicero, for example, were not of noble birth but they bequeathed prominence to their sons and nobility, too, if the sons had been willing to imitate the fathers' virtue. We today, however, derive nobility from membership in the knightly order, and we see men boast about the number of their ancestors who were knights. If they themselves had fought in battles and done great

131

deeds, as the title requires, I might grant them the nobility they claim, but as long as they loaf at home, far from any knightly enterprise, gold spurs and sword belts no more bestow nobility on them than bronze or silver. Gold, in fact, would seem a symbol, not of nobility, but of wealth.

"True nobility, I think, is not something peculiar to country estates, as the French and English think, or set among mountains and busy with robbery, as the Germans believe. For wise men do not think solitude, idleness, or even wealth confer nobility but only the pursuit of virtue does. Wise men judge that nobility is gained and exercised best in cities, among people, and less easily among wild beasts in solitude or in dealings with farmers. It seems utterly absurd, moreover, to imagine that princes can confer nobility, for they cannot make a man prudent, honorable, or wise. Nobility is not externally derived but springs from one's own virtue. The very great variety of criteria applied in the world only convinces me that what people call nobility is nothing but a sort of display and vanity devised by human folly and conceit.

"Let's put popular notions aside for a while, for on serious consideration I am convinced that this common word, 'nobility,' does not refer to nobility at all. Here is my own belief. All things may be called either good or bad or placed between the two, what the Greeks call 'indifferent.' No one has ever set nobility among bad things, for it would be absurd if something so much praised and admired were bad. But if it is a good thing, it must be either a mental or a bodily or an external good. It can scarcely be one of the gifts of fortune, for those who gain such gifts are not called noble, but rich. Nor do bodily advantages, such as health and beauty, bestow nobility, for if it lay in these, nobility would pass with the passing of wealth, beauty, or health. Non-noble persons would readily become noble and noble persons would readily lose their nobility. If there is nobility at all, therefore, it must pertain to mental assets, otherwise known as virtues; and these in turn, are either intellectual or moral. Now a person may be prudent by reason of his prudence, wise by his wisdom, just by his justice, moderate by his moderation, and similarly, virtuous according to the sum of his virtues, but we still don't know what will make him noble. No one virtue of itself makes a man noble, nor will even all the virtues together make him noble, though they will make him happy.

"Nobility is neither virtue nor vice, then, nor does it seem to be among the things which are said to be in between, since these are considered sometimes good, sometimes bad, according to their application. If nobility were now good, now bad, it could be considered both. It would follow that good persons and bad ones would be equally capable of acquiring nobility, which is utterly absurd. Nobility, it seems, cannot be an 'indifferent' thing. And another line of reasoning also leads here: for nobility, if it is something, is either to be sought or to be shunned. Ridiculous to call it something to be shunned, for then no one would desire it. It also does not seem something we ought to seek, for we ought to seek what reason and wisdom prescribe, honorable things and whatever makes us blessed and happy. Since nobility gives us neither virtue nor any good to make us better, richer, or more blessed, I fail to understand why it should be sought. It seems, then, that nobility is nothing at all. ✱

"It is the same if we consider whether nobility deserves praise or blame. Since it is much praised and sought by good men, it cannot belong to the things that ought to be blamed. But it belongs even less in the category of praiseworthy things, for anything praiseworthy arises from virtue. It is praiseworthy to live rightly, that is, virtuously, and this is because we ought to value virtue. But there is no virtue which is called nobility or from which nobility derives, nor ought extra praise to derive from the nobility of an honorable action. Nobility itself cannot be a thing that is praiseworthy.

"If nobility exists, moreover, it must lie in a man or in his goods. If in the man, it arrives there either by nature or by acquisition. If by nature, all are born equally noble, which no one even half-educated would admit. But if acquired, nobility must come through actions or work. But actions and works make men good, bad, prudent, learned, diligent and so forth, not noble—there is no work from which nobility is forged. If nobility were located in things, however, these would automatically bestow nobility on their possessor, as riches make a man rich. And for lack of these things, we would lack nobility. Nobility would leave us with our material possessions and return to us with them, as if going in and coming out of lodgings.

"Such arguments show that nobility is simply a kind of illusion, a form of insanity. Reasoning without that vanity, I fail to see why this empty tale has been so widely circulated, or what good or profit there is in it. Why is nobility so much valued? It makes us neither wise, nor learned, nor prudent, nor just, nor lucky, and it adds nothing to our health, our beauty, or the probity of our lives. Rather, like some dim shadow, it plagues our thoughts. It resembles dreams, which excite those who sleep with false visions that make no sense when the sleepers awake. I am often annoyed to see men who take pride in their nobility, yet are silly, coarse, and lazy. I no more esteem such boors than I do ballad singers who sing heroic tales on street corners but have no good in themselves beyond their ability to sing the praises of others.

"But we have talked enough now, and at this late hour, we should liberate our host from all this troubling conversation."

"Not at all," said Lorenzo, "You shall not escape, leaving your sting like a bee. You shall hear out my brief reply. If you refuse, you will seem very peevish—as I realize I myself must seem at this moment. I am not surprised at you, Niccolò, for you always oppose the conventional view—so here you go now, denying the existence of both kinds of nobility, the kind the general public believes in and the kind wise men have defined philosophically."

"I have said nothing about the wise so far," said Niccolò, "I have spoken only about the general public and the obsessive vanity of the nobles themselves, who, on the sole basis of empty ostentation and a conspicuous display of whimsey annoy us every day with hints of their nobility, yet have no idea by what means or with what skill it may be acquired."

"If you side with the philosophers," said Lorenzo, "or fail to refute them, you are bound to lose your case. For Aristotle, whose subtle genius exceeds that of all other philosophers, comes out against you, since he defines nobility and proves that it is something. His wisdom in all things is, in fact, so immense that anything that contradicts him is apt to seem foolish."

"I admit he is called the greatest of philosophers," said Niccolò, "yet no authority will stop my thinking and saying what seems to me closest to the truth."

"As you like," said Lorenzo. "Now you will see me, like you earlier, trying to oppose the view of another. But if your conscience prevents you from changing your mind, I won't insist. To return to Aristotle, however, he says in Book V of the *Politics* that nobility consists in in-

134

herited wealth.[14] And elsewhere he says that people are noble whose ancestors were outstanding in virtue and in wealth.[15] Aristotle, as you see, wisely and gravely defined nobility, not as the empty shadow you think it, but as something quite definite. Let there be no further doubt, therefore, that nobility exists and that the philosopher has rightly defined it."

"Nay," said Niccolò, "these words do not shake me at all. I believe that Aristotle wrote them, not from his own considered judgment, but from common opinion. For in the *Ethics*, where he expresses more what he truly feels, he calls *well-born* the man who is naturally inclined to distinguish what is true and to desire what is good; and this, he says, is the most excellent thing, since it is not received from another person nor learned.[16] A person born with that kind of character he calls truly and perfectly noble. And he seems inclined also to consider well-born the man who actively achieves virtue, having been predisposed that way from birth. Now, how could this great philosopher also espouse the ideas you just reported?

"He says that virtues combined with wealth equal nobility—does this mean that virtues without a mass of fortune's goods have no nobility? No one with even a slim education would consent to it, but for Aristotle's great name and established authority. What of the sons and grandsons of Valerius Publicola, of Fabricius, of Coruncanius, of Scipio Nasica (the last of whom was even buried at public expense because of his poverty), what of the children of Scipio Asiaticus (whose daughters' dowries had to be supplied from the public treasury), and many other outstanding men who remained poor while exercising the highest commands and offices and who brought glory, not only to Rome, but to the world? If the children and grandchildren of such men imitated them in being virtuous and poor, would they (to say nothing of their fathers) be devoid of the splendid nobility they inherited—all because of Aristotle's definition? If so, you could not call Aristides noble, the man who was uniquely nicknamed the "Just" on account of his great integrity and who was the only Athenian leader comparable to Themistocles. He could not qualify for nobility, nor could he bequeath nobility to his children, for this civic leader and celebrated man of virtue died so poor that he left scarcely enough to pay for his funeral. What could be more idiotic than to say that Aristides, Scipio, and the other great leaders of the

135

ancient nations lacked nobility because they cared more for virtue than for wealth, or to think that they barred the path to nobility for their children?

"Even suppose that, in line with Aristotle's definition, there is a man of virtue and wealth, derived from virtuous and wealthy parents, and consider the absurdity of it: since riches are dependent on chance and can be given or taken away, his nobility will depend on the turn of fortune and will vanish with prosperity to reappear when prosperity returns. Likewise when a rich man surrenders to vice, he loses part of his nobility. Such nobility would be a wandering thing, coming and going like boys at play, and held in no firm grasp. What of riches built on usury, plunder, booty, crime, and the condemnation of citizens, could such wealth possibly ennoble the owner? No more, I say, than it can make him honorable and good. Let riches have no claim to bestowing nobility, therefore, but let us call the owner of wealth rich and opulent, not noble.

"Yet, you will say, Aristotle adds virtue to wealth, and it is the combination he says ennobles the possessor. But how can these things ennoble the children of such a person? As the wise man has said, whatever existed before us concerns us no more than what will come after us,[17] and our parents' virtue no more belongs to us than our own to our children. I don't think Aristotle meant to imply that nobility is transmitted from one generation to the next, for he said nobility required virtue as well as wealth, and while wealth may certainly be inherited, virtue hardly ever is. Virtue consists in action, and actions belong to the doer of them; hence nobility based on virtue belongs to the doer alone. We do not call a horse strong and fair and swift because it is bred of a stallion with these qualities, but only because its own harmonious build attracts attention, its own strength carries the rider well, and it is itself roused by the trumpet. The offspring of famous fathers, likewise, I shall not call noble, but only the man who has lustrous virtues of his own. I judge a house beautiful, not because a handsome carpenter built it, but because it is magnificent and well-ordered in every way. Military science, horsemanship, and the liberal arts may indeed be taught to our children, but virtue does not come by parental instruction—only by some sort of divine favor and by the invisible movement of fate. We have, in fact, seen many evil and wicked men beget sons of outstanding

136

merit. We have also seen men of high renown cursed with sons whose disgraceful behavior has wrecked even their fathers' reputation. Here, as we see, the sons gain no virtue from their parent, but in other cases, sons transcend their fathers' crimes and achieve greatness nonetheless. Since vice or virtue is not inherited, then, everyone is the creator and framer of his own nobility, as of his own virtue. If nobility were really something transmitted by inheritance, a worthless slave who happened to be adopted by a rich man and to be made his heir would become noble, and no sane person would say that.

"Procreation, moreover, is the means by which sons are brought into the world, and if it be base or foul, through adultery, incest or rape, it cannot confer nobility, for neither virtue nor anything praiseworthy can come through evil. Such an outrage would invalidate all praise of a man's birth. The Aristotelian nobility you proposed, then, seems, first of all, not to exist, and second, not to be a thing one could inherit. Even if we accept his definition, we will find hardly anyone noble, or only a handful of men who would be noble only intermittently. It is rare, of course, for wealth to be combined with virtue, for virtue alone is rare and difficult, and even the virtuous can lose their good reputation through some public disgrace or because of one wicked act. Virtue dishonored would apparently shed its nobility.

"It is said of Themistocles (by far the greatest Greek leader in peace and war) that in his early years he had such a bad reputation for criminal behavior and for vice that his father disinherited him. Thus, by deserting his father's virtue, Themistocles lost his nobility. Later, when he chose a better way of life, he recovered his nobility by illustrious deeds and by the wealth that came to him from those. But this nobility was marred, for he still had been disinherited. Still later, when he was convicted of treason and exiled, and when he lost his fortune, his nobility left him again. He had befouled his great glory by plotting against his country. And what about Hannibal, the most famous of all generals? Born of a noble family and a famous father, he was renowned for his own deeds—but since, as Livy reports,[18] his vices were as enormous as his virtues, should we not deny all his claims to nobility? For a man whose vices and virtues are equal is neither noble nor ignoble. And the same argument applies to Pausanius, who wavered, they say, all his life between vice and virtue.

137

"I should like to ask Aristotle, Lorenzo, for the sake of our definition, what he would say was the source of nobility. If wealth, I should oppose him, for these transitory gifts of fortune would make nobility something transitory.[19] If wealth and virtue together, a man could leave his sons part of his nobility (namely his wealth) but would have to take his virtue with him. If the sons fail to live as virtuously and also squander the wealth, they will be ignoble; if they succeed to his fortune and have as much virtue, they will be noble. Yet in view of the vicissitudes that beset human life, it is likely that the grandchildren will be stripped of fortune's gifts and will have very different lives from the preceding generation, so that nobility will not come to them. The great-grandchildren may have the virtue and wealth of their grandfathers and great-grandfathers, and thus have nobility again. In the long run, a single family will produce some noble and some ignoble descendants in no sure and predictable order, and the family name will not be any guarantee of nobility. Nobility will be, after all, something unstable and outside of our control. We should prefer to see nobility as something which, based on our own judgment, is neither given to us nor taken from us without our own consent. I believe, in fact, that Aristotle, when writing about the state, followed popular opinion and gave more weight to riches than a philosopher should."

Then Lorenzo: "Well, Niccolò, you have talked a long time but I think you have said nothing worthy of your erudition. If you consider the meaning of the Greek word, it confirms Aristotle, I think: for what the Romans call *nobilitas*, the Greeks call *eugeneia*—'being well-born,' in Latin, *generositas*. Those born of an ancient family renowned for its virtues and deeds were thought well-born because of the fame of their family and tribe. *Generosus* means born of a notable tribe, '*genus*.'"

"It seems," said Niccolò, "that the Romans had a better name for this thing than the Greeks. While the Greeks consider nobility derived from birth, we call men *noble* for their own upright deeds and for the glory and fame they win by their own character. We seem to derive the word from ourselves (*nobismet ipsis*),[20] not from others. We think a man ennobled by some great deed that brings both wide renown and high esteem."

"Think what you will of the meaning of the word," said Lorenzo, "I shall remain Aristotelian and say that nobility derives, not only from virtue, but also from fortune's goods, family, and country and the blessings of health and wealth. Riches make possible magnanimity, the most welcome of virtues. In war, in peace, when expenditures are required, the glory that bestows nobility is won. Without the goods of fortune, moreover, we would not be able to practice magnificence, which greatly enhances our reputation and fame. And our homeland contributes to our nobility as well. Themistocles saw this, for it is said that a man from Seriphus complained that Themistocles owed his fame, not to himself, but to the glory of his country. To this Themistocles replied that, even if he were from Seriphus, he would not be ignoble, but the man from Scriphus would not be famous or noble even if he were an Athenian.[21] A peasant from some Italian hamlet, to be sure, does not have the same opportunities to gain glory as a Florentine, but neither can a Florentine achieve nobility just by being a citizen. Birth, too, is of great assistance. Commands have been entrusted, provinces allotted, and triumphs granted to people, not only for their virtue, as we read, but also and sometimes more, because of their glorious ancestors and the memories associated with their name—such appointments have provided individuals with the opportunity to become noble. Aristotle was right, then, that virtue supported by wealth is what produces nobility.

"Riches, of course, are neither good nor bad in themselves but become good or bad according to their use, but they do seem to make a good man more illustrious and to place him, as it were, in the place where his virtue may shine forth. He will use the gifts of fortune as a sort of means for his purposes in life, and his fortune will allow him to apply his virtues to the needs of his friends, to the building of his own magnificence, and to the defense of his country. Without wealth such virtues would be inadequate and weak, not strong enough to achieve their purpose. In maintaining the general good, what does Stoic generosity do? To the Stoics this virtue is a mental attitude, not an outer deed. Aristotle saw that wealth, wisely employed by a virtuous man, was necessary to a good public character, and he correctly deduced that wealth must be joined to virtue in order for a man to be noble. Though poverty is much praised, we know that both philosophers and other admirable men have preferred to lack that distinction rather than to lack material resources."

"The fault," said Niccolò, "is not Aristotle's, but belongs to human vice. Men are led, by Aristotle's teaching, to praise riches, and they are corrupted by the frailty of their own nature and led to despise poverty as a vile condition and one of the worst evils. Desiring wealth too much, they believe there is no way to virtue and right living without it. We are not interested in corrupt opinion, however, but in truth, and that, in my view, is a long way from Aristotle's definition. If you look at the facts of the matter, riches usually make men proud, headstrong, lustful, abusive, and more disposed to pursue pleasures and vices. Aristotle himself sensed this and wrote that men usually become worse because of riches; therefore riches are seldom associated with virtue, and even more seldom produce nobility.[22] He also admits it in the *Politics*, where he says that nobility and virtue are rare among the rich.[23] If riches did ennoble men, the owner would be less noble than his safe or wallet. I say that no prestige, no honors, no deeds, no public offices, no military commands, and no triumphal processions can bestow true nobility—unless virtue is there and is, in fact, the crucial element.

"Riches, to be sure, bring fame among the common people as a shadow of glory, but the high name of nobility is attained through virtue. Birth, nationality, and ancestry, as well as the other things you mentioned, are without virtue: they are like the sign of the tavern, which shows where wine is sold but does not add in any way to its quality. Virtue stands alone and, even without props, it can attain nobility. Marcus Cato the Elder was not raised up from his low station by nationality, birth, or riches—for he was born at Tusculum of an obscure family with slender means—but by his outstanding virtue. Gaius Marius of Arpinum, an obscure country boy serving in the army for small wages, attained nobility by his virtue and deeds alone. Sertorius of Nursia, as well, became illustrious and noble through his virtues. These and many others should prove to you that nobility has been granted to virtue unaided by riches or other external aids."

Then Lorenzo said to me, "As usual, our friend has demonstrated his ability to refute the ideas of others and disparage them. He condemns every view that is offered, but he says nothing to show us where *he* stands."

"That is your fault," said Niccolò, "since you have furnished the material for discussing what I don't think rather than what I do believe. Now if you ask my own opinion, the answer is simple, for I am not the famous Diogenes the Cynic, who mocked nobility as a veil for wicked-ness.[24] Nor do I agree with the masses and accept an insane idea of what is noble.

"I commend as truest the opinion of the Stoics. In all questions of right conduct, and in the matter of nobility specifically, they have drunk from the source of philosophy itself. They do not flatter the masses, but speak according to the dictates of truth, and they do not pursue fortune —a deceptive and uncertain kind of goal—but virtue, the sure way and the lord of right conduct. They put virtue and observance of the mean first, and subordinate everything else to the question of virtue. The highest good they see in virtue (*honestum*), for if you have this good and have law, you have something stable and abiding, while fortune's gifts pass like a flowing stream, solid nowhere and treacherous to all. In this, and in other things, the Stoics seem to have spoken most truly: nobility is born of virtue alone.

"They themselves, however, seem to have regarded Plato as the orig-inator and founder of their wisdom, and his wisdom in all things is considered unique and almost divine. As Diogenes Laertius says in his *Life* of Plato, the philosopher divided nobility into four categories.[25] The first kind, he asserts, belongs to those whose parents were famous, good, and just. The second kind belongs to those whose parents were very powerful men, sometimes rulers. The third belongs to those whose an-cestors were celebrated for their glorious deeds or for winning the prize at the public games. The fourth, however, is the most excellent, and it belongs to those who gain nobility not by another's virtue and greatness of soul, but by their own. These last alone he finds truly deserve the name of noble. ✳

"This division of Plato ends by considering the nobility based on vir-tue as the one that is true, genuine, and self-sufficient, for nobility is like some sort of radiance proceeding from virtue and illuminating those who possess it and raising them up from any station whatsoever. Now our ancestors' virtues, public offices, and glorious deeds and struggles pertain to them, adorn and distinguish them for their achievements, their labor and their determination. We earn our own praise and no-bility through our own merits, not those of others, and only through those actions which we perform by our own choice. For how do the actions of our forefathers, performed without our advice or assistance, reflect on us? Their deeds lent brilliance and glory to them and opened for us an opportunity. If we use the opportunity and follow their example, our achievements will be slightly diminished, as they would be if we were deriving support from inherited wealth, for our glory will be less than that of persons who take the path of virtue and glory without the advantage of a family precedent. Just as it is considered better to have built a house than merely to have inhabited it or decorated it, so it is more distinguished and fine to possess nobility created by oneself, not merely to preserve a nobility received from others. Better to shine by one's own strength and power than merely to display another person's. The palm of nobility, for this very reason, must go to virtue alone. Courtyards, furnished with ancestral busts, colonnades adorned with sculptures and paintings, splendid villas, newly built churches, and various decorations added to one's home evoke in spectators more wonder than respect for one's nobility.

"Antisthenes, following Plato, thought that nobility derives from virtue alone and that the pursuit of virtue was nobility itself.[26] The Stoics embraced Plato's opinion and regarded wise men as the only noblemen. These opinions are recorded in our own Cicero,[27] and Seneca, an eminent Stoic philosopher, often, but especially in a passage of, I believe, his forty-fourth letter to Lucilius, said that the source and origin of nobility lies in the virtues of the mind. Of nobility, he says:

> A good mind may belong to anyone; in this we are all noble. Socrates was not an aristocrat. Philosophy did not find Plato noble, but made him so. Who is well-born? The man naturally well disposed to virtue; this is the most important consideration. Now, if you turn back to antiquity, everyone comes from a time before which nothing existed, and if all are traced back to the very beginning, all are sprung from the gods. From the first origin of the world even to the present day, an alternating series has brought us forth, now glorious, now mean. Plato says there is no king who is not sprung from slaves, nor any slave not sprung from kings. A courtyard filled with famous* likenesses does not make one noble; no one has lived his life to give us glory. It is the soul which ennobles, and it can rise from any man's station and above his fortune.[28]

"These are Seneca's words, and this very wise man could, it seems, say nothing truer if he were to speak through the oracle of Apollo, than to state that nobility is possible only through virtue and wisdom, and

---

* The best texts have *fumosis* (sooty) for Poggio's *famosis* (famous).

those alone are noble whose virtuous conduct has brought them praise and dignity. Following reason, Juvenal, also, in one of his *Satires*, refutes with many arguments the general and popular idea of nobility, to show that it does not depend on the things you just mentioned; he agrees with Seneca that virtue, and only virtue, is nobility.[29]

"To me the philosopher Cleanthes (who sometimes himself drew water from the well for his garden) and the philosopher Demetrius (whom Seneca saw sleeping on straw and called, not a mere teacher, but a real witness to virtue and truth) were nobler than Pericles and Themistocles, who derived their nobility more from their country's glory and power than from their personal virtue.[30] For many had a share in the glorious deeds they did—they had allies, soldiers, fortune to make their virtue famous—while only he who has striven for those virtues which preserve and protect our lives has a share in philosophy, the sole guide to wisdom and the knowledge of the right. The man who lives prudently and wisely derives the good things of life not from outside but from within himself, and the praise he obtains comes through his own achievement only. He who has put his virtues into practice creates his own glory and for this, with no external aid, obtains the distinction of nobility."

Then Lorenzo said: "Though I admit that virtue pertains to nobility and has great importance in determining what it is, the whole of nobility does not seem to me located in virtue. To me it seems necessary, if a man is to merit the title of noble, that he also possess those external things you just rejected: the courtyards full of statues, the colonnades, the theaters and public entertainments, hunting parties, and other things by which we enhance our reputation. These things make men famous, and thus bestow nobility. Glory does attend virtue and upright character in action, but these things too have a certain splendor, produce a kind of fame beyond mere popular acclaim, something which people call nobility. The great deeds and the virtues of our family seem to give dignity to their descendants, and the honor of our fathers is like a light illuminating us and making us more worthy and notable. Who would really deny that the virtues of our ancestors make us nobler and more illustrious? If we want our own deeds to be praised and remembered by our posterity, the recollection and praise of parents must shine—as their portraits would—on sons. The parents wished to bequeath even their

143

personal glory. Many people say, therefore, that nobility is simply hereditary, that, like fortune's goods, it comes to us from our parents, and that it is up to sons either to reject or to preserve it. Whoever maintains the virtues and guards the heritage of his ancestors will match them in nobility, while whoever abandons himself to lesser pursuits and defiles his life with vices and crimes squanders their nobility, just as if he were extravagant and wasted his patrimony by prodigal spending. One should not deny the transmission of paternal nobility to sons, and that persons who are not yet seen as virtuous may be called noble. Cicero, in his oration *For Roscius*, says: 'You, too, youths who are noble, I shall stir up to the imitation of your ancestors.'[31] Thus wisest Cicero regards as noble even those who have not yet, on account of their youth, been able to emulate their fathers.

"In fact, to be frank, I would sooner call a man noble who could point to illustrious forebears, even though he was himself not especially distinguished for his virtue, than one of obscure ancestry but great and varied excellence. The first of these men can readily become famous because of his ancestors' renown, and in him even a little light of virtue will shine with their added splendor. The second, with no such advantage, will need great powers to illuminate the obscurity in which he was born, for it is more difficult to open a new way. One, with small effort, sustains a glory already won for him, while the other must fight against obscurity with time, effort, and persistent striving finally to gain the greatness and renown from which nobility arises.

"Your Stoic virtue, Niccolò, is too naked, needy, and almost disagreeable to come into our cities and seems to stand rather forsaken and solitary. It has been often praised, that's true, but few can be found who really desire it. Although they regard nobility as derived from virtue alone, they must admit that, unless they flee from city life, they will need many aids—health, wealth, nation, and other things within the power of fortune—else their virtue must shiver in the world, a lonely and needy thing. This virtue will not keep company with men in general, so that the 'nobility' it gives seems rather rustic and lacks all public status. For what is the nobility of a philosopher, content with his studies, living obscurely in a library where even he hardly hears of himself, or of a man who lives moderately, uprightly, chastely and wisely in a hidden villa, while no one talks about him or praises him. Virtue I would concede to them, but not nobility. I would call them lovers of virtue but not noblemen. Few seek the nobility of the Stoics, and fewer still attain it. I myself desire and admire the nobility which human custom enshrined long ago, and I don't think the Greeks or Romans knew so little of life as to use this term often in describing men if they had not meant something other than Stoic virtue could be considered noble."

"I won't deny," said Niccolò, the nobility of a high-ranking citizen who is a respected public figure, provided he also cares to protect honesty. Yet I would also include in the nobility a man who stood outside of public affairs and devoted himself to virtue, taking time for himself and striving to have a good conscience. The man who fights vices is no less brave than the one who wages war. One who steers his life toward the good, or who teaches good judgment, I would call as wise as one who manages the state and looks to her advantage only, in war and in peace. I would call not only noble, but most noble, the philosophers and scholars whose diligence and long hours of work have refined human life in various ways and who, though they shunned public life, have given us better character and helped, by their writing, to reduce human vice by their example.

"I grant—don't think me obstinate; I shall make some concessions—that a certain splendor and prestige comes from national and ancestral glory, and that one's descendants may be said to share in a small portion thereof. Yet when I think as rationally as I can, I fail to see what exactly this share is. To me, at least, this share seems like a sop given to lazy people, whose excuse for their own mediocrity is an exhibition of the glory of others, as if it were theirs. Fleeing the dust and sunlight of the struggle, they lurk in the shadow of others and recount the virtues of past heroes, with nothing to say for themselves. As for the nation, certainly it sheds light equally on all the citizens. The greatest individuals, too, have not left clearer paths for their sons to follow than for anybody else. The light of their distinction shines for all, but brightest for those who stand close, who imitate their glory and do not merely observe it. Thus the teaching and great wisdom of Plato and Aristotle benefited their sons no more than other men, and the virtues of the elder Scipio could give as much nobility to me—if I modeled my behavior on his—as to his sons. Theophrastus, who succeeded Aristotle in the academy, gained more of his noble heritage than Nicomachus, Aristotle's son, who

145

was inferior to Theophrastus in learning. For virtue may belong to anyone, and does belong to the man who grasps it. Lazy, indifferent, impious and perverse descendants of great ancestors ought to be considered, contrary to their own claims, even baser than other men, for they fail more conspicuously in maintaining the inherited standards. Cicero's freedman, Tiro, who adhered to his master's virtues, was indeed more noble than the son who abandoned his father's integrity.

"How wrong you are to see virtue without external goods as needy, rude, and somehow solitary. Virtue does not depend on wealth or the assistance of fortune, for she is perfect in herself, radiant in her own dignity, grace, and charm, like a queen enthroned, and her splendor illuminates the world. What need has she of outward things when she is content with what she has—and what she has is the greatest wealth, excelling all other treasures. She needs and wants no external support. To lack something seems a defect, but since virtue possesses everything needed for a good and happy life (being in herself perfect and absolute), she needs nothing else, for nothing can be added to make her more virtuous. The Stoics wisely regarded nobility as solely dependent on virtue, itself independent of external things. Those who think otherwise seem to follow, not truth, but common belief.

"The Stoic philosophy is not only truest, but it inspires the best conduct. For if men were sure that they could become noble through integrity and character, that true nobility comes through right conduct, and not from any outside source, they would surely be spurred to virtuous resolutions; shaking off sloth, we would not rest on the laurels of others, while doing nothing worthwhile ourselves; we would rise up and pursue the honor of nobility. See how the rich behave, if they have inherited their wealth. They are idle and less careful to guard it than if they had earned it by their own sweat. Thinking that nobility is theirs by inheritance, some people grow soft and sluggish. They smugly describe the greatness of their ancestors, and show no eagerness to pursue honor for themselves. But those who believe that only one's own virtue and merit can bestow nobility are kindled with ardent desire to do deeds of shining virtue. Whether they follow the example of their parents or pattern themselves after other models, they will achieve true nobility, a greater achievement, in my view, if not based on any inheritance, but simply on diligence and love of virtue.

146

"We must cherish virtue, Lorenzo, for it not only makes us noble, but blessed and immortal in the memory of men. From virtue, nobility; from virtue, glory; from virtue, our conduct should derive; from virtue comes all right conduct and the willingness to strive.

"But we have talked long enough. Which of us is right, let others judge, who have more talent. All are free to judge for themselves. But now that the afternoon has grown a little cooler, let's go for a walk outside town to see the stream our friend has often told us is so well stocked with fish."

NOTES

The following notes to classical sources, and the basic literal translation from the Basel edition of 1538 (with a few emendations), were provided by David Marsh, graduate student in the Classics Department of Harvard University.

1. The work is dedicated to Gerardo Landriani, Bishop of Como.
2. Cf. Diogenes Laertius, *Lives of the Philosophers*, V, 22; X, 1, 24.
3. *Commentariolum Petitionis*, 12.
4. *Tusculanae Disputationes* IV, 2.
5. *De Finibus* II, 49.
6. *Pro Archia* 11, 26.
7. *Ab Urbe Condita* XXII, 50, 1.
8. Ibid., XXIII, 47, 4.
9. The "hero," Lucius, in Apuleius' *Metamorphoses*.
10. Cf. Virgil, *Aeneid* VIII, 190ff.
11. *De Officiis* I, 42, 151.
12. *Epistle* CXX, i (Migne XXII = Hieronymus I, col. 984).
13. Giovanni di Bicci de' Medici (1360–1429), father of Lorenzo (1395–1440) and of Cosimo (1389–1464), was one of the richest bankers in Italy.
14. *Politics* IV (not V), vi, 1294 a 21.
15. Ibid., V, i, 1301 b 4.
16. Cf. *Nicomachean Ethics* X, ix, 1179 b 8ff.
17. Cf. Cicero, *Tusculanae Disputationes* I, 38, 91.
18. *Ab Urbe Condita* XXI, 4, 9.
19. The text actually reads "If virtues, etc." but this would so distort the logic of Niccolò's argument that it seems the text must be corrupt here, and that "wealth" is the correct word: *divitias*, not *virtutes* having been intended.
20. The etymology is fanciful.
21. Plutarch, *Life of Themistocles*, xviii; Seriphus is an island in the Cyclades.
22. Source uncertain; cf. Aristotle *Rhetoric*, II, 16, 1390 b 32ff.
23. Source uncertain; cf. Aristotle *Politics*, II, viii, 1273 a 31ff.
24. Diogenes Laertius, *Lives of the Philosophers*, VI, 72. The word in Greek is

kakía. Cicero explicitly rejected the Latin translation *malitia* and invented the technical term, *vitiositas*. *Tusc. Disp.* IV, 15, 34. Poggio, apparently preferring a more flowing Latin, used *malitia*.

25. Ibid., III, 88.
26. Ibid., VI, 11.
27. Cf. *Tusculanae Disputationes* 12, 34ff.
28. *Epistulae morales* XLIV, 2–5.
29. *Satura* VII, 20, and passim.
30. For Cleanthes, cf. Seneca, loc. cit.; for Demetrius, Seneca *Epist.* XX, 9.
31. Actually *Pro Sestio*, 65, 136.

Lorenzo de' Medici

Lorenzo de' Medici 1449–1492

Lorenzo de' Medici, ruler of Florence for over two decades, stands at the center of attention among this group of political writers. He says relatively little, but all of them, in some sense, talk about him. For some he is a hero; for others, a villain. In Poliziano's view, he was a well-loved ruler. Alberti enjoyed Medici favor also, and his account of restive Rome under papal control suggests the contrasting virtues of the Florentine regime: at least a party of native patricians, rather than foreigners, controlled the city. For Rinuccini and Savonarola, one with a secular, the other with a religious perspective, Lorenzo was a tyrant. Bruni and Poggio wrote of their political ideals before he was born, but one can say that Lorenzo became the man of whom they dreamed: a virtuoso of pen and sword and commerce, a leader of inherited status who greatly magnified that status by his own achievements, and last but not least, a discriminating and generous patron of art and letters. Some twenty years after Lorenzo's death, Machiavelli and Guicciardini stamped his reign with their magisterial approval and consolidated his reputation.

Lorenzo had a splendid training for public life. When he was five, he was dressed as a French child in honor of the visit of the Duke of Anjou, and it was observed that "his seriousness, foreign to the French character, showed that he was Lorenzo."[1] As a child of ten he headed a procession to welcome the visiting Duke of Milan. We recognize this boy in the painting by Benozzo Gozzoli which shows him, splendidly dressed and mounted on a gorgeously caparisoned horse, looking around in a grave and commanding

150

way. At sixteen he went to Pisa to welcome Frederic of Aragon, Prince of Naples, and accompanied him on a trip to Venice and Milan. Later he visited Naples and made a favorable impression on King Ferrante.

When Lorenzo was seventeen, Piero, his father, had to defend his position of leadership against a conspiracy of certain other magnates. Lorenzo was able to help his father avoid a deadly ambush. When Piero responded to the crisis by the time-honored device of calling a *balìa*, or mass meeting, Lorenzo, armed and on horseback, was in charge of the three thousand troops who lined the assembly. Protecting or intimidating? . . . that is always the question with the Medici. From that time on, despite his youth, Lorenzo sat on the political committees that ran the city. When his father died in 1469 he accepted the role of leader of the party. His motive, as he states in the account given below, was less to achieve glory than to preserve his own wealth and that of his friends: "for it is hard to be wealthy in Florence without political power."

After the Pazzi conspiracy of 1478, the Medici party changed the laws to make more certain than ever that all important functions of government were in their control. In 1480, when Florence had been at war for two years with the papacy and Naples, Lorenzo secretly left the city and sailed to Naples. He succeeded in persuading Ferrante to abandon his papal ally and arrange a peace. This act appeared daring, but not high-handed, to the Florentines; he had ended an unpopular war that many blamed entirely on him. Subsequently Lorenzo himself acted as peacemaker in the complicated shifting conflicts of Northern Italy. He seems to have been, indeed, a "consummate and dispassionate statesman."[2] Until his death in 1492, his power was unshaken. It was never absolute: As Wilcox sums it up, "Lorenzo's power lay largely in his ability to get along with the other families that formed the Medici party, not in his capacity to overawe them."[3]

Under Lorenzo's leadership, Florence in 1474 took from Volterra the alum mines of Val di Cecina, which were to be exploited by the Medici bank. Volterra rebelled, and the rebellion was violently repressed. Lorenzo is said to have regretted this violence. Later he acquired certain border towns to round out Florentine territory: Pietrasanta (1484), Sarzana (1487), and Piancaldoli (1488). He was able at the same time to maintain good relations with the two main Tuscan neighbors, Siena and Lucca.

In 1486 the breach with the papacy was well enough healed to allow Lorenzo to win from Pope Innocent VIII a cardinal's hat for his thirteen-year-old son. Twenty years after Lorenzo's death, this son, Giovanni, was able to restore the ousted Medici family to power in Florence with Spanish troops borrowed from the pope. The family remained rulers of Tuscany for the next three centuries, and two of their descendants became queens of France. Giovanni was also able to further the church career of his cousin, Giulio, son of Lorenzo's brother. Soon after Giovanni's death as Pope Leo X, Giulio became Clement VII. These achievements of the family were long-term results of Lorenzo's planning and bargaining.

It has been said that Lorenzo never understood business well and that he squandered money. Internationally, the bank declined under his leadership. In Bruges his agents lent money to Charles the Bold of Burgundy, who lost his dominion to France. In London they lent money to the Yorkists, who lost the throne. In Italy, with better luck, Lorenzo invested in land around Pisa and in building up the port; he also increased the Florentine presence there by founding a university. Lorenzo seems to have used the bank to further political aims, and he used the taxes of the citizens of Florence, sometimes with the consent of the Signoria, to pay the bank's and the family's debts.

Cosimo de' Medici had collected a great library and favored literary scholars, whom he viewed as philosophers, to be in his entourage. Marsilio Ficino was one of these, a Christian Platonist, who became one of Lorenzo's teachers. So did Cristoforo Landino, a Latin and Greek scholar, and Argiropoulos, the Greek refugee and Aristotelian. Lorenzo's mother, Lucrezia Tornabuoni, was his first teacher and a writer of religious poetry. Lorenzo carried on the tradition, collecting manuscripts, enjoying learned conversation, and writing poetry. He wrote a defense of the Tuscan language and encouraged appreciation of the great Florentine poetry of the previous century—manifesting his appreciation of literature and his patriotism. He himself wrote a wide variety of fresh, lively, sonorous Italian verse.

Lorenzo lived in a network of close relationships within the wider network of his relationships as a politician. When he was young he was much in the company of his *brigata*—a group of close friends, all male, with whom he went hunting, feasted, and enjoyed conversation and song. He was also married young, according to his father's wishes, to a Roman aristocrat, Clarice Orsini. She bore him ten children, of whom seven lived. As letters show, he took a great interest in his children and was well loved by them. As for Clarice, even in letters that show disagreement, she shows a spirit of confidence that her feelings matter to him. Lorenzo further speaks in his poetry of extramarital loves. Love he describes as desire for the "beautiful thing" and relates it as such to the Platonic idea of earthly love leading to greater love. At the same time he sees this desire as "ordained by nature for the propagation of human beings." He says it should not be distorted by considerations of wealth and family, but should be moved only by "a cer-

152

tain proportionality and appropriateness between the loved and the lover for the reproduction of the human species."[4] In addition to all this, the letters of Poliziano, who lived in Lorenzo's household for eighteen years and was present at his deathbed, have sometimes been seen as the letters of a lover. They do express immense devotion and dependency, and one can be sure that Lorenzo loved this preeminent poet and scholar. While nothing proves that Lorenzo had male lovers, we can see in Botticelli's painting of the "Gift of the Magi" (in the Uffizi) that Poliziano had a softly gracious and sensual appearance and that masculine homoeroticism was freely displayed at Lorenzo's court.

For posterity a good deal of Lorenzo's luster derives from his function as a Maecenas. He was the patron of Benozzo Gozzoli, Ghirlandaio, Verocchio, Pollaiuolo, Botticelli, Leonardo da Vinci, and Michelangelo. He was the patron also of writers, including Pulci, Ficino, and Poliziano. The intimacy among literary men and painters in his circle left its most conspicuous mark in the mysterious semiclassical allegories set forth visually by Botticelli. Generally, a combination of scientific curiosity and idealistic fervor permeates the style of both literature and art from Lorenzo's court.

Lorenzo, though nominally only the first citizen of the Republic, deliberately moved toward more and more power. Directly or indirectly, through the influence of Machiavelli and Guicciardini and others, he became a model for later Renaissance princes, helping them to realize how powerful they could be. The glittering image of his court had its continuation in theirs. One thinks of Henry VIII, Francis I, Queen Elizabeth, and even of Ivan the Terrible.

Unlike these hereditary monarchs, however, Lorenzo did not have power simply thrust upon him. Though his late memoir, given below, assures us that he was forced into leadership, it is clear that he worked for his reputation as a suitable leader and gladly committed himself to that kind of life. In a dialogue written by Landino around 1468, Lorenzo, then nineteen or younger, rejects with indignation the idea of withdrawing from politics, even for a time, to cultivate only one's own soul.[5]

The issue reappears in this letter from his former tutor, Marsilio Ficino, written in 1474. Lorenzo is twenty-five, Ficino is forty-three. Ficino speaks to Lorenzo as a philosopher to a rich young friend full of talent.

I beg you, my dearest patron, for God's sake, make frugal and wise use of even the smallest bit of this short time. Please set aside vain worries, superfluous games, unnecessary political business in order to hear the Socratic message: get away you wretched fiends, depart as fast as possible, evil of my soul!—These steal you from yourself little by little.—

Buy your freedom, I beg of you, from this miserable captivity, while you still can! You can only do it today, be your own man today![6]

While replying with friendship and admiration, Lorenzo lets fly one sharp observation: Loving and useful as are Ficino's thoughts, he says, they are the thoughts of a man very much afraid of death. Lorenzo, it seems, here suggests his distance as a man of action from Ficino's position.

There is an implication in all this that Lorenzo might have chosen to share his power more, to be less concerned with both the pleasures and the business of his worldly position.

Lorenzo's most famous lines are the refrain of a Carnival song:

> How lovely youth that flies us ever!
> Let him be glad who will be:
> There is no certainty of tomorrow.[7]

His late philosophical poetry, by contrast, breathes a certain world-weariness. His immense practical and social skill is not enough for him: He longs to escape the hypocrisy of the city, and he longs for religious peace of mind. The fact that he had gout, or arthritis, and suffered much pain in his last years, may have something to do with this. Sara Sturm however, having studied the corpus of his writings, makes a convincing intellectual reconciliation of its worldly and religious sentiments: "Life and youth and pleasure are celebrated within a context of fleeting earthly joy; it is the ever present sense of their impermanence and limitation which causes the poet to turn to philosophical speculation about the nature of human happiness, and finally to address himself directly to God."[8]

Giovanni, when he became pope, is said to have expressed a sentiment both far and not far from Lorenzo's spirit: "Since God has given us the papacy, let us enjoy it." The son of Lorenzo had a more passive approach to life than his father did, and probably less philosophical discrimination. But what unites him with his father and with Ficino, the unworldly Platonist, is the conscious thirst for happiness now. In the late letter to Giovanni given below, Lorenzo shows a skeptical humor about politics, but he also exhibits an ambition as lively as ever, backed by a lifetime of success.

NOTES

1. Emmy Cremer, *Lorenzo de' Medici*, Vittorio Klostermann, Frankfurt am Main, 1970, 11, citing A. Fabroni, *Laurentii Medicis Magnifici Vita*, Pisa, 1784, ii, 10.

2. G. B. Picotti, "Lorenzo de' Medici" in *Enciclopedia Italiana*, xii, 1934.

3. Donald Wilcox, *In Search of God and Self: Renaissance and Reformation Thought*, Houghton Mifflin, Boston, 1975, 149.

4. Lorenzo de' Medici, *Opere*, ed. A. Simioni, Laterza, Bari, 1939, ɪ, 16.

5. The dialogue is well described in William Roscoe, *The Life of Lorenzo de' Medici*, London, 1846, 98–100.

6. Cremer, op. cit. 93.

7. Translation of George R. Kay in *The Penguin Book of Italian Verse*, Harmondsworth, Middlesex, 1958, 142.

8. Sara Sturm, *Lorenzo de' Medici*, Twayne, New York, 1974, 87.

SUGGESTED READING

Cecilia M. Ady, *Lorenzo dei Medici and Renaissance Italy*, English Universities Press, London, 1955. An excellent brief but informative biography.

Raymond de Roover, *The Rise and Decline of the Medici Bank*, Harvard University Press, Cambridge, Massachusetts, 1963.

Hugh Ross Williamson, *Lorenzo the Magnificent*, Michael Joseph, London, 1974. Tendentious but interesting and splendidly illustrated.

William Roscoe, *The Life of Lorenzo de' Medici*, London, 1796. There are several revised nineteenth-century editions. A very detailed, still valuable and enjoyable narrative.

Sara Sturm, *Lorenzo de' Medici*, New York, 1974. A thoughtful and persuasive study of Lorenzo's poetry and literary prose.

A MEMOIR AND A LETTER

by Lorenzo de' Medici *

RICORDI OF LORENZO THE MAGNIFICENT, SON OF PIERO DI COSIMO DE' MEDICI

A brief narrative of the course of my life and of some other important things worthy of remembrance for the guidance and information of those who will succeed me, and especially for my sons. Begun this day, the 15th March 1472.

I find from the books of Piero our father that I was born on January 1, 1449 [1450]. By our mother Maria Lucrezia di Francesco Tornabuoni our father had seven children, four male and three female, of whom four are still alive. They are Giuliano my brother, aged . . . and myself, aged twenty-four, Bianca, wife of Gugliemo de' Pazzi, and Nannina, wife of Bernardo Rucellai.

Giovanni d' Averardo, surnamed Bicci, de' Medici, our great-grandfather, died on the 20th February 1428, at the fourth hour of the night. He would not make a will, and left property to the amount of 179,221 scudi *di suggello*, as appears in a record in the handwriting of Cosimo our grandfather in his red leather book on page 7. The said Giovanni lived sixty-eight years, and left two sons, Cosimo our grandfather, then about forty, and Lorenzo, aged thirty.

* From *Lives of the Early Medici as told in their Correspondence*, translated and edited, Janet Ross, Boston, 1911, 151–56; 332–35. Slightly amended for this edition.

Lorenzo had one son, Pier Francesco, born on . . . 1430, who is still alive.

Cosimo had two sons, our father Piero, born . . . and our uncle Giovanni, born. . . . On September . . . 1433 our grandfather Cosimo was imprisoned in the Palace, and in danger of losing his head. On September 9th he was banished to Padua, together with his brother Lorenzo, a sentence confirmed by the Balìa of 1433 on the 11th, and on the 16th December he was permitted to reside anywhere in the Venetian territory, but not nearer to Florence than Padua.

On September 29, 1434, the Council of the Balìa revoked the sentence of exile, to the great joy of the whole city and of almost all Italy, and here [in Florence] he lived until his last day as head of the government of our Republic.

Lorenzo de' Medici, brother of Cosimo our grandfather, quitted this life at Careggi on September 20, 1440, aged about forty-six, at the fourth hour of the night, and would not make a will; Pier Francesco, his son, was his sole heir. The property amounted to 235,137 scudi *di suggello*, as appears in the said book kept by Cosimo on page 13, which amount Cosimo kept for the use and benefit of the said Pier Francesco, and for Piero and Giovanni, his own sons, until they were of proper age, as appears in the books of the said Cosimo, wherein is a detailed account of all.

On December . . . 1451 the said Pier Francesco being of age, we divided the property according to the arbitration of Messer Mannello degl' Strozzi, Bernardo de' Medici, Alamanno Salviati, Messer Carlo Marsuppino, Amerigo Cavalcanti, and Giovanni Serristori, by whom a liberal half of our possessions was assigned to him, giving him the advantage over us and the best things. The deed was drawn up by Ser Antonio Pugi, notary, and at the same time we gave him an interest of one-third in our business, whereby he gained much more than we did as he had no expenses.

Giovanni, our uncle (*et hujus quidem ingenio et virtute, plurimum confidebat Cosmus, qua propter ejus interitu maxime doluit*), died on November 1, 1463, in our house in Florence, without making a will, because he had no children and was under parental tutelage. But all his last wishes were faithfully carried out. By Maria Ginevra degl' Alessandri he had a son named Cosimo, who died in November 1461, at about the age of nine.

Cosimo our grandfather, a man of exceeding wisdom, died at Careggi on August 1, 1464, being much debilitated by old age and by gout, to the great grief not only of ourselves and of the whole city but of all Italy, because he was most famous and adorned with many singular virtues. He died in the highest position any Florentine citizen ever attained at any period, and was buried in S. Lorenzo. He refused to make a will and forbade all pomp at his funeral. Nevertheless all the Italian princes sent to do him honour and to condole with us on his death; among others H.M. the King of France commanded that he should be honoured with his banner, but out of respect for his wishes our father would not allow it. By public decree he was named PATER PATRIÆ, and the decree and the letters patent are in our house. After his death much sedition arose in the city, especially was our father persecuted out of envy. From this sprang the parliament and the change of government in 1466, when Messer Agnolo Acciaiuoli, Messer Diotisalvi, Niccolò Soderini, and others were exiled, and the State was reformed.

In the year 1465 H.M. King Louis of France, out of regard for the friendship between our grandfather, our father, and the House of France, decorated our escutcheon with three Lilies d'or on a field azure, which we carry at present. We have the patents with the royal seal attached, which was approved and confirmed in the Palace with nine beans [votes].

In July 1467 came the Duke Galeazzo of Milan. He was fighting against Bartolomeo of Bergamo in the Romagna, who was vexing our State. By his own wish he lodged in our house, although the Signory had prepared everything for him in S. Maria Novella.

In February or in March of the same year Sarzana, Sarzanelle, and Castelnuovo were bought by the aid of our father Piero from M. Lorenzo and M. Tommasino da Campofregoso; notwithstanding that we were engaged in hot war the payment was made by Francesco Sassetti, our confidential agent, at that time one of the managers of the *Monte*.

I, Lorenzo, took to wife Clarice, daughter of the Lord Jacopo Orsini, or rather she was given (*i.e.* betrothed) to me in December 1468, and the marriage was celebrated in our house on June 4, 1469. Till now I have by her two children, a girl called Lucrezia, of . . . years, and a boy named Piero, of . . . months. Clarice is again with child. God preserve her to us for many years and guard us from all evil. Twin boys were born prematurely at about five or six months, they lived long enough to be baptized.

In July 1469 I went to Milan at the request of the Illustrious Duke Galeazzo to stand godfather as proxy for Piero our father to his firstborn child. I was received with much honour, more so than the others who came for the same purpose, although they were persons more worthy than I. We paid our duty to the Duchess by presenting her with a necklace of gold with a large diamond, which cost near 2000 ducats. The consequence was that the said Lord desired that I should stand godfather to all his children.

To do as others had done I held a joust in the Piazza S. Croce at great expense and with great pomp. I find we spent about 10,000 ducats *di suggello*, and although I was not highly versed in the use of weapons and the delivery of blows, the first prize was given to me; a helmet fashioned of silver, with Mars as the crest.

Piero, our father, departed this life on July 2nd, aged . . . , having been much tormented with gout. He would not make a will, but we drew up an inventory and found we possessed 237,988 scudi, as is recorded by me in a large green book bound in kid. He was buried in S. Lorenzo, and we are still at work to make his and his brother Giovanni's tomb as worthy to receive his bones as we can. God have mercy on their souls. He was much mourned by the whole city, being an upright man and exceedingly kindly. The princes of Italy, especially the principal ones, sent letters and envoys to condole with us and offer us their help for our defence.

The second day after his death, although I, Lorenzo, was very young, being twenty years of age, the principal men of the city and of the State came to us in our house to condole with us on our loss and to encourage me to take charge of the city and of the State, as my grandfather and my father had done. This I did, though on account of my youth and the great responsibility and perils arising therefrom, with great reluctance, solely for the safety of our friends and of our possessions. FOR IT IS ILL LIVING IN FLORENCE FOR THE RICH UNLESS THEY RULE THE STATE. Till now we have succeeded with honour and renown, which I attribute not to prudence but to the grace of God and the good conduct of my predecessors.

I find that from 1434 till now we have spent large sums of money, as appear in a small quarto note-book of the said year to the end of 1471. Incredible are the sums written down. They amount to 663,755 florins for alms, buildings, and taxes, let alone other expenses. But I do not regret this, for though many would consider it better to have a part of that sum in their purse, I consider that it gave great honour to our State, and I think the money was well expended, and am well pleased.

In the month of September 1471 I was elected to go as ambassador for the coronation of Pope Sixtus, and was treated with great honour. I brought back the two antique marble heads, portraits of Augustus and Agrippa, given to me by the said Pope Sixtus, and also our cup of chalcedony incised, and many other cameos which I then bought.

The following adjunct is written on the fly-leaf of a small codex in the archive in Florence without any date, but probably in 1483–5, containing a list of letters written by Lorenzo to various people, and above is written Ricordi di Lorenzo de' Medici. *All the first part is in a codex in the Nazionale Library, a copy of Lorenzo's* Ricordi, *the original of which seems no longer to exist. It differs somewhat from the version given by Roscoe, which he says was in Lorenzo's own handwriting.*

On the 19th day of September [1483] came the news that the King of France by his own free will had given to our Giovanni the Abbey of Fonte Dolce. On the 31st we heard from Rome that the Pope had ratified this and declared him capable of holding benefices, being seven years of age, and had created him a Protonotary. On the 1st June our Giovanni came from Poggio [a Caiano] and I with him. On his arrival he was confirmed by our Monsignore of Arezzo [Gentile Becchi] who gave him the tonsure, and thereafter he was called Messer Giovanni. These ceremonies took place in our own chapel, and in the evening we returned to Poggio. On the 8th June Jacopino, the courier from France, arrived about twelve of the clock with letters from the king, who has bestowed on our Messer Giovanni the Archbishopric of Aix en Provence, and after vespers the man was despatched to Rome about this business, with letters from the King of France to the Pope and the Cardinal of Macon, and to Count Girolamo, to whom we sent at the same hour letters by the courier Zenino to Forlì. God grant that all will be well.

On the 11th Zenino returned from the Count with letters for the Pope and the Cardinal of S. Giorgio, and we forwarded them to Rome by the Milan post. God grant that all will be well. On the same day after Mass in the chapel the daughters and sons of the house were confirmed, with the exception of Messer Giovanni.

On the 15th, at six in the evening, came letters from Rome saying that the Pope raised difficulties about giving the archbishopric to Messer Giovanni on account of his youth, and the courier was at once sent on to the King of France.

On the 20th came news from Lionetto that the Archbishop was not dead.

On March 1, 1484 (1485), the Abbot of Pasignano died and we at once sent off an express messenger to Messer Giovanni d'Antonio Vespucci, our ambassador at Rome, to do all he could to obtain this abbey for our Messer Giovanni. On the 2nd we took possession of the estate under the seal of the Signoria, by reason of the reservation made by Pope Sixtus to our Messer Giovanni, confirmed by Innocent during the visit of our Piero to Rome to do obeisance.

LORENZO DE' MEDICI TO HIS SON, CARDINAL GIOVANNI, AT ROME, IN MARCH 1492

MESSER GIOVANNI,—You are much beholden to our Lord God, as we all are for your sake, as besides many benefits and honours our house has received from Him it has pleased Him to bestow on you the highest dignity our family has yet enjoyed. Great as this is it is much enhanced by circumstances, particularly your youth and our condition. Therefore my first recommendation is that you endeavour to be grateful to our Lord God, remembering every hour that it is not by your own merits or solicitude that you have attained the Cardinalate, but by the grace of God. Show your gratitude to Him by leading a saintly, exemplary, and honest life. You are the more bound to do this because during your youth you have shown a disposition which gives hope of good fruit. It would be indeed most shameful, contrary to your duty, and to my expectations if at a time when others generally acquire more reason and a better understanding of life, you should forget the good precepts learned as a boy. It is incumbent on you to try and lighten the burden of the dignity you have attained by leading a pure life and persevering in the studies suitable to your profession. I was greatly pleased last year to learn that without being reminded by any one you had been several times to confession and to communion, for I conceive there is no better way of obtaining the grace of God than by habituating oneself to persevere in these duties. This seems to me the best advice I can begin with. I know, as you are now going to Rome, that sink of all iniquities, that you will find some difficulty in following it, as bad examples are always catching, and inciters to vice will not be wanting. Your promotion to the Cardinalate, as you may imagine, at your age and for the other reasons already mentioned, will be viewed with great envy, and those who were not able to prevent your attaining this dignity will endeavour, little by little, to diminish it by lowering you in public estimation and causing you to slide into the same ditch into which they have themselves fallen, counting on success because of your youth. You must be all the firmer in your stand against these difficulties, as at present one sees such a lack of virtue in the College. I recollect however to have known a good many learned and good men in the College, leading exemplary lives. It will be well that you should follow their example, for by so doing you will be the more known and esteemed as being different from the others. It is imperative above all things that you should avoid as you would Scylla and Charybdis the reputation of being a hypocrite and of evil fame. Be not ostentatious, and have a care to avoid anything offensive in conduct and in conversation, without affecting austerity or severity. These are things you will in time understand and practise better, I conceive, than I can write them. You know how important is the position and the example of a Cardinal, and that the world would be far better if the Cardinals were what they ought to be, for then there would always be a good Pope, from whom emanates, one may say, peace for all Christians. Make every effort therefore to be this, if others had done so we might hope for universal good. Nothing is more difficult than to hold converse with men of various characters, and in this I can ill advise you; only recollect when with the Cardinals and other men of rank to try and be charitable and respectful in your conversation, weighing your reasons well without being influenced by the passions of others; for many desiring what they cannot attain turn reason into abuse. Satisfy your conscience therefore by taking care that your conversation with every man should be devoid of offense. This seems to me a general rule most applicable in your case, for should passion by chance make an enemy, as his enmity would have no reasonable cause he may sometimes return with more ease to the old friendship. It will be better I think on this, your first visit to Rome, to use your ears more than your tongue. To-day I have given you entirely to our Lord God and to Holy Church; it is therefore essential that you become a good ecclesiastic, cherishing the honour and the State of Holy Church and of the Apostolic See above aught else in this world, and devoting yourself entirely to their interests. While doing this it will not be difficult for you to aid the city and our house, for the city being united to the Church you will represent the solid chain, and our house is part of the city. Although it is impossible to foresee what may happen I think it is likely that a way will be found to save, as the proverb says, the goat and the cabbages, always keeping steadfastly to your abovementioned duty of setting the interests of the Church above all else. You are the youngest Cardinal, not only of the College, but the youngest that has hitherto been made, it is therefore most necessary that where you have to compete with the others you should be the most eager and the humblest, and avoid making others wait for you in Chapel, in Consistory, or in Deputation. You will soon learn who has a good or an evil reputation. With the latter avoid any great intimacy, not only on your own account, but for the sake of public opinion; converse in a general way with all. I advise you on feast-days to be rather below than above moderation, and would rather see a well-appointed stable and a well-ordered and cleanly household than magnificence and pomp. Let your life be regular and reduce your expenses gradually in the future, for the retinue and the master being both new at first it will be difficult. Jewels and silken stuffs must be used sparingly by one in your position. Rather have a few good antiques and fine books, and well-bred and learned attendants, than many of them. Ask people to your own house oftener than you accept invitations to theirs, but do both sparingly. Eat plain food and take much exercise, for those who wear your habit, if not careful, easily contract maladies. The rank of Cardinal is as secure as it is great, men therefore often become negligent; they conceive they have done enough and that without exertion they can preserve their position. This is often prejudicial to character and to life, and a thing against which you must guard; rather trust too little than too much in others. One rule I recommend to you above all others, and that is to get up betimes; besides being good for health one can meditate over and arrange all the business of the following day, and in your position, having to say the office, to study, to give audiences &c. you will find it most useful. Another thing absolutely necessary to one in your station is to reflect, particularly at this, the commencement of your career, in the evening on all you have to do next day, so that an unforeseen event may not come upon you unawares. As to speaking in the Consistory, I think it would be more seemly and becoming if you refer all that comes before you to His Holiness, alleging that as you are young and inexperienced you consider it your duty to submit everything to the most learned judgment of His Holiness. You will probably be asked to intercede in various matters with our Holy Father. Be cautious however at the beginning to ask as few favours as possible and not to bother him; the disposition of the Pope is to be grateful to those who do not break his ears. Bear this in mind in order not to annoy him. When you see him, talk about amusing things, and if you have to beg, do it with all humility and modesty. This will please him and be in accordance with his nature. Keep well.

Angelo Poliziano

Angelo Poliziano 1454–1494

Alessandro Perosa's splendid edition of Poliziano's *Commentary on the Pazzi Conspiracy* provides not only a correct text but also notes that clearly show its shortcomings as history.[1] Poliziano wrote within three months of the events described, taking part as a favorite of Lorenzo's in a battle of propaganda. He heaps abuse on the villains who had attacked his patron. Five years before, Poliziano had tried respectfully to win for his poetry and himself the patronage of Francesco Salviati; now he presents Salviati, one of the chief conspirators, as a totally repellent scoundrel whom no honorable man could ever have liked. Jacopo Poggio, another conspirator, had been for years a member of the same learned circle around the philosopher, Marsilio Ficino, as Poliziano himself; Poliziano presents him only as a pretentious bore and an irresponsible spendthrift. Several members of the Pazzi family, especially Renato, had enjoyed public esteem, but Poliziano assures us they were all universally hated. The head of the family, Jacopo, was not in actuality much in favor of the conspiracy, but of this hesitation Poliziano does not write. In dealing with the Pazzi and Salviati, Poliziano tries to show hardened criminals, not angry aristocrats, at work. He reduces their political opposition to mere envy and financial greed. Fear of poverty, in fact, is his explanation for practically every participant's willingness to join the conspiracy. The psychology of those who revolted against Lorenzo may be as truthfully reflected in this outrageous caricature, however, as in any presentation of their side, such as Alamanno Rinuccini's, which would make them disinterested defenders of liberty.

168

After vigorously maligning the conspirators and understating their popular appeal, Poliziano tells of an armed invasion accompanying the internal revolt but quickly dealt with by Lorenzo's troops. In actuality, the invading captains retreated without fighting as soon as they heard that Lorenzo was still alive. Thus Poliziano distorts the military facts for Lorenzo's greater glory.

He also tries to suppress all signs of the basic cause of the conspiracy—a long-standing political conflict between Lorenzo and Pope Sixtus IV. There are few and veiled references to the pope and to his nephew, Duke Girolamo of Riario, whose territorial ambitions had collided with Lorenzo's. When Poliziano describes the role of Archbishop Salviati in the conspiracy, he presents him, not as a representative of the pope, but as "the Pisan leader." When the writer speaks of his summary execution—an obvious breach of clerical privilege—he stresses that even before the Florentine authorities hanged him, Salviati had been beaten half to death by a mob. He thus minimizes the international issues, causes and consequences of the situation as much as possible, and he appears, if we ignore his motives, to be incapable of political analysis.

Poliziano structured his story by beginning with profiles of the villains and ending with a eulogy of their victim, Giuliano de' Medici. Between these contrasting portraits lies an account of armed conflict, riots, and the government's successful calming of civic disorder. Crowds gather and act in various ways under the influence of events and leaders. Yet there are no speeches. Speakers—who might have given a classical clarity to the issues—are shown only as they affect crowds. The pictures of crowds follow each other: the frightened crowd in the church where the assault took place, the crowd that failed to come out of their houses for all Jacopo Pazzi's hoarse cries (that he cried "Libertà" Poliziano does not mention), the crowd that tore Salviati and his followers apart, the crowd that loudly cheered Lorenzo, the soldiers who flowed in and out of the city, and finally the crowd of children—monstrous in their fierce imitation of adult hatreds—who dragged Jacopo Pazzi's exhumed corpse around the city. Perhaps the naïveté, the absence of specific political motives and political analysis, was due not only to Poliziano's cunning as a propagandist but also to a certain vision which he, as a poet, had of the reality. In a Florentine crisis, the fulcrum of politics was the crowd.

Poliziano was a sophisticated scholar and poet, yet he exhibited here no concern with rational analysis. Despite models like Sallust and Tacitus, he reduced events almost entirely to the sensual level. Some forty years later Machiavelli combined the descriptive power that was Poliziano's with the fair-minded analytical seriousness introduced into Florentine historiography by Bruni: the result in his *History of Florence*, for instance, was both vivid narrative and interesting ideas about power.

NOTE

1. Angelo Poliziano, *Della Congiura dei Pazzi (Coniurationis Commentarium)*, ed. Alessandro Perosa, Antenori, Padua, 1958.

THE PAZZI CONSPIRACY

by Angelo Poliziano

[Translated with David Marsh]

I shall proceed here to give a brief description of the Pazzi conspiracy, for this was one of the most memorable evils committed in my time, and very nearly overthrew the whole Florentine Republic. While the affairs of the city depended on the willing support that all good men gave to Lorenzo, Giuliano and the rest of the Medici house, only the Pazzi as a clan and some of the Salviati began, first secretly and soon quite openly, to form an opposition. They were very envious and wanted, if they could, to undermine both the Medici's civic power and their private position.

The Pazzi had made themselves unpopular with both the citizens and the humble folk for, besides being very avaricious, they were all unbearably stubborn and insolent; the head of the family, Jacopo Pazzi, a knight, spent night and day gambling, cursing gods and men when his luck was bad, and sometimes throwing the gambling table or whatever else came to hand at the nearest person. He was pale and weak, and had a habit of tossing his head all the time; the way he expressed himself with mouth and eyes and hands revealed his lack of stability. Two great vices were characteristic of him, vices that surprisingly seem incompatible with each other—consuming avarice, on the one hand, and, on the other, a mania for spending. He tore down the magnificent home of his father and started to build anew. He made much use of day laborers but did not pay them their full wages; thus the poorest sort of men who live by their manual labor were cheated by him, and he tried to make

171

them take their pay in rotten pork. He was always widely disliked, therefore, and his ancestors had enjoyed no greater popularity. But he lacked legitimate children, and was much courted by relatives who hoped to inherit from him. This man had no sense of responsibility, least of all towards his own family. The way he lived made bankruptcy foreseeable, which spurred him on to plan the crime and gave him the burning desire to carry it out. For this insolent, ambitious man was not prepared to bear public disgrace as a spendthrift. He planned instead to burn himself and his whole country in one great fire.

Francesco Salviati, on the other hand, was a man who had just come into good fortune by being raised to the position of archbishop of Pisa. He had barely understood himself and his luck; he simply basked in his pleasant situation and promised himself all kinds of further gains through his own efforts and his luck. This Francesco was, as gods and men know, devoid of knowledge of and also respect for the law, divine as well as human. He was involved in outrageous and criminal acts, lost in sensuality and disgraceful intrigues. He too loved to gamble at dice; he was a great flatterer, very lightheaded and vain, with a bold, aggressive, calculating and impudent spirit; by these means he had gained the position of archbishop (so shameless was Fortune) and now he vowed to storm heaven itself.

Together with Francesco Pazzi, whose deep-rooted vanity filled him with high hopes, Salviati had made plans long before, at Rome, it is said, to kill Lorenzo and Giuliano and to take over the Republic. Now in the suburban villa of Jacopo Pazzi, a place called Montughi, the whole faction was sworn to the crime, and Salviati himself drew up the oath.

The main leaders after him were Jacopo and Francesco Pazzi. Francesco was the son of Antonio, Jacopo's brother, and as he was naturally stubborn, he had grown fixed in his passion and arrogance. He was incredibly angry that the Medici family outshone him. He was always disparaging and underhandedly betraying Lorenzo and Giuliano in various way, sparing them no slander and no shame, stopping at nothing to do them what harm he could. He had spent some years at the Pazzi bank in Rome, for he felt that in Florence he had no standing compared to the Medici brothers, who were known for their goodness and strength of character. He shared the peculiar Pazzi irascibility to a surprising extent. His stature was short, his body slender, and his color pale. He had blond hair, which he was overly concerned to keep well groomed. The mannerisms of his face and body revealed his prodigious insolence, and his great efforts, especially in first encounters, to cover this up were not very successful. He was a bloodthirsty person, besides, and the sort who, once he desired something in his heart, would go after it undeterred by considerations like honor, piety, fame, or reputation.

Jacopo Salviati, meanwhile, was the kind people find charming, with a smile and a joyful welcome for everyone at all times. He enjoyed the company of prostitutes and low company, but he also managed business deals with plenty of zeal and shrewdness.

There was a third Jacopo, too, involved in this affair, the son of Poggio, the well-known eloquent writer. This Jacopo, because his own resources were meager and his debts immense, and also because of a certain innate vanity, was eager to see an insurrection. His outstanding gift was for speaking ill of people, in which respect he even rivaled his venomous father. Thus he was always attacking the leaders of the city, or railing without discretion about everyone else's behavior, or mercilessly tearing apart some learned man's work. He was inordinately proud of his store of historical knowledge and his considerable eloquence, and paraded these talents in every circle of his acquaintances, to the point of boring his audiences. He had totally squandered his father's ample legacy in a few years, and thus was driven by poverty to become wholly devoted to the Pazzi-Salviati cause. Basically he remained what he had always been: for sale to any buyer.

There was a fourth Jacopo in the conspiracy, the brother of the archbishop, an altogether sordid and obscure person. Besides these there was Bernardo Bandini, a wicked, bold and shameless man, likewise driven by bankruptcy to plunge into any crime.

These were the seven citizens who undertook the deed. Add to them Giovanni Battista from the town of Montesecco, who was of the household of Duke Girolamo. Also Antonio of Volterra, who was drawn to the group either by the hatred of his people [Volterra had been sacked by permission of Lorenzo] or by a certain frivolous and unthinking tendency to follow others. The priest Stefano was another, the secretary of Jacopo Pazzi, a shameless fellow and one of whom all sorts of evil things were said. He lived in the household of Jacopo performing a not very honorable function, as tutor to Jacopo's only daughter, conceived in adultery.

Renato and Guglielmo Pazzi, according to reports, were not unaware of the conspiracy. Guglielmo was married to Bianca, the sister of Lorenzo de' Medici, and had raised with her numerous children, so that he thought, as they say, he could straddle the fence. He was the older brother of Francesco, whom we have already described. Renato, on the other hand, was the son of Pietro, a man of knightly rank and a brother of Jacopo and Antonio. Renato, therefore, was a cousin on the paternal side of Guglielmo and Francesco. He was far from stupid, and he hid his great hatred and wrath, but his was a passionate nature, and though he was not bold, he would act decisively when it came time to do what he had been storing in his heart. He was tightfisted and avaricious, for which reason he was not popular with the masses. A member of Guglielmo's household called Napoleone Franzesi, furthermore, played no small part in the proceedings.

There were a number of more obscure participants in the crime, some from the archbishop's household and some from that of the Pazzi. Among them was a certain Brigliaino, a man of the lowest class, and Nanni, a wicked and quarrelsome Pisan notary.

But the one who played the largest part among the foreigners in this affair was Giovanni Battista, whom we have mentioned, from the household of Duke Girolamo. He had set the uprising, which was planned a full half-year before, for April 26, 1478, the Sunday before Ascension. He was a man of intelligence and foresight, a good planner and not inexperienced in these things. Salviato and all the conspirators had great faith in him.

The story itself requires that we now set forth the conspirators' plan.

The Medici family, splendid and magnificent in its style at all times, is especially so in the entertainment of notable visitors. No well-known man has visited Florence or Florentine territory but he has been offered magnificent hospitality by that house. When Cardinal Raffaello, therefore, the son of the sister of Duke Girolamo, had sojourned for a while at the country house of Jacopo Pazzi, where we noted that the conspiracy itself was sworn, the conspirators seized this opportunity for their great crime, and they sent word to the brothers in the cardinal's name that they wished to be received at the Medici's suburban home in Fiesole. Lorenzo and I myself and Lorenzo's son Piero went there. Giuliano was kept away by illness and stayed at home, and that postponed the affair to the day we have mentioned. Again, they sent a servant to say that the cardinal would also like to be invited for dinner to the house in Florence—he wished to see the way the house was decorated, the draperies, the tapestries, the jewels and silver and elegant furnishings. The fine young men did not suspect a trap; they got their home ready, exhibited their beautiful things, laid out the linens, set out the metal and leather work and jewels in cases, and had a magnificent banquet ready.

A group of the conspirators appeared somewhat early, asking, "Where is Lorenzo? Where is Giuliano?" The servants said that both were in Santa Riparata, and that is where the group went, the cardinal out of sight in the choir according to custom. While the mass was being celebrated, the archbishop and Jacopo Poggio and the two Jacopo Salviatis, as well as some other companions, slipped out to go to the Signoria, there to oust the lords of Florence from their stronghold and to take over. The others stayed in the church to carry out the crime. Since Giovanni Battista, who had been appointed to kill Lorenzo, had refused the job, Antonio of Volterra and Stefano undertook it, while the rest got ready to fall upon Giuliano.

When the priest had taken the wine, the signal was given, and Bernardo Bandini, Francesco Pazzi and the rest of the conspirators clustered around Giuliano, encircling him. Their leader Bandini took his sword and ran it through the young man's breast. Giuliano, though fatally wounded, retreated a few steps; the others followed; he lost consciousness and fell to the ground; as he lay there Francesco struck him repeatedly with his dagger—thus they killed the noble youth. The servant in attendance on Giuliano, fainting with terror, rushed shamefully into hiding.

Meanwhile the assassins appointed to kill Lorenzo attacked him, and Antonio of Volterra first of all laid his hand on Lorenzo's left shoulder, aiming a dagger for his throat. Terrified, Lorenzo took off his cape and wrapped it over his left arm, drawing his sword from its sheath. As he was freeing himself, however, he suffered a wound, for he was cut in the neck. Then he turned on them, a powerful and furious man, sword in hand, facing his enemies and glancing about in readiness. They were afraid and fled; nor were Andrea and Lorenzo Cavalcanti, who were his immediate attendants, slow to guard him. Cavalcanti's arm was wounded; Andrea came through unharmed.

It was amazing to see the crowd in confusion—men and women, priests and boys were running wherever their feet led. The whole place resounded with cries and moans, yet no words were clearly distinguishable; there were people who thought the church was collapsing.

Bernardo Bandini, the murderer of Giuliano, was not satisfied with that but now went after Lorenzo, who had rushed with a few others into the shelter of the sacristy. Pursuing Lorenzo, Bandini attacked Francesco Nori, a wise man and the manager of the Medici business, and gave him a fatal wound in the stomach with a single thrust of his sword; Nori's body, still breathing, was quickly dragged into the sacristy to which Lorenzo had retreated.

Having fled to the same place, I together with some other persons then got the bronze doors shut and so we held off Bandini. While we guarded the doors, some within feared for Lorenzo because of his wound and were anxious to do something about it. Antonio Rodolfo, the son of Jacopo Rodolfo, an impressive young man, sucked out the wound [in case there might be poison]. Lorenzo himself gave no thought to his own safety but kept asking how Giuliano was; he also made angry threats and lamented that his life had been endangered by people who had hardly any reason to attack him. A crowd of young men loyal to the Medici were pounding on the sacristy doors with their swords. They all shouted that they were friends and relatives: let Lorenzo come out, come out, before the other side returns with reinforcements! We inside were fearful and unsure whether these were friends or foes, and we kept asking whether Giuliano was safe. To this, they never replied. Then Sigismondo Stufa, a splendid young man and one who from childhood had been attached by bonds of great love and loyalty to Lorenzo, quickly climbed a ladder to a look out point, the organ gallery, from which he could see down into the church, and at once he knew what had been done, for he could see the body of Giuliano lying prostrate. He could also see that those who stood at the doors were friends, so he gave orders to open up; thronging around Lorenzo, they made an armed bodyguard for him and took him home by a side door so that he should not run across Giuliano.

Going out through the church towards home myself, I did come upon Giuliano lying in wretched state, covered with wounds and hideous with blood. I was so weakened by the sight that I could hardly walk or control myself in my overwhelming grief, but some friends helped me to get home.

There [at the Medici palace] armed men were everywhere and every room resounded with the cries of supporters, the roof rang with the din of weapons and voices. You saw boys, old men, youths, clergy and lay-men all arming themselves to defend the Medici house as they would the public welfare.

The Pisan leader [Archbishop Francesco Salviati] meanwhile sum-moned Cesare Petrucci, the "Standard-Bearer of Justice" (as he is called), into a conference without witnesses, intending to kill him but saying that he wanted to tell him something on behalf of the pope. Certain Perugian exiles who had been aware of the plot had come to the Signoria and gathered in the chancery, which they thought a suitable place. They had closed the doors of that room but when the time came, they found that they could not open them [without a key]; thus they could be of no help to themselves or to their friends. Now, when Petrucci observed Salviati's nervous manner, he suspected some trick and called the guards to arms. Salviati was afraid and burst out of the room. Petrucci, in pur-suit, ran right into Jacopo Poggio and had the courage to grab him by the hair and throw him to the ground, calling on the guards to hold him. The next minute Petrucci, with a small band of the Signori, had taken refuge high in the palace tower. There he guarded the door with a spit seized from the kitchen, (for fear and anger had made him seize this weapon), and so fought as best he could for his own and the public safety. Others too fought bravely for their lives. The palace of the Signoria is full of doors, and by closing many of the passages, the guards were able to separate the leading conspirators and channel them into many small currents lacking the original impact. The whole time all those of the Signoria were in an uproar within the building, while few citizens came to the spot.

Meanwhile, when Jacopo Pazzi realized that his hope of killing Lo-renzo had been disappointed, fully aware of the seriousness of the crime in which he was involved, he struck his own face with both hands, then rushed home from the church and collapsed on the floor in anguish.

Seeing that the whole matter was still in crisis, however, he went forth to hazard his fortune and, with a few relatives, proceeded to the piazza and called the people to arms. He had no success, for everyone scorned him as a criminal (whose fear made him scarcely able to call out in a steady voice) and abominated his wicked deed. Seeing no help in the people, he trembled and completely lost heart. Those who had betaken themselves to the highest parts of the Signoria were throwing huge stones and lances at Jacopo. Terrified he returned home, and Francesco, who had been seriously wounded in this fray, abruptly fled with him.

Lorenzo's men, meanwhile, regained control of the Signoria. After the Perugians had broken down their door, they were cut down. Then the fury turned on others of the conspiracy. They hanged Jacopo Poggio out a window, and having seized the cardinal, they took him with a large guard to the Signoria, protecting him with difficulty from the attacks of the populace. Several of his former associates were killed by the people, and when they were completely stripped, were foully mutilated: soon a human head fixed on a lance appeared at Lorenzo's gate, and part of a shoulder was brought forth. Everywhere there was nothing so clearly to be heard as the voices of the people shouting, "Palle, palle," (the emblem of the Medici).

Jacopo Pazzi made up his mind to flee: at the exit known as the Gate of the Cross, he and his armed followers demanded passage and burst forth.

At the Medici palace, meanwhile, the people gathered full of marvelous zeal and love for the Medici, driving traitors to the place of execution, sparing no curse or threat as they herded the criminals to their punishment. The house of Jacopo Pazzi was barely defended from looters, and Pietro Corsini's men took the naked and wounded Salviati, who was already close to death, to the place of execution; it was no simple or easy matter to rein in the furious people. The Pisan leader was soon dangling from the same window as Francesco Pazzi, and his body hung above the other's lifeless corpse. When he was lowered, by chance or in mad fury he sank his teeth into the corpse of Francesco Pazzi (a marvel seen, I think, by everyone there and soon reported throughout the city), and even after the rope had choked him he kept his teeth fixed in the other's breast while his eyes stared madly. After him, the two Jacopos from the Salviati family were hanged also, their necks broken by the rope.

I remember going to the piazza myself later (for things were already quiet at home), and seeing a multitude of lacerated corpses scattered here and there, visibly the objects of popular abuse and execration, for the Medici house was, for many reasons, in favor with the people. All abominated the murder of Giuliano, calling it an outrage that this outstanding young lord, the darling of Florentine youth, should be slain by trickery, crime and treason, cut down by persons who had least excuse for such an act and who belonged to a violent and sacrilegious clan hateful to both gods and men. The crowd was spurred by the recent memory of Giuliano's excellence, for only a few years earlier, he had won acclaim in a jousting tournament where his conspicuous prowess had won him the victory and the trophy. This was a feat to endear him greatly to the hearts of the crowd. There was, moreover, the enormity of the outrage, for one could not name or conceive of any crime to rival the hideousness of this. Everyone was indignant that a pious and innocent youth should have been cruelly slain at the altar, while taking part in a sacred rite. Religion and hospitality had been violated and the church polluted with human blood, while Lorenzo, himself, on whose single person the whole Florentine Republic depended, in whom the hopes and the resources of all the people were concentrated, had been attacked by armed men. Against all this there was deep indignation.

Soon, from all the various towns near the city, a large force of armed men streamed into the piazza of the Signoria, the other piazzas, and especially the Medici palace. Everyone was eager to show his own personal zeal—people flocking with their children and retainers to offer their help, protection, and support. All men declared that on Lorenzo alone their public and private well-being depended. For days you could see a continuous stream of arms pouring from everywhere into the Medici palace, as well as bread and meat and whatever else was available in the way of provisions. Neither his wound nor his fear nor his great sorrow for his brother's death prevented Lorenzo from overseeing his affairs. He received all the citizens, thanked them individually and exchanged greetings with them all. Since the public was anxious about his health, he had to appear often at the windows of the palace. Thereupon the whole people would acclaim him, cheer and wave, rejoice in his safety and revel in their joy. He in turn was determined to expedite all that had to be done, and never faltered in courage or in wisdom.

While this was the situation at Florence, it was reported that Giovan-Francesco da Tolentino, governor of the town of Forli, had crossed the border of Florentine territory with a picked troop of cavalry. Lorenzo Giustini, likewise, as many letters and messengers warned us, had come from Città di Castello and was invading from Sienese territory. But both were repulsed by our forces and retreated to their homes. Throughout the city, guards were posted during the dark hours of the night, also Lorenzo's house was carefully guarded, and there were armed men posted at the piazzas, in front of the Signoria, and all around the city. On the following day, Giovanni Bentivoglio of Bologna, a knight and lord of his own republic, who was closely allied by many favors to the Medici, came to Mugello with some squadrons of cavalry and many companies of infantry. The whole city had begun to fill up with infantry, but the Eight, fearful lest the soldiers begin rioting for loot, first picked a force to direct the protection of the city, and then ordered the rest, as soon as they had entered the city, either to return home or to go wherever they determined that they would be useful.

Renato Pazzi, meanwhile, who had retreated the day before the crime to his villa in Mugello and surrounded himself with soldiers, was taken captive with two brothers, Giovanni and Niccolò. Giovanni Pazzi, brother of Guglielmo and Francesco, was caught in a certain garden near his house. Abandoned now by all those who had followed him, Jacopo was pursued and captured in the village of Castaneto. The first to pursue him was a certain farmer named Alexander, a little over twenty years of age. He grabbed hold of him, and although Jacopo offered him seven pieces of gold in a plea to let him kill himself, he could not persuade him. When he continued to argue and plead, Alexander's brother beat him with a staff. Then the terrified man saw the truth of the saying: "Fate guides the willing man, and drags the unwilling." [Seneca *Ep.* 107, 11.] Taken thence to Florence with an armed escort from the Eight to keep the crowd from tearing him apart, he was brought to the Signoria and confessed the whole crime without being tortured; he was hanged a few hours later. Even as he faced death, he did not abandon his mad and furious ideas. He was giving up his soul to the devil, he cried. After him, Renato was executed, and the other brothers were put in chains. The youngest, Galeatto, who was still a boy, tried in his terror to escape in the guise of a woman, but he was recognized and thrown into jail with the rest. Not much later, Andrea Pazzi, Renato's brother, was brought back from attempted flight and thrust into the same jail.

As he fled, Bandini encountered Lorenzo Giustini and by joining his ranks, escaped to Siena. Napoleone Franzesi arranged his own escape, aided by the knight, Piero Vespucci. Giovanni Battista of Montesecco was executed a few days later. Antonio of Volterra, the man who had wounded Lorenzo, and Stefano, the priest, hid for some days in a Florentine monastery. When their whereabouts were learned, the people flocked to the place and almost laid hands on the monks, whose religious scruples had prohibited their betraying the fugitives. They seized the assassins at last and foully mutilated them. Their noses and ears were cut off and they were severely beaten until, after confessing to the crime, they were dragged off to the gallows. Later, rewards were decreed and announced by the town crier for anyone who should kill or capture Bandini and Napoleone. Guglielmo Pazzi, who had taken refuge in Lorenzo's own palace hoping the bonds of kinship would save him, was exiled together with his children to a zone at least five miles but not more than twenty miles outside the city.

When Piero Vespucci's role in helping Napoleone Franzesi was uncovered, he too was immediately seized. (He had been dissipating his parents' property since earliest youth and was therefore denied his inheritance by his father's will. Poor at home and in debt to others, he was discontented with the status quo and eager for a change of government. As soon as Giuliano had been murdered, he was ready to praise the Pazzi crime, so abrupt and precipitate was his judgment. Soon afterwards, seeing the whole people and all the citizens on Lorenzo's side, he rushed out to plunder the Pazzi palace. There he encountered some soldiers who were gazing hopefully at the place with thoughts of looting, and he would—had not the remarkable young Pietro Corsini opposed his barbarities—have greatly endangered the whole city, with all its secular and religious establishments, so rabid and urgent was his attempt to incite the mob and soldiers to start looting.) He too was finally thrown into prison, and his son, Marco, was exiled to a distance of five miles from the city.

Many other deaths followed, and all the conspirators were either killed or put in chains or exiled.

When the news reached Rome, there was great sorrow, numerous embassies from all quarters, and extraordinary general relief that Lorenzo was safe.

The funeral of Giuliano was very magnificent and the solemn obsequies were celebrated in the church of San Lorenzo. Many youths dressed in mourning. Giuliano himself had been stabbed in nineteen places. He was twenty-five years of age.

A few days later, when heavy rains had come, a vast crowd of men from all parts of the country suddenly came into the city, crying that Jacopo Pazzi should not have been buried in sacred ground. The reason it had rained so long was that such a wicked man as he, who even in dying had shown no regard for religion or God, had been buried in a church, contrary to custom and sacred law. According to an old superstition of the peasants, this would hurt the grain, which was just filling out, and (as is the way with such things), all the people started repeating the assertion. The crowds finally gathered at Pazzi's tomb, exhumed the corpse, and reburied it near the edge of town.

The next day, monstrous as it seemed, a vast crowd of boys appeared as if inflamed by the mysterious torches of the Furies, and again exhumed the buried man, and almost stoned to death someone who tried to stop them. They seized the corpse by the rope that had choked him and dragged him through the entire city with taunts and jests. Some ran ahead and mockingly ordered the streets to be cleared for a great and special knight; others beat the cadaver with sticks and goad, chiding him not to be late since the citizens expected him in the Piazza of the Signoria. Then they took him to his own house and made him knock his head on the door, while calling out, "Who is within? Who will receive the lord returned with his train?" Forbidden to enter the Piazza, they moved on to the Arno and threw the body in. As it floated along, a large group of peasants followed it along the banks shouting insults. Someone is reported to have remarked, not inaptly, that he would have succeeded beyond his wildest dreams if, when alive, he had had the popular following he had in death.

By this upheaval and these changes I was repeatedly reminded of the instability of human fortune, and most of all was I struck by the incredible grief of everyone for the death of Giuliano, whose physical appearance, character, and habits, I shall briefly sketch. He was tall and sturdy, with a large chest. His arms were rounded and muscular, his joints strong and big, his stomach flat, his thighs powerful, his calves rather full. He had bright lively eyes, with excellent vision, and his face was rather dark, with thick, rich black hair worn long and combed straight back from the forehead. He was skilled at riding and at throwing, jumping and wrestling, and prodigiously fond of hunting. Of great courage and steadfastness, he fostered piety and good morals. He was accomplished in painting and music and every sort of refinement. He had some talent for poetry, and wrote some Tuscan verses which were wonderfully serious and edifying. And he always enjoyed reading amatory verse. He was both eloquent and prudent, but not at all showy; he loved wit and was himself quite witty. He hated liars and men who hold grudges. Moderate in his grooming, he was nonetheless amazingly elegant and attractive. He was very mild, very kind, very respectful of his brother, and of great strength and virtue. These virtues and others made him beloved by the people and his own family during his lifetime, and they rendered most painful and bitter to us all the memory of his loss. Yet we pray to Almighty God that he may not forbid "this youth's helping our suddenly stricken generation." (Virgil *Georg*. I, 500.)

Alamanno Rinuccini

To introduce Rinuccini, I want briefly to describe his career, the beliefs he expresses in *De Libertate*, and the value of this dialogue. His career was admired, not least by Rinuccini himself, as of *duplex foelicitatis genus*, combining the active and the contemplative life. His political and his scholarly activities were certainly related. He used his writings to gain influence and his influence to encourage scholarship. The ideas in *De Libertate* are largely classical, yet combined in a creative way, and applied with precision to the actual contemporary situation. The dialogue has special virtues, in fact, for it compresses into one short, clear exposition the essential heritage of Florentine civic humanism. At the same time it openly discusses some of the major political issues debated in Lorenzo de' Medici's Florence, issues carefully veiled in most writings from Lorenzo's circle.

Rinuccini wrote *De Libertate* a year after the Pazzi conspiracy; he was fifty-three, a long time member of the Medici party now embittered by the turn politics had taken in his country.[1] He wrote both as a humanist and as a member of the Florentine hereditary ruling class. Since the thirteenth century, as he reminds us, members of his family had enjoyed wealth, status and public office in Florence. His own career, though this is something he does not make clear, had always been dependent on his friendship with the Medici. At various times, however, he had shown himself critical of their growing power. He enjoyed a small patrimony, and he devoted his youth to scholarship, not, like his brothers, to getting established in business. When his name was first placed in the lists from which public officials were chosen by lot, it was withdrawn because of his youth (1433). Later, when he was reentered and actually chosen for the office of prior, or member of the Signoria, he could not hold office because, it seems, he was in debt for taxes (1454).[2] At this time, however, his scholarly translations and participation in philosophical discussions earned him certain eminent friends and a reputation. He and his friends formed an "Academy"—the direct model for Ficino's later and more famous Neoplatonic group. Rinuccini, in 1456, urged Cosimo de' Medici to bring to Florence the noted Byzantine teacher, Argyropoulos. Argyropoulos saw as an integrated whole the history of ancient philosophy from Socrates to the Alexandrians, and thus he shaped the later humanist perspective on the classical heritage. Cosimo arranged for him to hold a professorship in the new university at Florence. Rinuccini, in various writings dedicated to the Medici, expressed his enthusiasm for Cosimo's quiet political coup of 1458, when he put an end to the organized opposition of some eminent patricians. Rinuccini viewed this coup as a public boon and as a peaceful, viable compromise.

In 1459 Rinuccini was again entered on the lists of those eligible for the highest offices. He became a prior in 1460, a member of the committee called "Twelve Good Men" in 1462, a member of the Squittino, or board of scrutiny, which controlled the lists of possible officials, in 1465. In 1466 he was a member of the balìa, or *ad hoc* council with full powers, which exiled Piero de' Medici's opponents, and greatly tightened his control. Rinuccini, however, seems to have voted against this increase in Medici power. Suddenly, thereafter, he found himself entirely without public office—a state that lasted until 1472. Such unemployment may have given him more time to study, but it surely meant financial hardship as well as anxiety about his social status.[3] In 1469 Piero died.

Rinuccini's relations with young Lorenzo seem to have been good, and he played a part in facilitating the succession to power of Lorenzo and Giuliano.[4] In 1471 Rinuccini's name was drawn for the highest office in the state, the position of standardbearer among the priors, or Gonfaloniere di Giustizia. He could not actually hold the office because his brother was a prior at the time, but simply to have been drawn for it gave one prestige and meant that a promising career lay ahead. Starting in 1472, in fact, Rinuccini became a member of the five-man board of trustees of the growing Florentine university. In 1475–76, however, he took on, rather naively, an important but dangerous post as ambassador to Rome. He was caught in the cross fire of the feud between Sixtus IV and Lorenzo de' Medici. When he reported in too great detail to the Signoria a papal tirade against the first citizen of Florence, he won the enmity of Lorenzo. He was not again deprived of all offices, but he was delayed for a while from reentering Florence and then was confined to administrative work outside the city itself. In the first years after the embassy, he was sometimes entirely unemployed. He approved of the Pazzi revolt, as he tells us, and saw it defeated—presumably in silence. War taxes greatly reduced his private wealth, while he privately considered the war an expression of Lorenzo's tyranny. In 1479, moreover, he also lost his only son to a plague, which took, during those years of civil conflict, a recorded 18,000 Florentine lives.[5] In a mood of bitter grief, therefore, Rinuccini wrote his *De Libertate*, dated April 10, 1479.

Though he wrote as though he would never more serve the Medici, he again received and accepted offices from 1480 on. He sat that year in the *balìa* which created the Council of Seventy, a new ruling group designed to give Lorenzo more absolute political control. Rinuccini did not like this creation and probably voted against it. Lorenzo, however, did not always mind a show of opposition, as long as it was ineffectual. He gave back to Rinuccini the position that best suited his wishes and talents, perhaps, for he again made Rinuccini one of the trustees of the University. This position, which he had held from 1473 to 1477, was his again, with the power of hiring and firing professors and planning development, from 1480 to 1484. After this, he was given a series of minor administrative posts in various Tuscan towns under Florentine control. Perhaps the overthrow of the Medici in 1494 brought Rinuccini satisfaction. Certainly it brought him an important position in the new government of the Republic. He became a member of the Council of One Hundred, which oversaw the administration of taxation. He remained politically active until his death in May 1499.

The story of Rinuccini's life shows that he was not one of the most consistent opponents of the Medici. Yet the *De Libertate* is "the most vehement and merciless indictment of Lorenzo's politics written by any of his contemporaries."[6] As Vito Guicciardini also suggests, ". . . in Rinuccini the conflict between an inherited dependence on the Medici and the old idea of *libertà* is much more visible and impressive than in his contemporaries, who experienced similar things. . . ."[7] It may also be true that Rinuccini simply wrote down what many others thought and said. How many people were like Alitheus in the dialogue, who knew very well what Rinuccini meant when he began to complain about Florence? The *De Libertate* seems to Nicolai Rubinstein to express the viewpoint of the conservative republican opposition, a viewpoint found in the Signoria debates of 1466 and probably implicit in the Pazzi revolt.[8] How many patricians, however, were like Rinuccini's friend, Microtoxus, dupes of propaganda who still considered Florence a citadel of freedom? Rinuccini complains furiously of citizen

188

apathy. Donato Acciauoli, his close friend and fellow humanist, distinguished himself in 1478 by his visible loyalty to the Medici.[9] One must realize, however, that by this means alone, he avoided exile and the confiscation of his goods. Rinuccini's own withdrawal and counsel of silence to other dissidents kept him, too, safe, and could well have looked rather weak to, for example, a Pazzi. It seems possible that a good many Florentine citizens were simply waiting for an assassin to eliminate Lorenzo.

What sort of political faith did Rinuccini have? He gives us a clear idea of it in Alitheus' long speech in the latter half of the first book of *De Libertate*. He believed in the Republic and its institutions as he thought they had been in the days of Leonardo Bruni and as Leonardo Bruni had described them. Citizen equality ought to be the basis of liberty. Equality would mean equal justice in the courts, equal and effective protection for life and property. Justice would hold the rich and poor in their respective places. The government ought to rest on wide participation—citizens to qualify by being taxpayers, hence pillars of the state.[10] Freedom of debate should really exist, producing wise decisions in the governing councils. No clique, obviously, should seize all the profits of government and drive opponents into exile. The result of true liberty, moreover, would be the protection and extension of the common good, the Florentine empire. And Rinuccini, through Alitheus, narrates a good part of the history of Florence's wars, justifying all her conquests and taking pride in her vigorous defense of her gains.

Rinuccini shared, not only Bruni's essential program, but also his feeling that Florence was or ought to be as related to the Athenian as to the more obviously relevant Roman ideal. In Athens there were not only law and empire and a republican form of government, but also a stress on the individual citizen's power to reason, hence on diversity. As Athens was Bruni's model in his *Laudatio*, a work based on Aelius Aristides' *Panegyric* of Athens, so in Rinuccini one can see the influence of Pericles' funeral oration, particularly where the humanist claims that the justice of the Florentine courts used to attract many foreigners to them, and where he speaks of the stability formerly achieved through rational debate.

In giving a philosophical basis for his own view of liberty Rinuccini begins with the idea of the *summum bonum*, leaning on Cicero and also on Leonardo Bruni's *Isagogicon*, which compares Aristotelian and Stoic ideas of happiness.[11] The *summum bonum* is happiness, but, philosophy teaches us, real happiness depends on virtue. This virtue may be a style of action achieved by moderating and balancing one's desires, or a static condition of the soul achieved by eliminating passions and needs entirely. In either interpretation, as Rinuccini says, virtue requires ethical choices. *Libertas* must

189

be achieved on two levels: first, as an outer precondition allowing the individual to make choices at all, and second, as an inner state of self-discipline. (In our translation, the first kind of *libertas* tends to appear as "liberty," the second as "freedom.") Full liberty belongs only to virtuous men, and these, by definition, wish to serve their fellow men—a willing service, not a bondage. Hence the virtuous man does participate in politics. Only when his own ethical freedom is threatened thereby, will he withdraw from politics, and then reluctantly. (The great and ancient question whether virtue can be politically imposed simply does not appear for Rinuccini.)

Following, possibly, Xenophon's *Hiero—On Tyranny*,[12] Rinuccini stresses that the effect of tyranny is to surround the tyrant with dishonest people. Both he and they live in constant anxiety, but are driven on by greed as well as by fear itself. The effect is to undermine not only philosophical liberty, but also the traditional Florentine patrician standards of honesty in transactions and personal dignity, *onestà*.

At this time, Rinuccini says, withdrawal seems best to him. If he could overthrow the tyrant, he says, he would gladly do it, but too many citizens are complacent. Since he feels he cannot change the government, he does not want to stay in Florence even as a merely private man. To do so would involve seeing things that it is painful even to hear about. He may be referring to the persecutions that followed the Pazzi revolt—persecutions described in a different spirit by Poliziano—and to the war with all its costs, which he considers a private crime of Lorenzo's.

As soon as Rinuccini—who in forced retirement, prescribed retirement—was offered a position by Lorenzo, he in fact abandoned his villa and returned to the city. Perhaps he was satisfied to think that his own role in Florence would be opposed to the general direction of the regime. As he says in *De Libertate*, the refusal of good men to hold office under a tyrant makes the tyranny worse.

One of the great virtues of the dialogue is its concreteness. Rinuccini directs himself especially to Microtoxus, the man of limited vision. When Microtoxus says that, "Really all generalizations, or, to use the philosophical term, universals, do completely and wholly contain the particular truth spoken of, but just the same such conceptions are not easy for everybody to grasp,"[13] he points to the need for a nonscholastic explanation. Rinuccini then moves toward the methods of modern fiction, for he tries to capture and convey the quality of an individual's experience in a specific situation. This technique is meant to clarify, not to undermine, philosophy, though a certain hostility to philosophy as logic-chopping (the philosophy of the scholastics) is quite apparent. In effect, however, Rinuccini transcends the

190

weaknesses of his own moral and political philosophy by creating a clear expression of his ambivalent and difficult state of mind.

The ideas and experience of Rinuccini are startlingly modern, and this is true although his vocabulary is classical and his experience that of a patrician in a pre-modern city-state. His ideas on freedom and virtue, on the need for tolerance and lawfulness in political processes, seem indispensable still. And many modern liberals, too, are prevented by the patrician roots or cast of their thought from observing that the rule of law in an oligarchy is undermined, not just by a few unscrupulous men, but by the underlying need of such a state to oppress its neighbors and to keep its masses in silent subjection.

NOTES

1. The facts of Rinuccini's career as given here are taken from the meticulous work of Vito R. Giustiniani, *Alamanno Rinuccini, 1426–1499* (Böhlau), Cologne, 1965, especially 1–35, "Das Leben."

2. This, at least, is the usual meaning of being *a specchio*, as the records show that he was. (Guicciardini, 30). Cf. Nicolai Rubinstein *The Government of Florence under the Medici*, Oxford, 1966, p. 64, note 4.

3. Most of his writings date from 1455 to 1475. (Guicciardini, 30). From 1466 to 1471, only seven short letters are preserved (Guicciardini, viii) which suggests that political inactivity did not stimulate writing.

4. He sat in the balìa of 1471 which arranged for greater control of offices by the two young Medici. It is clear that he manifested his support for them because he was immediately named the head of the "Brotherhood of the Three Kings," an organization of Medici supporters. Guicciardini, 25–6.

5. Guicciardini, 30.

6. Ibid.

7. Guicciardini, 25.

8. Rubinstein, 196.

9. Eugenio Garin, *Medioevo e Rinascimento*, Bari, 1954, 231.

10. *De Libertate*, below, "It is considered best for liberty and justice if all those who aid the republic privately by payment of taxes are also given a chance to participate in its rewards and advantages."

11. Leonardo Bruni, *Humanistisch-Philosophische Schriften*, ed. Hans Baron, Leipzig, 1928.

12. A literal translation and close analysis are given in Leo Strauss, *On Tyranny*, Glencoe, New York, 1963.

13. *De Libertate*, below.

LIBERTY

by Alamanno Rinuccini

Preface to his brother, Alessandro:

When I took up a way of life, my beloved brother, not much different from the one you yourself profess, I was encouraged by your advice and that of certain friends, but I know full well that my decision met with disapproval from some who envied me and some, perhaps, who did not understand. They did not like to see me give no further consideration to practically any of the affairs of the city and devote myself, almost like an exile, solely to the cultivation of this little house and farm. They did not approve of my leaving all public concerns and all unnecessary personal ones. We can silence their criticism, of course, by calling on the testimony of various famous men, but you alone seem enough of an example. You lived in the great English city of London, representing the richest and most eminent company of all that were there and enjoying the favor and good will of your superiors. The way you did business made it clear that only lack of desire prevented you from amassing an enormous fortune. All these things you put aside, however, and what is more, relinquished your considerable personal inheritance, in order to live a kind of life you thought would give you leisure with dignity and undisturbed tranquillity. I could not do the same, for I was already committed to the care of wife and family, but I chose the nearest approximation, a life far from the crowded city and innumerable anxieties associated with the greed and ambition which it fosters.

193

I have been unable to avoid some well-meant reproaches from friends, however, and I have made, as you will see, a rather long answer to their objections. Rather than let them change my determination in the least, I won them over to my own opinion. After the grievous loss of my only son, I was living sorrowfully in the villa he himself had frequented and was avoiding the company of men. Two persons of our academy came to see me at that time on a visit of condolence. I shall not put their names in writing lest, if some of the talk that took place among us seems to attack a certain person, these men might have reason to complain that I published the freely spoken words of a friendly conversation. So I have invented names appropriate to their characters and sentiments, which I think suggest them both well enough. If you recognize them, I look forward to your comment on that. But if you cannot give me your opinion on the choice of names, I would still appreciate it on the substance of the discussion at least, and I look forward to hearing whether you agree.

This is how it all happened: they were returning from the Casentine and went out of their way to visit me. By chance they found me at home, reading something or other, and after the sort of things customarily said when friends first meet again, they spoke at length on the themes of comfort and consolation. Finally Alitheus, hoping to distract me from the oppressive grief that weighed on me, suggested to Microtoxus that he say in my presence what they had been saying about me on their trip. So he began as follows.

DIALOGUE ON LIBERTY BEGINS:

Speakers: *Alitheus* (the Truthful), *Eleutherius* (the Lover of Liberty), and *Microtoxus* (the Short-Range Shooter)

Microtoxus: This little house and the land around it remind me of the Curii or Cincinnatus. The farm is beautifully cultivated though it looks to me basically quite small. Clearly all this delights you no end, Eleutherius, yet it provokes me to laughter or amazement. For up to now, when you stayed out of town so much, I always thought you were busy either in agricultural pursuits or in the enjoyment of a more beautiful house. I could easily understand your desire for open air and for escape from the prison-like confinement of the city house. After all, your very name, Eleutherius, indicates a love and zeal for liberty. But now I see your fields are well kept up and that your country house is much smaller than your city residence; I really don't see what has kept you away so long. I can't believe that you hate the city, like some people, who are lazy and want to enjoy a passive leisure. You abound in skills that not only keep you active in the city but bring you honor. And I think Alitheus agrees.

Alitheus: Frankly, Microtoxus, I am not as surprised as you at Eleutherius' decision to live in the country. And what is more, I admire his frugality and modesty, for he has set the limits of both farm and house to make them economical and to provide for all necessities, not to fulfill luxurious designs. When I consider his former life and character and especially, as you say, his name, I feel he has not set himself these limits just by chance but rather that he has chosen a life style. I think he has made a wise decision. If he wanted freedom to lead a good life, I think it is indeed more possible here in isolation than in the city.

Microtoxus: You have strange ideas, Alitheus. Why should he alone, among so many thousands, be unable to find freedom in the city? And particularly in the one city which professes to uphold liberty most among the states of Italy! She has spared neither treasure nor risk to defend not only her own freedom and the freedom of her citizens but also the freedom of many other Italian cities. All that I could easily prove on historical evidence, but to set it forth to you seems superfluous. You have given your attention to the talk of our elders and also to books, so you know these things very well.

Alitheus: Very true, Microtoxus. In all Italy, I think, there is no city that has so energetically and enduringly championed the cause of liberty. Nor is there any place where it has flourished in so pure and ample a form. For if you go from the beginnings to the present, you will find that this country's liberty has never been crushed by a foreign people or a tyrant. There is only the isolated case of Walter [of Brienne], duke of Athens, who was called in by a popular revolt and reigned as a tyrant through deceit and the support of a faction of the nobility, but he did not rule long, nor could he long suppress the fruitful tree of liberty, if I may so express myself. I am not sure, in fact, whether this whole episode is not perhaps greater proof of the native Florentine love of liberty than a totally uninterrupted history of freedom would be.

Consider what you said and what I said too: doesn't it make your crime and the crime of men like you even more serious and less pardonable? You received a treasure of such magnitude and magnificence from ancestors who, at the greatest cost of labor and money, preserved it and passed it on to you—and you, lazy, apathetic, and enfeebled by your blinded intelligence, let it slip through your fingers. I don't know, in view of all this, whether to blame your slowness of mind and coarse sensibility, if it happened without your even knowing it, or, if you did bear and suffer such losses consciously, to condemn your degenerate and effeminate softness. These are things to be avoided even at the sacrifice of one's life; for to me it is clear that an honorable death is preferable to a life of disgusting shame.

This truth did not escape the truly magnanimous mind and noble character of Jacopo and Francesco dei Pazzi and of the various heads of that family. Though they were flourishing, possessed ample wealth, had intimate connections with the most eminent citizens, and enjoyed popularity and the good will of the people as a whole, they scorned all these advantages in the absence of liberty. Thus did they undertake a glorious deed, an action worthy of the highest praise. They tried to restore their own liberty and that of the country. You know that Fortune foiled their plans, as is often her way. Their resolution, however, and the action on which they embarked, deserve praise forever. Men of sound judgment will always rank them with Dion of Syracuse, Aristogiton and Harmodius of Athens, Brutus and Cassius of Rome, and in our own day, Giovanni and Geronimo Andrea of Milan.[2] But I don't know why this discussion has wandered so far from its starting point. The greatness of these men and of what they attempted certainly demand, not a little digression from us, but the full attention of an eloquent historian.

Microtoxus: Are you quite in the possession of your senses, Alitheus, saying such things to us and completely forgetting what I just said?

196

Alitheus: And what was that?

Microtoxus: I said that the state of Florence was always zealous in the pursuit of liberty, always remarkable among other states in this respect. That is why the word liberty is actually written in gold on one of her banners.

Alitheus: Let's think about that, Microtoxus. It seems to me the fine words and the golden letters clash with the facts. This sort of argument only adds to my sorrow, indeed, for I see so many of my fellow citizens are fooled and are wholly detached from reality. What could be stupider than to think you are what you are not? Or to imagine you possess what is completely out of your reach?

Microtoxus: I would like to hear something clearer and, if I may say so, more explicit, if you are going to talk about these things. I admit my comprehension is rather slow. Really all generalizations, or, to use the philosophical term, "universals," do completely and wholly contain the particular truth spoken of, but just the same such conceptions are not easy for everybody to grasp. These general statements are not fitted for practical application, since action must deal with particular things in particular situations. From you, therefore, I long to hear what liberty is and how we have moved away from it in the way we live, as well as how the way our friend, Eleutherius, lives is particularly free.

Alitheus: You must realize that you have just thrown the whole burden of this discussion on me. If some of what has to be said is unpleasant, it will be up to me to say it. Well, whatever comes of it, I am not going to be afraid to say what I really think among good friends. I shall answer as well as I can both the first parts of your question. Of the way of life Eleutherius has chosen, however, I think it is only fair that he himself should speak. No one can set forth better than he his reasons for living in isolation and what he hopes to gain thereby. It would be better actually if he handled all this talk of liberty, since, as you said in your first speech, liberty herself gave Eleutherius his name.

Eleutherius: This is not right. Since you two started the argument, I think you should finish it. I shall, like an honorable judge, keep watching to see which of you comes closer to the truth, and I may on occasion give my own opinion.

Microtoxus: Well said, Eleutherius. But we don't want you to get away without even getting your feet wet, you know, especially when the whole discussion began on account of you. So let's take the divisions just made by Alitheus, and leave to you the explanation of your total retirement to the country and of the philosophy behind your life style. You have been listening to us in cunning silence, while we seemed to be guessing, as it were, at your secrets, but now we won't do that any-more. I suppose you were laughing to yourself while we tried to under-stand someone else's mind by our own interpretation rather than by asking him questions directly.

Eleutherius: Your talk concerned things that are most worthwhile, and was very interesting—so I was happy to have served as the object of some speculation. Now I am really eager to hear Alitheus' ideas, which he promised us. For I think he will take his speech from the heart of philosophy. I know how hard he has been studying, especially these last years as a good student of Johannes Argyropoulos.[3] Like a good many of our friends, moreover, he has even kept a written journal on the lectures. I won't, as Microtoxus puts it, escape without getting my feet wet. If any need is felt for a word from me, I shall tell you whatever you want to know. Now let's listen to Alitheus. I noticed already how well he defined the parts of our topic.

Alitheus: I don't see how I can put off any longer fulfilling my promise to you. I do suggest, though, that we go sit in that grove over there, for this is a lovely time of day, especially in spring, and the walk through flowering vines and trees, and over blossoming flowers and grasses, seems to call to us. I know that it's just the work of nature, but this landscape—in its dimensions, its relation to the sun, and its shape —looks like the work of an artist. The grove is just far enough from the house so that if you go back and forth while you're reading or meditating, you get some exercise. The gentle slope offers a lovely view, and makes your walk not overstrenuous and fairly quick.

198

Microtoxus: What good ideas you have. The mild weather urges us to stay outside, not under a roof, and the very topic of our discussion suits the open air and not a walled-in place. Not to cross the space from the house to the woods in idleness, however, let Eleutherius recite for us, on the way, one of the poems of Theocritus' *Bucolics*.

Eleutherius: I shall, and it's a pleasure to do for you what I so often do even by myself. For I almost never wander through these places without a book of poetry. I shall begin, then, and when I fall into barbarisms, as they used to say in Attica, please correct my mistakes. You know how hard it is for a man used to Latin to speak Greek correctly. But be that as it may, I shall begin.

* * *

Microtoxus: A lovely poem and most suited to our bucolic surroundings. You spoke so well that you seemed a very Greek. Now, as you see, here we are at the wood. Let's sit or lie, whichever we prefer, beneath this spreading oak, and listen to Alitheus.

Alitheus: As you please. But hearing this poem delighted me so that I could have walked unawares all the way to Florence. I was enthralled by its sweetness and occupied also by thoughts of what I should say. To begin with that now, I shall use the method developed by Plato and define the subject of our discussion so that it is clear to all the participants. I think you will indulge me if I take rather many words to state with some precision what that subject is. There is no such thing in actuality, as an absolute and perfect definition composed according to the method of the philosophers, by stating first the category to which the thing belongs and then the essential differences that mark it off from other members of that category. They themselves admit that, because of the paucity and inaccuracy of words, there are many more things than there are words for things, hence always ambiguities. I think I may say roughly, though, that liberty is a kind of potential for enjoying freedom within the limits set by law and custom.[4]

199

Microtoxus: Right, but it hasn't taken you many words, Alitheus, to state the extent of this potential. Still, since we aren't trying to match the sharp wits of the dialecticians and their verbal parsimony, but really want the amplitude of the orator, I hope you'll explain each of these points more extensively and completely.

Alitheus: I'll be glad to, if Eleutherius doesn't mind.

Eleutherius: On the contrary, nothing could be more to my taste. I long to hear some words on this subject, which often concerns and troubles my mind. For I see a lot of people who neglect and utterly scorn this precious gift of God. Yet the love of liberty and longing for freedom are natural not only to man but even to the animals. The very brutes prefer poverty and hardship, accompanied by freedom, to a life of comfortable servitude. But too much of this, I see Alitheus is ready to speak.

Alitheus: You've heard my definition of liberty, as brief as I could make it. It seems reasonable to call liberty a kind of potential or capacity, for the man who is called free is able, at will, to use or not to use this capacity. If he is indeed free, nothing prevents him from leading the life of a slave, which he can do through ignorance or by a conscious, if perverse, choice. Such is the case, for instance, of men addicted to lust or avarice or some such vice; they voluntarily give up the use of their liberty. For who would call a man free if he's subject to avarice, anxious night and day, bending every effort to the pursuit of money by fair means or foul? Neither his body nor his mind is ever free from labor.

Shall I continue and also consider the people who get entangled in shameful love affairs? At the nod of a lover, they vacillate a thousand times an hour—now filled with foolish delight, now tormented by horrible anguish. Shall I talk about ambition too? Tossed about by vicissitudes, ambitious men constantly attempt to command undistinguished little wretches. And, for the appearance of being in command, they actually subject themselves to men even worse than they are. Let's not list all the kinds of vice that enslave men and oppress them. I shall just cite the Stoic paradox, which is as true as it is elegant: "Only the wise are free."[5]

Only the wise, as the Stoics say, have extinguished the passions; or, in the language of the Peripatetics,[6] moderated them. Empty of conflict and distraction, they live in peace and tranquillity and are directed by their own free will. Their senses, their reason, and all the powers of their soul agree in directing them to certain ends, and these they steadily pursue. This is not just the source of liberty, but of happiness, the goal praised and desired by philosophers. Perhaps its nature was best expressed by the writer who called it εὐθυμία,[7] a state of spiritual well-being, a state I would suppose, of peace and tranquillity. The man whose mind is in this state truly is free and can live exactly as he wishes. It seems that liberty does not differ much from happiness. From these remarks it is clear, I think, why I defined liberty as a kind of potential. Now let us—if you do not object—look at the other parts of this definition.

Microtoxus: You have made amply clear that liberty is some kind of potential. Now it would be nice to know whether you think this potential is innate or acquired by training and practice, like running and jumping and wrestling.

Alitheus: A good question, Microtoxus. I too think this potential is much like any human faculty. Its basis, like that of any tendency or inclination, is a natural gift found in any well-endowed human being, and it may be perfected by the liberal arts and good education. Its origins, since it is actually also a certain appetite, I think are quite like the origins of the affections. It is like love, hate, anger and other such things, to which some men naturally incline and which others naturally shun. For I won't deny that some people are, by nature, more inclined than others to cherish liberty. Such is the character of all affections.

Eleutherius: My own observations confirm the truth and wisdom of what you say. I have seen plenty of men, not in the least attracted by any definite advantage, subordinate themselves to the vilest persons. Yet others could not be induced by bribes or terrible threats to make themselves the inferiors of their peers. In this sense liberty might reasonably be classed as a kind of fortitude. Even Cicero seems to think so in his

201

book *De Officiis*, where he says of fortitude: "It makes anyone of a naturally strong mind unwilling to obey another unless his commands are just and legitimate and serve a useful purpose."[8]

I could give you many examples, both Florentine and other. But not to go far from home, Alitheus is such a man and, I admit, so am I. We have often talked about it in the past. I don't see why I should subordinate myself to men who are inferior to me in family and character, men who owe their higher status only to the depraved judgment of knaves and to the bold whim of fortune. But I don't know if we should even call it high status to hold offices that are awarded, in many cases, not for merit or education or good character, but by arbitrary choice, or for a price, or for reasons of shameful corruption. I am holding up Alitheus' discourse unduly, however. I am eager to hear his explanation of the rest of his definition.

Alitheus: I was very glad of your critique of these times. I found in it a kind of reply to certain thoughts that often torment me. But of that I shall find occasion to speak later. Now let us move on. We have defined liberty as a kind of potential for living, meaning by "live" to act and do things. I don't use the term here as Aristotle does where he says that to live is simply to be among the living. Such life is fully present not only in animals but in plants and in grass and in anything that has a vegetative soul. Here, however, I am calling life something that consists of action and is granted to animals, especially to men. For human life, as the philosopher says himself, consists of a kind of action.[8] What I said of the potential for living, therefore, is the same as if I had said the capacity to act and do things. I think we do well to call this a free capacity, moreover, if it is not limited by force or by consideration of externals, but acts in accordance with the dictates of right reason.

In the senate, or in court, or in any place of judgment, a man may be inhibited by fear or desire or something else from saying openly what he thinks. But would he then be free? He must dare to speak and to act. Hence, as I said before, liberty has quite reasonably been seen as part of fortitude. Both the free and the strong man reveals himself most clearly in action. We praise a man's strength, however, when he with reason exposes himself to bodily danger, while we admire his freedom when he is speaking and giving counsel. Frank and noble spirits must possess both virtues, it seems, for they neither yield to present dangers nor are terrified by threats. In states where liberty exists, these qualities are most useful, for there the citizens speak without subterfuge and give advice to the Republic based on their real convictions. I think it was right, therefore, to call this power to live liberty. Or do you perhaps disagree?

Microtoxus: I don't feel that anything has been introduced here altogether superfluously. Furthermore I won't take offense at anything you say or that I hear said about myself, as long as you'll please go on with the discourse you started. Even if I seem to know already what is coming, I still want to hear you explain what is meant by "within the limits of law and custom."

Alitheus· I noticed long ago, Microtoxus, that nothing worries you more than to seem to be hearing something for the first time. Let me tell you what I think though.

I would not call anyone unfree merely because he had to obey the law of his country. Obedience to the law is, as Cicero says, the truest liberty. So, we obey the law in order to be free.[9] Many actions can, in fact, be prohibited without diminishing personal liberty. I would not call it lack of freedom not to be allowed to strike one's fellow citizen with impunity, or to take his wealth by force, or to rape his wife. Then there is a myriad of things not prohibited by law but forbidden by the customs and conventions of the city. Anyone who does those things risks suspicion of madness. This, in my view, is not a threat to liberty either. I don't consider a man unfree because, if he wants to keep his reputation for sanity, he can't unlace his boots or eat his dinner in the piazza—that is, if he's a citizen of Florence, for these same things are tolerated in travelers. Custom likewise does not let a respectable man cavort or sing in the market place, though there is no law against it. I would not describe a man as less than free because, for fear of disgrace, he abstained from such activities. Would you?

Microtoxus: Not at all. What you say seems absolutely true, and nothing could be truer. I see how wrong I was not to understand the need for these last points in your definition. They are really no less

important than the rest. Since you have done justice to the first part
of our problem, now, and explicated your definition part by part, I am
only waiting to hear you on the other half of the question. Please go on
and explain in what ways we at present live without liberty, for this
point I scarcely believe you can prove.

Alitheus: You are asking me to contemplate again a very sad situation. These things are painful to remember, let alone discuss. Dear
friends, I cannot think about this subject without tears. It makes me
ashamed, for I too was born in this city, and I too belong to our time.
And I see the people who once commanded most of Tuscany and even
some of the neighboring peoples, bullied today by the whims of one
young man. Many noble minds and men of eminent seniority and wisdom wear today the yoke of servitude and hardly recognize their own
condition. Nor, when they do see it, do they dare avenge themselves.
They become, and this is worst of all, the unwilling adversaries of those
who try to liberate them.

We have degenerated so much in our time from the virtues of our
ancestors; I am convinced that if they came back to life, they would deny
we ever sprang from them. They founded, cherished and increased this
Republic. They gave it excellent customs, sacred laws, and institutions
that further an upright way of life. Our constitution, as anyone could
see, equaled or surpassed in its protection of the people's liberty the
ancient constitutions of Lycurgus, Solon, Pompey, and the rest. The
results proved it. As long as our state lived in accordance with its own
law, it enjoyed preeminence among the other Tuscan cities in wealth, in
dignity, and in power. All that time this city was a model, not of power
alone, but of moral principles. Now I see the same laws despised by
everyone till nothing stands lower. The desires of a few irresponsible
citizens, instead, have gained the force of law.

Consider the facts, really. Isn't it well known that the basic principle
of all liberty is citizen equality? This is a fundamental to keep the rich
from oppressing the poor or the poor, for their part, from violently
robbing the rich. On this basis everyone keeps what is his and is secure
from attack. Judge for yourselves how secure things are in our country.
Shall I describe the sale of justice? Most carefully, as long as our state
was free, was justice kept clear of corruption. Now it is managed in

a way that is sickening even to talk about. I cannot recall without great sorrow how no one dared, by word or vote, contradict the charges which, backed by plenty of false denunciations from certain individuals, were thought to be in line with the wishes of one powerful man. It came to the point where I considered it one of Fortune's gifts, and not one of the lesser ones, if a man could find some honorable reason not to participate in judgment. And yet at one time our state was well known for justice, and men from distant countries brought cases to be tried in Florence. Now when cases arise in the city, they are never judged but after long delay and great expense. The play of ambition and bribery or the wishes of the powerful are always involved. As a result the sentence often favors, not the man with right on his side, but the one with influence. There are many to tell how they have been forced out of their houses and lost their inheritance. They have been despoiled by force and fraud of their homes, their money, and all that they possess.

Why compare the freedom of speech that used to prevail in the senate and in all public meetings with the present silence? There once did shine the wisdom, the eloquence, and the fervent patriotism which graced some of our best citizens. Serious and responsible men used to consider all sides of any proposal freely, and soon got at the truth of things that way. There were not many errors made in council then. Once a decree was passed, it was not repented of the next day and changed to its opposite. Now, on the other hand, as there are just a few Catos sitting in consultation on the weightiest questions, we often see resolutions passed one day and reversed the next by the same body, perhaps because they received a word of warning from someone. Our state has been robbed of the advantage or convenience which Aristotle noticed in free republics—that they are one body served by many heads and hands and feet.[10] For it is practically the same as not to possess something, if, having it, you do not wish to use it.

Thanks to the arrogance of a few overbearing individuals and the apathy of the rest of the citizens, these few today usurp the power of all. Their impulses and ambitions decide everything, while almost no authority is left to the councils or the people. Silent is the voice of the herald so eloquently praised by Demosthenes, that used to be empowered by our government to call all citizens to a council.[11] If, for custom's sake, it does occasionally still ring out, everyone knows it is meaningless. For men are too intimidated to give free and open counsel.

Consider, too, the undeniably important power of the state to punish malefactors. Irresponsible criminals, whom no shame, no sense of right and wrong, no love of honor can deter from crime, can be coerced by fear of the judge and of punishment. Unless their boldness is curbed by that fear, no crime is horrible and cruel enough to make them hesitate. The absence of threats is for them an invitation to crime. And what do such scoundrels have to fear today? What holds them back, when the bribes and the influence of wicked leaders whom they delight to serve assure them of immunity and rewards? Men actually condemned to exile or prison openly walk the streets in front of everybody, released, not on the order of an official, but by the words of one citizen. Men condemned by the Committee of Eight to perpetual imprisonment are removed from jail on the whim of a private person, or rather of a tyrant.

And what about the way public officials are chosen these days? You know as well as I that, in free states, offices are filled by chance selection from certain lists. It is considered best for liberty and justice if all those who aid the Republic privately by payment of taxes are also given a chance to participate in its rewards and advantages. But now all the positions that bestow some dignity on a man and yield some profit are filled, not by lot, but by appointment. The result is that no good men, no men noted for prudence and nobility are chosen, but satellites of the powerful or servants of their desires and pleasures who will unquestioningly obey them and act as humble as ever they can. This, of course, lessens the authority of the legitimate government, or rather destroys it. Good men, furthermore, and men fitted for public affairs, react with the natural indignation of free persons and refuse to hold any office. This gives still more license, however, to the small group of criminals who harass and ruin the Republic. I could go on much longer, protesting against these disgraceful abuses, but my own grief, by God, and the repulsive character of the crimes involved, makes me want to stop.

I cannot simply ignore, however, the most terrible abuse of all. This is an evil all our citizens should be trying to stop like a plague. While Italy in general has enjoyed great peace in recent years, what could be more shameful than to find that all our citizens, but for a few, have been drained by heavy taxes? These resources, moreover, collected on the excuse of purchasing agricultural surpluses or on some other stupid pretext, have all been diverted to serve one man's pleasures. No need to wonder, now, how they get all the money for urban and rural building at once, or where the money comes from to feed such crowds of horses, dogs, birds, actors, sycophants, and parasites. So much spent in so few months does in itself invalidate the impression of private wealth he supposedly wants to give. And he openly admits that he does not have to pay his debts. He has always extorted money on any pretext from all sides, from friend as well as stranger. He has always assumed that Fortune will always favor him, so that he can freely use the wealth of others, public or private, as his own.

These facts and others like them, Microtoxus, in my judgment simply undermine liberty. Liberty has been uprooted and thrown away. To hate such an undignified and corrupt condition like the plague is only natural. But I find the situation even more unbearably bitter when I reflect on what I have learned from the talk of older men and from books about our ancestors' long struggle to preserve liberty and citizen equality. They used to have periodic inquiries to expose wild behavior or, in legal terms, to uncover public scandal. Those who were convicted they exiled. This custom of ostracism goes back to the Athenians and has always been characteristic of free republics, for people knew that citizen equality is basic to the preservation of liberty. I am sure the fact has not escaped you, for instance, that Giorgio Scala received the death penalty. He was a noble knight and a very distinguished man who held high public office, but he had removed his follower, Scatiza Assecla, from the prefect's prison. The knight, Verius Circulus, was exiled for claiming a position above his fellow citizens. Curtius Donatus was expelled from the city because he took to wife the daughter of Uguccione Fagiolano. The people attacked him, and later he was defeated and killed in battle. Once he formed a connection with a tyrant, the people suspected he might have some sort of tyrannical designs. In those days there was real concern for liberty among the people. They wanted, that is, to keep things under their own control and to govern the Republic themselves. Now, on the other hand, the people seem to despair of themselves. They submit to an alien will and let the wishes of certain people subvert their lives.

This is not the result of natural and honest ignorance, but of coercion by force and threat. They dare not vindicate their rights. Yet this same people once fought powerful republics and great tyrants. They defended their liberty with success, first by sacrifice of blood and second by expenditure of vast wealth. We know how boldly, with what might and military cunning they made war against their neighbors when they saw themselves invaded or when, goaded by injuries and excessive provocations, they crossed the borders of others. They fought Volterra, Pisa, Arezzo, and Pistoia until all these cities came under their rule and dominion. They made Siena, Perugia, and Bologna suffer so much in war that by finally demanding peace, they were granting a boon. To speak of Lucca, it is true, is somewhat embarrassing. We repeatedly conquered that city but we never could hold it, and though it has often come under Florentine government, for some reason it has always slipped through our fingers again. It really has seemed like a dragon that annually devoured Florentine money and blood.

It would take too long to list all the tyrants and princes the Florentine people have fought. They carried on long and bitter wars rather than suffer the loss, if only in name, of their liberty. They fought Manfed at Arbium and again at Benevento, where he died defeated.[11] Love of liberty made our ancestors, much as they always cherished the Christian religion and the cult of the church, unhesitatingly take up arms against a wicked pope. Such was Gregory X, who for three years denied our city the sacraments.[12] Later they made war against the Emperor Henry, who pitched his tents as near as the monastery of San Salvi.[13] For similar reasons, they fought Uguccione Fagiolano and Castruccio of Lucca.[14] These tyrants could do great damage to our city but they could not destroy our liberty. The same thing with Guido Tarlato,[15] who was leader and tyrant of Arezzo. Even Louis of Bavaria, coming to be crowned emperor of the Romans, tried in vain to subjugate Florence.[16] Mastino [della Scala, of Verona], that perfidious tyrant, took over Lucca and made her drop her obligations as a Florentine ally. He not only held that city against all law and custom, but also waged war against Florence. Again his strategems and onslaughts, Florence made a marvelous defense.[17] Following Mastino's example the Milanese leader, Biscio of the Visconti, tried to drag the Florentines into his empire. He used no less fraud than force but in the end he grew weary of the struggle and was glad to sue for peace.[18] Then there was the greatest and most expensive war, the one against the terrible governors of the Papal States. They disregarded divine and human law. First by starvation, and when that didn't work, by war, they tried to rob us of our liberty. At that time Gregory XI ruled from Avignon, and the Florentines, led by the Eight appointed to wage the war, were able to make many papal cities revolt against the rule of the church.[19]

Not much later there was a full-scale war against Gian Galeazzo Visconti, the tyrant of Milan. That was a war that put us in great peril. It staggers the imagination to consider how much money it cost. For many years the Florentines waged that war without obtaining a true peace settlement, made in good faith. In the midst of peace the duke was setting traps for the Florentines and preparing further war. So they summoned Duke Robert of Bavaria into Italy on the promise of 40,000 gold pieces, and in a single night, they collected all that and more as the citizens carried their contributions to the magistrates. Such was their hatred of tyranny, such their love of liberty and country.

Great and mighty war was waged against Ladislas of Naples, that perfidious king, with the Florentines pouring out money: some spent on armaments and some intercepted by the treachery of the king. Yet they did purchase Cortona from that same king, and increase their dominion.[20] Later there were wars, not one but several, with Filippo Visconti, the duke of Milan.[21] That wicked tyrant and sewer of all crime used force and all sorts of cunning tricks to destroy our liberty. But our forefathers stopped him, and gave him occasion to do some worrying about keeping his own domains. Should I remind you of the wars with Alfonso, King of Sicily? Under the influence of Pope Eugene and the Sienese, he attacked the innocent Florentines, who were most loathe to fight, and waged a cruel war. Finally, he conspired with the Venetians so that he and they both expelled our ambassadors. Then he sent his son Ferdinand at the head of a huge army and himself invaded our borders. What happened? On both fronts the armies came back to their kingdom without loot, wholly disgraced, and ravaged by hunger and exhaution.[22]

But the war we are now waging against Pope Sixtus and King Ferdinand[23] leaves me at a loss as to what to say. Both of them clearly declare in speech and writing that they do not seek to take away but to restore the liberty of the Florentine people, and that they war, not against the

Florentines, but only against Lorenzo de' Medici. Everywhere they speak of him as a tyrant, not a citizen, and they have hurled at him alone the full range of ecclesiastical censures. I don't really know whether the struggle of those who oppose these attacks ought to be viewed as a defense of liberty or of servitude.

I wanted to review all this briefly, however, and to demonstrate by a quick summary of past events how great was our ancestors' concern always to preserve and guard liberty. They gave their blood, insofar as it was their business to fight, and later, when they waged their wars with foreign armies, they spent enormous sums. Nor were they satisfied with Italian forces; they brought to their side various transalpine princes. They called kings and emperors into Italy, such as Charles, king of Bohemia and emperor of the Romans, against the power of the bishop of Milan. Similarly against Ladislas of Sicily, they called in Louis of Anjou from France, and together with Pope Alexander V, arranged a friendly alliance with him. On the same principle, they paid heavily to get the count of Armenia to cross over into Italy and oppose what Gian Galeazzo was trying to do. They labored with special zeal, though not with success, to incite Robert, duke of Bavaria, elected Roman emperor, to come and fight that same Gian Galeazzo. And not to harp on ancient history, in our own day we have seen René, the alternate king of Sicily, called down from Provence to carry on against the Venetians the campaign of Francesco Sforza, duke of Milan, with whom we had become allied and associated. King René, to keep a presence in Italy as long as there was work to be done, left behind his son, John, styled the duke of Calabria. He lived a long time in Florence and avenged the city against the unprovoked onslaught of Alfonso and Ferdinand [king of Sicily and duke of Calabria of the actually reigning Aragonese house] when they tried to destroy her liberty.[24]

These things I had to say, excellent friends, concerning liberty. I am afraid I may have seemed to run on and on. But, by God, the subject drew out my talk beyond what I intended almost without my noticing it. If it bored you, I beg your pardon, but if it gave you some joy and pleasure, thank liberty herself, whose very name is a delight to the ear. Now, not to let ourselves be cheated of what was promised us, I think we may fairly expect to listen to Eleutherius while he gives us his reasons for living as he does.

Eleutherius: Your demand is just, Alitheus, and I can't in honesty evade it, much as I was hoping to. I had convinced myself that the seriousness and magnitude of the problems we have been discussing would make you forget my trivial and foolish concerns. But I do think it best to put all this further talk off till tomorrow. The sun, now inclining to the west, and the breath of a gentle breeze so pleasantly cooling the air remind us to think of our health. You know how good it is to take some moderate, not overstrenuous exercise before supper. That's what the doctors say. So, with your approval, let's go look at the various trees in that grove. It's just far enough from here to let us walk there and return home in time for supper.

Microtoxus: A wholly delightful and happy thought, Eleutherius. Nothing you could have suggested would do us more good. We wander through tall grass in the shade of the trees' green roof, we are surrounded by the varied songs of birds, and we approach a pleasant destination. These very delights, this abundance of honest pleasures, might even alter my opinion if I did not know you for a man destined to do greater things. Well, we shall argue about that later. Let's go now, and continue our little journey until we arrive at home. Then we shall see to our bodily refreshment, and surrender to rest and sleep.

BOOK TWO

Eleutherius: The next day, as dawn was breaking, I went to see my friends. They were already up and taking a stroll in the garden, where it was cool. When we had exchanged the usual words of greeting, I turned to Microtoxus and said, "Well, Microtoxus, did this night change your mind? Would you agree now that one is happier living in the fresh air, among wide fields, amidst the gratuitous bounties of nature? Or would you still prefer to be walled in on all sides by the city, to live as if in prison, and hardly to breathe freely?"

Microtoxus: We shall talk about these things later. Let us go slowly down the road which encircles the farm and sit in the meadow shaded by great oaks. You may follow me there now, and I shall be your leader.

211

Alitheus: Microtoxus, you made a fine choice of place. The heavy growth of oaks on the east provides shade and the field, surrounded by grapevines, is better furnished for our comfort with its soft grass and flowers than any room full of drapes and rugs.

Don't hold back any longer, Eleutherius, fufill your promise to speak. Redeem your pledge now and tell us your reasons for your way of life. Though I agree with you and approve of your life, I still want you to say something convincing to Microtoxus here.

Microtoxus: I myself, before Eleutherius begins, would like to state my objections to his retirement. I don't want you to think I am afraid to state my views. Also, I don't see the need for a lot of repetition in case Eleutherius wants to rebut my arguments.

Alitheus: Wise words. I admit it is folly to try to judge a cause unheard. So state your position. We are ready to listen.

Microtoxus: I've always believed that a man of natural talents, especially if he has further profited by education, ought as far as possible to be useful to society. He ought to communicate to others what he has developed in his own life. Architas[25] is right, you know, when he tells us that we are born, not for our own sakes, but for our family, country, and friends, and that we are only in some small part our own. But a man who lives only for himself, who withdraws into solitude and occupies his mind with private affairs, neglects his duty. I might concede the privilege to persons defective in mind or body, and therefore unable to do their duty as regards society. But I think withdrawal is least permissible to a man whose limbs are unhurt and who possesses an aptitude for speech and for observation, especially a man whom long study of literature has made still more intelligent. Such a person would be useful to his fellow men in the city.

Nor can you reasonably be deterred by shame or modesty, Eleutherius, as if you were some outsider newly invited to take part in government. Long ago your ancestors were already contenders for the honors of the city. In time of grave danger they aided the state with large financial contributions, being second to no other family or to few. I find in the public records that when the office of prior was only eighteen years old in our city, one Senro Rinuccini was awarded this highest dignity. Do not imagine, for the records show clearly that it was not so, that men of humble station or condition or men without proven ability and character were elected to the highest office in the Republic in those days. Until 1347, as it happens, I find no others of the clan raised to this dignity; perhaps those who lived then overlooked them, or perhaps it was the paucity of men, always a problem in your family. In the year I mentioned, however, Eleutherius, an ancestor of yours named Francisco was made prior, and he held that office five times before 1368. Between the last and second to last time, he was also made a knight by Niccolò d'Este, then prince of Ferrara. He and Maffeo Pillio were sent to that prince as orators from the Republic, and he elevated them both to knightly rank. After these events, Francisco was created one of the Eight with undefined powers. It was a dangerous time for the Republic, for Bernabò, the tyrant of Milan, had occupied the fort of Miniato with connivance of a noble faction. The Eight appointed to direct that war by their full efforts and with the support and cooperation of the people of Miniato took it back from the tyrant. Thus it returned to Florentine jurisdiction and control. After that, however, your family, along with the nobles in general, was excluded from the government of Florence by a rabble of scoundrels who cruelly vexed all the good men except those who paid them off.[26] Not much later, nonetheless, Giovanni, his son, was made a knight by the people and became a prior as well. Your house did not again enjoy that dignity for sometime, until Francisco, son of Cino and nephew of your father, the knight Francisco, was elected to that office in the year 1437.

I remind you of these things, Eleutherius, which you know better than anyone, of course, only to make you see that, if you sleep or live in leisure and rest on your wealth, you disgrace your family. You accepted your dignity from your ancestors, I remind you, and it is up to you not so much to guard the ample fortune which they bequeathed to you as to carry on their official role and likewise gain public honors, which are just as desirable a heritage.

Eleutherius: You, Microtoxus, have certainly given us a lot of information about my ancestors and about our whole family. I am filled with admiration for your diligence. You have managed to put together facts I thought were known to few persons beside myself. For while these things are all true, still, being old truths, they have been generally forgotten. I know them partly because my father, Fillipo, told me, and partly from certain old documents. I carefully keep those documents, which I sorted out after much labor from numerous bundles of papers, for such things are often lost through the negligence of the very people they concern. This makes it easy for me to accept your rather freely spoken criticism. I shall answer your points one by one, as briefly as I can. I don't want to go into too much detailed exposition and bore you. When it comes to the actual reasons for my own decisions, however, I shall state my arguments at more length.

I won't deny, good friends, that I have spent my whole life in the study of books and have, as I believe, made the best of my education. For I did not limit myself, as many people do, to what is done by the faculties of grammar and rhetoric at universities; I did not devote all my time to the poets and orators and historians, though I read enough in them. But equipped with this kind of knowledge, I turned to philosophy, a study which merits the name of guide to life. I applied my mind and worked hard to get from my studies not just an ornamental polish or some honest intellectual pleasure but also guidance to right living.

There is much acute controversy among the best philosophers, as to the nature of the ultimate good. Plausible reasons are poured out on every side of the issue, but all do seem to agree on one point, that happiness, or synonymously, the highest good, is found in whatever makes men, as far as humanly possible, similar to God. According to all the best thinkers, moreover, whether our own theologians or pagan philosophers, in God there is no passion or motion. Whatever, therefore, makes the mind tranquil and free of passion, that, they admit must bestow happiness. If we agree with Aristotle's conviction that happiness lies, not in passivity but in action,[27] we shall conclude that tranquillity is the essential foundation and basis of happiness because it allows us to devote ourselves properly to either action or contemplation.

I do not think it foolish to point this out because I have so often seen people mistakenly suppose that anything productive of tranquillity itself is the dreamed-of goal, happiness. Thus there are people who say that

214

wealth or status or some combination of external advantages is happiness, thinking that one of these can guarantee peace and tranquillity. This, I think, is far from true. For desires and possessions, as is well known, plunge the soul into perpetual agitation and anxiety. The opinion of the Stoics may not be unfounded when they say that only virtue, a right spiritual disposition or condition, is happiness.[28] This is a hard doctrine, for the soul so disposed is, by habit or by the condition of virtue, emptied of all passion. What are generally esteemed excellent things such men have learned simply to scorn. They live as though they had no sensual capacities, or as though, having them, they had no use for them at all. That is what the Stoics ask. If anyone actually should reach this state of mind, I would consider him, not a man but a mortal god.

Aristotle, however, speaks more plausibly and more in line with every day experience.[29] He grants that men may have passions within moderation, with the proviso that their feelings must obey rather than oppose reason. Thus we may in moderation seek honors, wealth, and some pleasures. Since he considers happiness an active pursuit, however, he seems thus to allow us very little of it. For, weighed down by the body and its needs, we are obviously prevented from cultivating happiness and can give only snatches of time to contemplation. In this regard the Stoics' ideas seem better to fit the case, for they declare that happiness consists simply in the quality or condition of being virtuous. These problems really require more extensive treatment and subtler argumentation, however, so let's leave them to people who inquire into the fine points of this kind of discussion more for the sake of argument than with a view to application.

We'll let it suffice to draw the following conclusion from their arguments: Man's first concern is to seek inner peace and liberty and tranquillity, and furthermore, he may do so in either of two ways—avoiding anything he might desire to possess, or learning so to moderate his desires as to have them diverge only minimally from the dictates of virtue and right reason. Having thus gained the mastery of our passions, we may live happily and well. A moderate worldly fortune will easily suffice us. We differ widely, then, from the foolish opinion of the mass of men, who think that the highest good, the goal that all should seek, is great wealth or the vulgar fame awarded and sought by the general public. Happiness is truly what the Greeks called εὐθυμία, a word we might translate "spiritual well being," or simply tranquillity.[30]

How I have hoped to attain this condition myself you shall hear. But I don't want you to think that I am trying to give other people a set of rules by which to live. I am not telling you what others ought to do, but simply what I have done and for what reasons. That is what you asked me.

When I read in the best authors that to a wise man nothing is so important as his own moral guilt, I understand this to mean that one should bear with equanimity whatever happens to one through no fault of one's own. Fault or guilt is properly defined as of two kinds: faults of ignorance, that is, and faults of wickedness or vice. Since by our own efforts we are able to avoid both classes of guilt, I have always believed that we are also obligated to avoid them both. It seems to me Cicero expressed it well and truly: "I have always wished," he said, "first to deserve honors, second, to be thought to deserve them, and only third —what many people consider the first thing—actually to obtain them."[31] With this philosophy in mind, I have mainly tried not to be barbarous, stupid, and ignorant concerning the customary activities of men living the common and civic life. I have tried to make absolutely sure that no one could ever justly call me a thief, a robber, a liar, a scoundrel, a slanderer, or an unjust man. Secondly, I have tried to give some evidence of my character to my fellow citizens, most easily, I thought, by service in office. I took the trouble, therefore, to fill, first the highest office of prior, and, not much later, that of member of the Eight.

I don't know what others thought of me, but this is what happened: without my asking or even suspecting it, I was appointed along with some most distinguished citizens, to the post of prefect of grammar schools, and I was soon sent as an envoy on an important mission to the pope. There, if I had preferred private advantage, or rather foul disgrace, to the public interest, I might have had what people call a very successful career. But I would rather lose every possession I own than enrich a certain private person at the expense of the Republic. Through all vicissitudes, I have maintained this principle always: nothing could make me an abject careerist, a servile creature, a man with no dignity. I would not buy anything with deals and favors. I saw it all

done so often and so shamelessly that I was embarrassed for these ignorant souls who wanted to be preferred above others and therefore
acted so obsequiously towards their natural peers as to fill them with
vast and unjustified delusions of grandeur. Too late these people themselves saw the mistake they had made. Then it was useless, for the disease
was too advanced for cure.

This is why up to a certain point I did try to participate in government, though I considered it a wise precept that says "do not get involved in politics." Such, we know, was Plato's view, the Prince of
Philosophers, when, in his old age, he saw the Athenians apparently
gone mad.[32] The same can justifiably be said today of the Florentines,
whose prolonged and bitter servitude has made them lay aside a long
time ago all sense of honor, all moral sensibility, all manly vigor and
love of liberty. Instead scoundrels and criminals, men one wouldn't want
to call citizens, have reached such a pitch of audacity that they unhesitatingly overturn and betray and undermine everything for their own
purposes. With virulent hatred, moreover, do they persecute anyone
they think knows of their crimes but refuses to be a tool or accomplice.
The result is that good men who do obtain a position in the government
along with them live in great danger and acute anxiety. For to serve
their greed would be vile and criminal, but for one to resist the power
of a whole group is impossible. And the greatest horror of all is seeing
crimes committed in one's presence which one could not even hear described without distress.

Although I am far from that wisdom which reached its height in
Plato, still the little knowledge of literature that I have has freed me
from the disease of avarice and ambition and taught me that the happiness all men seek is not to be found by amassing wealth, nor by
gaining what the crowd thinks are honors, but by living in tranquillity
and freedom of spirit. I speak now of the sort of happiness to which
a person placed in civic life can aspire in this valley of tears. Not that
I have ever wanted to live passively in a state of idleness. An inactive and
slothful life weakens the nerves of body and brain. But I have aimed
for the middle way which would make me every day a better man. I
am always learning something and becoming potentially more useful,
should the state ever require my services. Since, as I remarked before, it
is less painful to hear than to see things you cannot approve of, I spend

much of my time alone, in converse with my own mind or with the books you have seen here, and I enjoy the liberty I wholly believe in. I have apportioned my time so that not a particle of it is wasted. I am always attending to my bodily health by taking exercise, or concerning myself with domestic matters, or cultivating my mind by reading and meditation. For nothing worth writing has come to my mind, seeing how much there is already in the way of all sorts of books, and how well they have been written in both ancient and modern times. If Nestor or Titonus were to return to life and devote all his years to reading, I think he would hardly find time for my contribution—if I wrote.

If something were occasionally to bring me friends like you, therefore, to visit me here, I would not exchange my life for the life of those the poets call blessed, who inhabit the Elysian fields. Whatever it may be, I think my life is more blessed than the life of a city person, burdened by constant anxiety, humiliated by being unable to move a finger of his own will. Good men and loyal friends, now you have heard my philosophy. Perhaps I went into more detail than you bargained for. Whatever others may say, these sentiments will remain mine if you approve them. I so much respect your judgment that, if you agree, I shall consider myself armed against all criticism. If something seems amiss to you, however, I shall not refuse to change the present direction of my life.

Alitheus: The model of your conduct already impressed me before, but now, after your discourse, I feel convinced that no other is so conducive to happiness. Although I do not at present live so very differently from you, I shall after this strive to go more often to the country and enjoy solitude.

Microtoxus: Right, Alitheus. For, the ideas of Eleutherius have changed my mind so that I can think of nothing truer. Yet really I still don't believe that a man should shrink from work and from feelings of indignation, and should live for himself only. You turn your back on others and abandon your country, which should be your dearest concern. Aside from what we owe to immortal God, we owe our best to our country.

Eleutherius: This new plea, Microtoxus, and your freer discourse earlier tend to the same end. So I shall reply to both at once. First, consider whether that accurate list of the highly honorable offices held by my ancestors is not really an incentive to choose as I have chosen rather than to take the path you urge upon me. Who could justly reproach me for having enough pride to refuse to become a suppliant, begging from those wicked usurpers for my rightful inheritance and that of other good citizens? I should not remain long without public honor if I could regain it by recourse to justice or to arms.

What you said about the duty of a citizen, Microtoxus, was well and truly said. I too have thought long and hard about this, and therefore did serve my country as long as I could. I chose to act so as to be of some use to the state, and to show myself ready and willing to obey its orders with alacrity. Not my country but the criminals whose force took over all her laws and authority ignored my willingness to render good service. They sensed, of course, that I was repelled by their ways, or rather by their vices. Since that was so, why waste my time and effort? To coerce them by force was impossible, but to gain their approval by conforming to their way of life and to their crookedness would have been beneath me, I know, and totally dishonest. Should I have pleaded with them and flattered them to get what they owed me by law? And should I thus have humbled myself before men who had perverted all law and every sacred thing, who, to the great sorrow and indignation of good citizens, had usurped all authority and honor in the Republic? It is true, as once was said, good deeds done in a wrong context should be accounted villainy.[33] Likewise, in my view, honors won by foul means are blots on honor and degrading.

I did not believe that, as long as my own conduct had not disqualified me by immorality or weakness or lack of judgment from even the highest offices, I ought to seek office in a manner unworthy of my ancestors. I have met the standards of the best citizens of our time and the most eminent. They have judged me worthy of the highest honor of standard bearer, a grade no one of our family attained before. This makes me feel that my ancestors and even I have won sufficient honor. Of the three levels of honor mentioned by Cicero, I have at least attained two. And if I am excluded from the third, it is not my own fault, but on account of the unjust hatred and envy of malevolent men.

What excuse can they give for excluding me from the government? I carried out my mission, though in vain. They cannot say there was some flaw in my conduct, some contravention of orders, something done that was not in accordance with their orders. I had been given, by order of the people, full power to make binding agreements. I never used that power, however, unless specifically directed to do so by the highest magistrate. I can prove all this easily from public documents. I knew very well the duty of a good envoy and a loyal citizen. That man, elevated by Fortune's bold hand and by the imprudence of the foolish citizens, complained that I wrote publicly to the magistrate on great affairs of state, rather than privately to him. This does not bother me one bit. I shall always remember and declare that I was sent forth, not by one private individual, but by the whole people, by the highest public office, by the Republic itself. What right did he have to complain when, for friendship's sake, I even gave him a private report on the main points at the same time I handed in my official one? But with his usual arrogance he scorned this report, and left me without even the honor of a written acknowledgment. I would be dishonest not to admit that these things were somewhat upsetting.

When the pope in the council of cardinals, therefore, formally pronounced sentence against our Republic, I made a private report to him as well as a public one to the highest magistrate. Then he wrote and censured me for having spoken as I had in a public document. It is true that, both before and after my return, I did not hide my indignation. When the pope had left Rome on account of the plague and was traveling around, to the great discomfort and danger of his court, since he was no longer deliberating on matters that concerned us, I asked permission to return home. First I asked the magistrate and then him privately, but he kept denying my request. Shortly after, when without his knowledge I got permission from the Eight, he used the excuse that I came from plague-ridden parts to make the same Eight bar me from the city. I omit many details, I don't want to seem overconcerned with trivia.

The fact is I would have taken these blows calmly and not let them disturb my mind, had not far greater crimes and more serious evils inflicted by him on the Republic aroused my deep disgust. He accepted tyranny as a legacy from his grandfather, but exercised it much more severely than his grandfather did. He was more insolent than his father.

220

He did not get reasonable advice from the citizens, nor did he listen to his own reason. He did everything according to the impulses of his willful spirit, and he dragged down the poor country. Spoiled in part of her wealth and altogether of her dignity, she has become the mockery of all Italy for enduring such a destructive and cruel tyranny.

Even certain princes, remembering our former dignity and glory, have come to pity our distress. It has reached the point where they use their resources to war on Florence only partly to avenge their own injuries at his hands, but partly to restore to the Florentine people their former liberty. This Florentine Phalaris has now gone so far in insolence that he considers himself greater than the greatest princes of Italy. When he receives favors from them in his need, he esteems those something owed to him by right.

This gives you some idea of his cruel oppression of the citizens, his fantastic audacity and incredible arrogance. He taxed them enough in recent years, while there was peace from external enemies, to vex and wound them. Now he has involved them in a war that is grave indeed, dangerous and pernicious. This war—as not only rumor but public letters sent by the pope and king to all peoples make clear—was undertaken not against the Florentines but against Lorenzo de' Medici, the tyrant of Florence, for the liberty of the people. This man, whose insolence, temerity, and ingratitude had wounded the most powerful princes of Italy, implicated the state in a grave and calamitous war, conducted by them, as they declare, not against the Florentine people but for their liberation from Lorenzo's fierce tyranny. It is a shame and a misery, altogether, to see the many fields laid waste, the villages and farms devastated, the many men taken prisoner, the many victims reduced to indigence and beggary. One might well sing to us the song of Hesiod:[34]

πολλάχι δε συμπασα πὸλισ κακου ἀνδροσ ἀπήυρα.

Often the whole city suffers through one bad man.

If I am unwilling to adore, to flatter and to bow before this man, can you blame me?

These, good friends, are my answers to the arguments of Microtoxus.

221

I don't scorn the honors won by my ancestors nor do I lack the desire to follow in some modest way along the same path, if I may do so in liberty. I do not shirk labor and trouble. I would take on work, and danger too, for my country. But the truth is that I cannot peacefully tolerate our ungrateful citizenry and the usurpers of our liberty. I live, therefore, as you see, content with this little house and farm. I am free from all anxiety. I don't inquire what goes on in the city, and I lead a quiet and free life. There's never a day when I fail to read or write, and, except when it rains, I always take some exercise outdoors. If only I could have your company here, therefore, I should consider myself in paradise.

Alitheus: I think you have done very well, Eleutherius, and I myself, persuaded by your thoughts, shall try to see you and talk with you often.

Microtoxus: On such journeys, I promise to be your constant companion. But since we have talked enough now, let us dedicate the rest of the day to our health. Walking and talking, let us get ourselves a good appetite for dinner.

NOTES

1. Translated from Francesco Adorno's edition in *Atti Colombaria*, vol. 22 (N. F. 8; 1957), 265–303, previously published by him in E. Grassi, *Colleción Tradición y Tarea*, (losada), Santiago, Chile, 1952. Footnotes to classical sources are with one small exception his.

2. Giovanni and Geronimo Andrea seems to refer to two members of the Olgiati family who, in 1476, took part for idealistic reasons in the assassination of Galeazzo Maria Sforza, Duke of Milan. Cf. Jacob Burckhardt, *Civilization of the Renaissance in Italy*, New York, 1950, 37–38.

3. F. Adorno thinks this is a reference to Donato Acciaiuoli's still extant Commentary on the lectures of Argyropoulos. It is even possible that Alitheus may be Rinuccini's fictional name for Donato, and not just for one of his friends.

4. Cicero *Paradoxa* V, I, 34.

5. Cicero *Paradoxa* V.

6. Cicero *Tusc. Queast.* IV, 17–19.

7. Cicero *De finibus* V, 8, 23; V, 29, 87.

8. Aristotle *Ethica Nic.* I, 1097b–1098a.

9. Cicero Paradoxa V, I, 34.

10. Aristotle *Politica* III, 1281b, cf. 1279a.

11. Battle of Benevento in February 1266 ended the Hohenstauffen line in Italy.

12. Florence lay under the interdict from September 1273 till January 1276.

13. Henry VII in September 1312.

14. Uguccione Fagiolano was a Ghibelline leader who became tyrant of Pisa after Henry VII's departure. He defeated Florence at Montecatini in August 1315; he was overthrown by Castruccio in the spring of 1316. Florence warred against Castruccio from 1320 till his death in 1329. Florence took Pisa and could not be dislodged by the Emperor Louis of Bavaria in 1329.

15. Guido Tarlato, appointed Bishop of Arezzo in 1313, led that city in collaboration with his brother, Piero. Arezzo expanded its territory by conquest and Florence responded by conquering Arezzo and its domains in 1336.

16. Cf. note 14.

17. Pisa, rather than Florence, finally took Lucca from Mastino in July 1342.

18. In 1351 Florence repelled the invasion of her territory by Milan, ruled at that time by Archbishop Giovanni Visconti.

19. In the War of the Eight Saints, fought in 1375–78 against Gregory XI, the Florentines sent representatives to papal towns and urged revolt. They carried a banner inscribed with the word, *Libertas*.

20. The wars with Ladislas went on from 1408 till his death in 1414. The purchase of Cortona, according to Schevill, occurred in January 1411, when Florence "abandoned its allies and was rewarded for its treachery by the cession of the town of Cortona." Ferdinand Schevill, *History of Florence*, New York, 1961, 349.

21. 1422–28; 1440.

22. Alfonso's invasion of Tuscany in 1447 provoked a joint Florentine and papal policy of equilibrium in Italy and thus led to the Peace of Lodi of 1454. Peter Partner, "Florence and the Papacy," in Nicolai Rubinstein, *Florentine Studies*, London, 1968, 401.

23. This dates the present dialogue to the period from the summer of 1478 to the end of 1479. It seems unlikely that Rinuccini was writing after Lorenzo had set out for Naples in December 1479, a spectacular mission which did bring peace by February 1480.

24. Rinuccini's attitude to Florentine diplomacy based on calling in foreigners to the peninsula is most unapologetic, compared to the Florentine ambassadors' speech in Bruni's *History*, Book XII. Cf. Schevill (391): "the descent of the French was for many decades suspended like a portent over the peninsula, filling all its states, large and small alike, with alarm, but at the same time exercising a curious, hypnotic fascination." In 1495 Savonarola would convince the Florentines that Charles VIII of France was both a scourge of God falling upon them, and, after negotiations, an ally who would eventually help them regain control of Pisa.

25. Plato *Ep.* IX 358a; Cicero *De Officiis* I, 7, 22.

26. Reference to the Ciompi revolt of 1378 which greatly democratized the government till the counterrevolution of 1382.

27. Aristotle *Ethica Nic.* I, 1098b–1099a.

28. Cicero *De finibus* V, 79; cf. *Acad. Post.* I, 38.

29. Cicero *Oratio pro Murena*, 63.

30. Cicero *De finibus* V, 8, 23; V, 29, 87.

31. Cicero *Pro Cneo Placio oratio* XX, 50.

32. Plato *Ep.* V, 322ab; cf. *Ep.* VII, 325–6, 331d; *Resp.* VI, 496 c–e. Also *Apology* 31d, 32a.

33. Ennius *Scenica* fragm. 409 (Vhalen); Cicero *De Officiis* II, 18, 62.

34. Hesiod *Op.* 238. Quoted in Liddell and Scott as ξύμπασα πόλις κακου ανδρὸς απηυρα.

Girolamo Savonarola

Girolamo Savonarola 1452–1498

So far in this anthology, we have gathered writings on liberty or related topics by authors of a single continuous line: Florentine humanists. They mostly studied and practiced the arts of government. Only Poliziano neither studied law nor practiced administration, and he did live in the Palazzo Medici. They all cultivated the knowledge of classical texts and languages by a process of reading, translation, direct commentary, and more independent writing. If they did not constantly live in Florence, they considered it their home. They talked together, read each other's work, and passed on the torch of their aspirations—literary and political—through the fifteenth century. Among them, even adversaries such as Alamanno Rinuccini and Lorenzo de' Medici were closely acquainted and worked together. One way or another, gladly or reluctantly, they belonged to the ruling Medici circles within the Florentine mercantile aristocracy.

Girolamo Savonarola is somewhat different. He came to questions of government from immersion in biblical studies and theology. A Ferrarese Dominican preacher, he first visited Florence in 1482, when he was thirty. He came again, at Lorenzo's request, in 1489, to fill the office of abbott in St. Mark's monastery. While he certainly entered into cordial relations with the Florentine establishment—both political and cultural—he did so as an indignantly critical outsider. Eventually, aided by the invasion of Charles VIII with a French army and by the anti-Medici conspiracy of some Florentine patricians, Savonarola fomented and helped to guide a revolution. After this revolution the aristocracy was obliged to accept participation in

226

government by numerous independent members of the middle class, and new men rather than the men of the Medici faction stood out as leaders.[1] Savonarola actively favored this change. He differs from our other authors, then, in many ways—he was a churchman with a religious vocation, he came to Florence as a critical outsider, and he was, despite attachments to established power, a revolutionary. It only dramatizes the difference to add that he considered himself a prophet in the line of Amos and Jeremiah, that he became the object of a lasting religious cult, and that there are still authors who wish to see him promoted from the ranks of the officially "blessed" to the position of a canonized saint.

In contrast to the "divine" style of Bruni and "divine" magnificence of Lorenzo, the "divine" powers of Savonarola expressed themselves in self-mortification, prayer, visions of moral reform, and preaching. His hopes for a total *renovatio* in Florence are not wholly different from those cherished by the humanists, but they date from the change of government in 1494 and they involve leadership by means of popular sermons, asceticism spreading in the community, persecution of those who indulged in "vanities" and sexual "immorality," and a general pervasive spirit of communal sacrifice which was to unite the city. The Florentines as a political people, as architects and artists, and as investors, had long been distinguished both by their pride in the church and by their indignant anticlericalism. In Savonarola, who described them as an especially religious people, they found for a time religious inspiration and the hope of church reform from within.

During five years of preaching and teaching before the upheaval of 1494 Savonarola personally influenced the religious life of many of the most eminent humanists, artists, and merchants of the city, as well as of lesser folk. After 1494, through sermons and personal interviews, he influenced the leaders of the new Florence as they reshaped her constitution and made laws. These were years of trouble in foreign relations and in economic life. In 1497 Savonarola's quarrel with the Borgia pope, Alexander VI, threatened to bankrupt Florentine merchants through various possible papal measures against them. Meanwhile a growing part of the population was tired of his demands for austerity and moral strictness. Savonarola's reputation for sanctity had long aroused hatred from rival preachers who were now gaining a greater following. A spectacular ordeal by fire was planned to decide between the authority of Savonarola and that of some Franciscan opponents; but the ordeal, because of prudent delays and a drenching rain, failed to take place. The next day a mob killed Savonarola's chief secular ally, Francesco Valori, and besieged the priest in San Marco. He was taken to prison and tortured to obtain evidence that he had conspired illegally to tamper with the government and that he had falsely claimed to speak by divine inspiration. The Signoria of the moment willingly took up the role of executioner for the papacy and hanged for heresy the man who had been the most respected friend of the Signoria for three and a half years.

Passionately religious, proud of his own mission, highly intelligent in his assessment of Florentine political needs, Savonarola was a great popular leader during his few years of power. The *Trattato* was written during the last months of that period, while Savonarola was obeying the papal command to give no more sermons. Here his mature political ideas found the driest and most compact form of expression he could muster, lacking the allegorical dreams and visions and the topical allusions of his words from the pulpit. Only in the second book of the *Trattato*, where he expounds on tyranny in ways that clearly refer to his former masters, the Medici, does he rise to a crescendo of personal emotion. Even there he links what he is saying to a coherent total theory.

The theory is designed, of course, to justify practice—to argue for the current revolution in Florence. Nor is it free from contradictions. The groundwork, as spelled out particularly in the first book, derives via St. Thomas and his continuator, Tolomeo of Lucca, from Aristotle: it classifies the forms of government, considers monarchy the best, yet insists that theory must be balanced by empirical considerations and that for some peoples, such as the Florentine, the republican form is the only good one. In the remaining books of the *Trattato*, Savonarola's discussion of the dangers to be avoided and the goals to be pursued becomes more and more clearly apocalyptic. Bad government is totally evil and leads to doom and damnation; good government involves angelic inspiration and leads to a heavenly city with the probability of a worldwide empire guided by Christ. Yet in his concept of what can be done in Florence and how it can be done, the author attends closely to Florentine history and institutions. Building on the traditions of Florentine civic humanism, especially the ideas of Bruni, Savonarola takes the existence of factions as the worst ill of Florentine politics and puts great emphasis on the ideal of liberty.

Savonarola, as Weinstein has put it, "came to regard the practise and enjoyment of liberty as an indispensable component of the common good."[2] For him as for the humanists, moreover, "liberty was freedom from arbitrary rule protected by a broad, but not an equal, degree of participation in the electoral and legislative processes. . . . The main source of his idea of republican liberty, and he himself insisted on it, was Florentine tradition."[3]

It is a somewhat strange mix, this combination of abstract political thinking by which the world is to be judged and sifted, apocalyptic vision by which men are to be urged to immediate and extreme action, and Florentine republicanism, a source of specific institutional reforms. Savonarola had come as a prophet and stayed as a political conscience. The change in his thinking, which culminates in the *Trattato*, is summed up by Weinstein: "starting from a position of radical dualism, in which the world had to be destroyed in order to bring about the victory of the spirit, he had come to believe that the agencies of religion and the Florentine state could unite to achieve the victory of the spirit in this life. This in itself was a major departure from his earlier views, but there was a still further step—the identification of that spiritual victory with the apotheosis of Florence, and such an identification he spelled out in [book three of] the *Trattato*."[4]

Weinstein faults the circular reasoning that would base political reform on a spiritual renewal, yet promises that the reform itself will bring about the required spirit. Weinstein is also critical because he finds that, "Nowhere in his sermons or in his writings does [Savonarola] concern himself with the details of the new order (an omission, it may be observed, which is characteristic of millenarians of all times.)" Both these criticisms, it occurs to me, are characteristic of the conservatives of all times. One cannot complain, after all, I think, that Savonarola did not *try* to propose a specific program and to link it with his general ideas. He did so in practical politics and in the *Trattato*. No doubt, and unfortunately, there is a gap between the program and the intended heavenly city.

How great, however, is that gap? The Florentine Republic redesigned under Savonarola's influence still included violent mobs as well as immoral politics, and these two forces destroyed Savonarola himself. Yet as a system and a way of life it came close to fostering civic liberty as well as religious seriousness, and the Republic did not fail, before and after Savonarola's death, to show great powers of cohesion and creativity. It resisted the return of the Medici until 1512 and resisted again, most furiously, in its short period of renewal, 1527–30. What felled it, after all, was the superior force of the feudal yet centrally organized nations of Spain and France as well as the manipulations of the papacy. In response to these pressures came the great search for heroes and the extraordinary last efforts at diplomatic autonomy (no totally binding alliances) and military fortifications of every kind. Savonarola, it is true, was forgotten as the Republic struggled on. Machiavelli looked back at him with scorn as an "unarmed prophet," and despised his leadership as he did clerical leadership in general. Yet when we look back from the perspective of later centuries, including the Reformation and later

229

revolutions, we cannot despise the formula that combines an ideal of partic-
ipatory self-government with an atmosphere of enthusiastic religious repression.

NOTES

1. The degree of democracy in Savonarolan Florence and the politics behind
it are discussed by Nicolai Rubinstein, "Politics and Constitution in Florence at the
end of the Fifteenth Century," *Italian Renaissance Studies*, ed. E. F. Jacob, London,
1960, 148–83. Cf. Donald Weinstein, *Savonarola and Florence*, Princeton, 1970,
247–88.

2. Weinstein, 305.

3. Weinstein, 307.

4. Weinstein, 311.

TREATISE

ON THE

Constitution and Government

OF THE

City of Florence

BY GIROLAMO SAVONAROLA

FIRST TREATISE

Chapter I

Government is necessary in human affairs; on good and bad government.

The all-powerful God who rules the whole universe infuses into his creatures the excellence of his rule. He does so in two ways. Creatures lacking intellect and free will, he permeates with certain strengths and virtues so that they will naturally incline to take the right means toward the proper ends, making no mistakes unless, as rarely happens, something blocks their path. These creatures, therefore, do not govern themselves but are governed by God and by the nature he has given them, so that they achieve their proper purposes. Creatures endowed with intellect, however, such as man, are governed by him in a way that also requires their governing themselves; for he gives them intellect by which they can judge what is useful to them and what is not useful, and free will freely to choose what they like. But the light of intellect is weak, especially in childhood, and therefore a man cannot rule himself perfectly without the help of others. The individual person is by no means self-sufficient and cannot provide for his own physical and spiritual needs. Nature, we see, provides food, clothing, and weapons for all animals, and when they are ill they instinctively find their own medicines. None of this is provided for man; but God, who governs all things, has given him reason and the use of his hands to let him provide for himself. Because of his bodily weakness, moreover, man needs almost infinitely many things for his nourishment, preservation, and growth, and many arts in order to provide these things. Thus it was made necessary for men to live together and to help each other, some practicing one skill and some another, so as to form a body perfectly equipped with arts and sciences.

It is well said, therefore, that the solitary man is either God or a wild beast: for he is either so perfect a man that he is like a God on earth, having like God no need of anything or of anyone's help—such were St. John the Baptist, and St. Paul the first hermit, and many others —or he is like a beast, totally deprived of reason and hence without concern for clothing, shelter, cooked and prepared food, and the conversation of his fellow men, following only animal instinct. Since very few people are so perfect or so bestial, the rest are obliged to live with others, in cities, in castles, in country homes, or elsewhere.

Since the generation of men is very inclined to do evil, especially when there is no law or fear, they have had to find laws to restrain the aggressiveness of bad men, so that those who want to live well may safely do so. No animal, indeed, is more dangerous than man without law. The gluttonous man eats more avidly and insatiably than any other animal, not satisfied with the foods and kinds of cooking he knows, seeking, not the satisfaction of nature, but the gratification of unbridled appetite. Similarly in sexual matters, he does not obey seasons and nature's commands, but does things it is abominable to think of, let alone to hear about, and which no animal even thinks of. He also outdoes beasts in cruelty, for they do not make cruel war on each other, especially not on those of their own species, while man even invents new instruments for hurting others and new devices of torture and death. Aside from all these things, men have within them pride, ambition, and envy, and from these spring quarrels and intolerable wars. And yet, because men have to live together and want to live in peace, they have had to find laws by which the bad will be punished and the good rewarded.

But because only a superior authority can be a source of laws and because people can only be made to observe the laws by someone who has power over others, it was necessary to constitute some in authority, to care for the common good and to exercise power over others. For while every individual person pursues his own good, if none were there to care for the common good, society would be destroyed and the whole world would fall into confusion. Some men gathered together, therefore, to choose one individual to take care of the common good and to rule all others. This kind of government was called kingship and the one who ruled was called king. Certain other people, whether because they could not agree on one ruler or because it seemed better thus, set up a group of the chief persons and best and wisest in the community, to have them govern and hold public office in rotation; this was called aristocracy. Still others wanted the power of government to stay in the hands of all the people, who would distribute and rotate offices as they thought best. This form of government was called civil government, because it belongs to all the citizens.

The government of the community was created, then, to take care of the common good and to let people live together in peace, so that they might devote themselves to what is good and more easily pursue eternal happiness. A government is good, therefore, which uses all its strength to maintain and increase the common good, and to induce the people to be virtuous and live righteously, with special concern for religion. And a government is bad if it neglects the common good and cares for the private good of its members, careless of the character of the people and the way they live, except where this impinges on the particular needs of the rulers. Such government is called tyranny. We have made clear, then, the need for government among men, and what kind of government, generally, is good and what kind is bad.

Chapter II

Although the government of one good man is best
by nature, it is not good for every community.

While that government is good which concerns itself with the common good, spiritual as well as physical, it may be administered by one or by the principal citizens or by all the people, and we must realize that, in principle, the civil form of government is good, aristocracy is better, and kingship is best. Given that the aim of government is the union and peace of the people, this union and this peace are much more readily attained and preserved under the rule of one than under more than one, and under the rule of a few rather than a crowd. For when all the men in a community must respect and obey one man alone, they do not form factions, but are all bound together in love and fear of that one. When there are more than one, however, some people respect one and some another; some like one, and others another, and the people are not so well united as when one alone rules. They are less sure to remain united the more people govern them. Unified power, moreover, is more effective than dispersed power, as fire is hotter when all the fuel is burning in one place than when it is scattered and burns here and there.

It is clear then that the power of government will be able to act in a more unified way if it is concentrated in one man than if it is given to more than one; it follows that the rule of one, when he is a good ruler, is by nature better and more efficacious than any other. What is more, the rule of the whole world and of nature is the best government, and as art follows nature, the more a human government resembles that of the world and of nature, the more perfect it is. Obviously since the whole world is governed by one ruler, and since all natural beings that manifest some kind of government are also governed by one (for example, bees are governed by a king, and the various spiritual faculties by reason, and the limbs of the body by the heart, and so on), it follows that human government by one ruler is by nature the best. Hence our Savior, who wanted to give the church the best kind of government, made Peter head of the faithful, and he established in every diocese, as in every parish and monastery, the rule of one, placing all the lesser rulers under a single ruler's authority, that of his vicar.

Speaking absolutely, therefore, the government of one when the ruler is good is preferable to all other forms of good government. Every community should, if possible, be so governed, that is, that the whole people will peacefully make one man prince, who is good and just and wise, and whom everyone will have to obey. But we must note that this form of government is not good and not possible and ought not to be attempted in every community, because it often happens that the one who rules absolutely is not good, but rather, in a certain place or with a certain specific ruler, bad. The case is parallel with that of spiritual life, which is lived in the religious state, and this in principle is the best state, yet it is not a state to be imposed on all Christians, nor should that be attempted, nor would it be good, for many could not bear it and would make schisms in the church. As our Savior says in the Gospel: "One must not patch old cloth with new, for the old will tear and become more torn than before, and one should not put new wine in old wineskins, or the old will burst and the wine be lost." Sometimes we see a food which is good in itself and even the best of foods, harmful as poison to a particular person; and a climate which is considered perfect may be harmful to certain constitutions. The government of one likewise is best in principle but to certain peoples, who are inclined to quarrel, it will do harm and be the worst sort of government. Among them the prince will suffer opposition and even assassination, which will lead to infinite evils, for his death will be followed by the division of the people into factions, and then by civil war with a variety of chiefs, and if one of them does win, he will become a tyrant, so that finally, as we shall show, the common good of the city will be wholly ruined. If a prince wishes to attain security and stability while ruling such a people, he will necessarily have to become a tyrant, he will have to exile the powerful, to expropriate the rich, and to irritate the people with heavy-handed oppression; otherwise he will never be safe.

Certain peoples, then, who by nature are such that they cannot tolerate the rule of one unless it is accompanied by great and unbearable oppression are like certain men, who are really used to living in the open and who, if they decide to live in good, well-heated rooms and wear good clothes and eat delicate food will soon grow ill and die. Wise men, therefore, if they must institute a government, will think first about the nature of the people concerned, whether their temperament and habits are going to let them accept the rule of one. If so, that is the government to be established. But if not, wise law-givers will try to give them aristocracy. And if that too will not be tolerated, they will institute the civil form of government with such laws as suit that people's character. Now let us see which of these three good forms of government suits the Florentine people.

235

Chapter III
Civil government is best for the city of Florence.

There can be no doubt (if anyone gives serious consideration to what we have said) that if the Florentine people would tolerate the rule of one, it should receive a prince, not a tyrant, who will be prudent, just, and good. But if we examine the opinions and ideas of the learned, we shall quickly see that, considering the character of this people, such a form of government does not suit them. For it is said that this form of government suits a people who are servile by nature, a people lacking either in vitality or in intelligence, whichever it may be. Those who have plenty of vitality and are physically strong and daring in war, nonetheless, if they lack intelligence, are easily subjugated by a prince. It is easy to trap them through the weakness of their minds, and they will follow their prince as the bees follow their king, and as we see the people of Aquileia do. Those that have brains but lack vitality, being cowardly, easily accept a single prince and live quietly under him, as do the oriental peoples. When a people lacks both, of course, the rule of one is doubly easy. But a bold people who abound in intelligence and in vitality cannot easily be ruled by one man unless he is a tyrant, for they are always plotting against their prince, using their cunning, and since they are daring too, they readily put their plots into execution. Italy, we know from past and present experience, has never kept long under the rule of a single prince. Indeed we see this little province divided into as many principalities as there are cities, and those cities are almost never at peace.

The Florentine people, however, is the most intelligent of all the peoples of Italy and the most farsighted in its undertakings. It has, as its history has shown again and again, a vigorous and audacious spirit. For, though this people is devoted to commerce and appears a quiet people, nonetheless, when it enters into civil or external war, it is very terrible and full of spirit. This the chronicles show when they relate its wars against various great princes and tyrants, where Florence has absolutely refused to yield and finally, in self-defense, has carried away the victory. This people's character, then, will never tolerate the rule of a prince, even though he be good and perfect, for the bad citizens always outnumber the good, and here, through their cunning and courage, they

236

would either overthrow or kill him (since they are most inclined to ambition). Alternatively, the prince would have to become a tyrant. If we consider the matter further we shall conclude that this people not only finds the rule of one uncongenial, but it also could not accept aristocracy. Habit, indeed, is second nature, and as the rock's nature is to fall and it cannot alter this and cannot be raised except by force, so habit too becomes nature, and it is very difficult if not impossible to change men, especially whole peoples, even if their habits are bad, for their habits spring out of their character.

Now the Florentine people, having established a civil form of government long ago, has made such a habit of this form that, besides suiting the nature and requirements of the people better than any other, it has become habitual and fixed in their minds. It would be difficult, if not impossible to separate them from this form of government. And, indeed, while they may have been governed by tyrants for many years, nonetheless, the citizens who usurped the principate in this period did not tyrannize in such a way as freely to deny the sovereignty of the whole. With great cunning they governed this people without attacking their temperament and their habits. They left the form of government as it was and all the usual offices, but saw to it that only their friends held those offices. The form of civil government has long been unchanged, therefore, and the people finds it so natural that to try to change it and give Florence another form of government would be no less than to run against their nature and against their ancient habit. This would generate such unrest and anger in this community that it would soon risk losing all its liberty. History shows this clearly, and experience is the teacher of all arts. Every time Florence has been governed by a small group of leading citizens, there have been great divisions among the people and no peace until one party or the other was thrown out, and some one citizen became a tyrant. This citizen, then, usurped the liberty and common good of the people, and their hearts remained discontent and restless. If Florence was divided and discordant in the past, through the ambition and rivalries of the leading citizens, moreover, it is still more so at present. Were it not for the grace and mercy of God, there would recently have been much bloodshed, the destruction of many houses, and fights and civil wars within as well as outside the walls, for the citizens who were exiled at various times by those who governed from '34 on have returned, and they had mostly nurtured various hatreds in themselves during this period because of the harm done to their houses and families. What happened with the arrival of the king of France, as anyone who was here and capable of judgment knows, should have been the death blow for Florence; but the council and the civil government then founded in Florence were not created by men but by God, and helped by the prayers of good men and women within the city, this government became an instrument of divine virtue, and it preserved the city's liberty. No one not wholly deprived of his natural judgment by his sins could consider the dangers that have threatened the city for the last three years and deny that it has been governed and preserved by God.

We conclude, therefore, that in the city of Florence the civil form of government is best, although in itself this is not the best form, and we assert this both because divine authority created its present civil government, and because of the reasons given above. The rule of one, though in itself best, is not good, let alone best, for the Florentine people, any more than the state of perfection through life in holy orders, though best in itself, is best or even good for many of the Christian faithful, while some other state of life which is not in itself best is best for them. We have made our first point clear then; that is, we have shown what is the best form of government for the city of Florence. It is time now to make the second point, and to show what is the worst kind of government for the city.

SECOND TREATISE

Chapter I

The rule of one, when he is a bad ruler, is the worst form of government, especially if the ruler rose to become a tyrant from the status of a mere citizen.

The rule of one, if he is a good ruler, is the best of all forms of government and the most stable. It is less likely to turn into a tyranny than the government of more than one for the more people are in power, the more easily divisions appear among them and generate wider divisions among the people. Nonetheless, as this form is perfect and stable when it is good, so when it is unjust and bad, it is by nature the worst of all the bad forms of government. First, because evil being the opposite of good, and the worst the opposite of the best, so the government of one, being best when good, logically must be worst when bad.

Secondly, as we have said, united power is more effective than power dispersed; so when a tyrant reigns, the power of an evil government is concentrated in a single person, and as there are always more bad men than good and everyone likes those who are similar to him, all the bad people will try to follow this ruler. Those who seek rewards and honors will follow him with special zeal, and many more will follow from fear, and those who are not altogether depraved but simply love earthly things will come along either from fear or from love of what they desire; those who are good but not altogether perfect, moreover, will follow from fear and lack of courage to resist while few are perfect, or rather perhaps none are. So all the power of government will be concentrated in one man. This one man, however, being a bad and unjust person, will carry every evil enterprise to perfection and easily pervert every good thing. When a government consists of several bad men, one will get in the other's way, and they will not be able to do as much harm as they would like, nor as much as a single tyrant can do.

Thirdly, a government is worse, the more it leaves aside the common good. The common good, indeed, is the purpose of good government, and the closer it approaches that purpose, the better it is, while the more it departs from that, the worse it is, for everything gains its perfection by approaching its end, and by separating from that end, becomes imperfect. But it is clear that bad government by many departs from the common good less than does bad government by one, for if those who rule usurp the common good and divide it among themselves, divide, that is, the city's opportunities and honors, nonetheless being given to more than one, the common good remains to some extent common. But when all the common good is channeled to serve only one man, it does not remain common at all, but is altogether private. The bad government of one, therefore, is of all governments the worst. It departs most from the common good and is most destructive of the common good.

Fourthly, duration contributes to these arguments. The government of one is by nature more stable than that of several men and cannot, though it is bad, be as easily hindered and stopped as that of many, for all the members take their orders from the head and they have much difficulty in rising against it. Under a tyrant it is very hard to find a leader who will rise against him, for he is ever on the watch to destroy such men, and he prevents his subjects from gathering and generally is vigilant to stop all opposition. When a group of people constitute a bad government, they are easier to overthrow, for it is easier to gather good men around the one in the group who does well. And it is easy to sow dissent among the bad, to prevent their unifying, because each of them is only seeking his own private good, which makes it natural for them to quarrel. The bad government of one, in this respect too, is the worst of all; it is a hard thing to oppose and end it.

But although by nature the bad government of one is the worst, yet sometimes the worst miseries attend the bad government of a group, especially towards the end of it; for when such a government is bad, it quickly divides into factions, the common good and the public peace are torn apart and finally, if no remedy is found, one faction will have to win and to oust the other. From this event innumerable evils, temporal and bodily and spiritual, will follow. The worst and most important result will be that the government of a group will become the rule of one. From having been a mere citizen, the one who has most popular favor will rise to become a tyrant. And the rule of one who is bad is the worst of all governments (as we have said) but there is still a big difference between the government of one natural and true lord who has become a tyrant and the government of a mere citizen who has become a tyrant. The latter will do more harm than the former, for if he wants to reign he must destroy by death or exile or other means not only those citizens who actively oppose him but all who are his equals in nobility, wealth, or fame. He must get rid of all those who could possibly harm him, and this means vast suffering. The natural lord does not have to do this, because there is no one who is equal to him and the citizens, accustomed to being his subjects, are not likely to be conspiring for his overthrow. He does not live in the state of universal suspicion that characterizes the tyrant who started as mere citizen.

Peoples who have aristocratic governments will discover that, through the quarrels men readily start and through the ubiquity of bad men and gossips and slanderers, division may easily come and precipitate them into tyranny. Such peoples, therefore, ought to take precautions and to make most vigorous and severe laws to prevent any individual from trying to make himself a tyrant. They should punish him with the extreme penalty, not only if he has spoken of doing it, but especially if he has been trying to do it. While they should show mercy to any other criminal, moreover, in this one case they should show no mercy, except that the soul of the criminal should always receive assistance. They should never diminish the penalty but rather increase it as an example to all, so that every person may learn, not only never to attempt it, but not even to think of it. Anyone who is merciful in this situation or negligent in punishing such a case sins gravely before God, for he fosters the tyrant's beginning, and from his rule come the innumerable evils we shall talk about later. When bad men see that the punishments are light they become bold, and little by little they move towards tyranny, as a drop of water little by little hollows the stone. He who has failed to punish this crime seriously is responsible for all the evils that follow through the tyranny of such citizens. A people that has civil government should be more willing to tolerate any other evil and inconvenience arising out of civil government with its imperfections than to let a tyrant arise. And to help everyone understand the evil that comes from tyranny, although we have preached of it at other times, still we will speak of it in the next chapter, to make the dangers better known. We will touch at least on the major points, but if we wanted to tell all the ommissions and abuses and grave crimes and evils that follow from tyranny, it would be impossible, for these are infinite.

Chapter II
The wickedness of tyrants and the evils of tyranny.

Tyrant is the name given to one of evil life, the worst kind of man in the world, who wishes to rule all others by force, especially if that man was once a mere citizen. First, it must be said that he is proud, since he desires a position above his equals, and even above those better than himself, whom he should more justly have to obey. He is envious, likewise, and suffers whenever other men gain any glory, especially when citizens of his own city achieve high renown. He cannot bear to hear others praised, though he often pretends pleasure and listens with

241

pain. He delights in his neighbors' disgrace, and longs for every man to be slandered so that he alone may stand in high honor. He lives beset with fantasies of grandeur and with melancholy and with fears that always gnaw at his heart; therefore, he is always looking for pleasures as medicine for his condition. There is hardly a tyrant, perhaps there never has been one, who is not lustful and devoted to fleshly delights. Since he cannot maintain himself in that state or give himself all the pleasures he wants without plenty of money, however, he necessarily also yearns, with inordinate passion, for property. Every tyrant, therefore, is greedy and rapacious and a thief. He not only steals sovereign power, which belongs to the whole people, but also steals the property of the community, as well as whatever he desires to take from individual citizens. Sometimes he uses cunning and hidden means, and sometimes obvious ones. It follows that the tyrant commits virtually all the sins there are. He is steeped, first of all, in pride, sensuality and avarice, the roots of all evil. Secondly, once he has taken power, which was the whole object of his desire, there is nothing he will not do to keep it. There is no crime which he is not ready to commit when it is a matter of keeping power. Experience confirms that the tyrant stops at nothing and spares no one when it is a matter of keeping his position. In mind, therefore, or in actual practice, he commits all the sins in the world. Thirdly, because from his perverted kind of government all the sins of the people follow, he is himself responsible for all, as though they were his sins. It follows that his soul is totally depraved. His memory always reminds him of injuries and desires revenge, while he instantly forgets the favors of friends. His intellect is always busy plotting fraud and treachery and other wickedness. His will is hate-filled and perverse in its desires. His imagination is crowded with false and wicked visions. All his exterior senses are ill-used, whether to satisfy his concupiscence or to wound and deride his neighbor, in expression of his overflowing rage and scorn. All this comes to be because he has made it his purpose to hold such power as it is, in fact, difficult if not impossible to hold for long, for nothing violent can last. He is thus trying to maintain whole by force something which naturally breaks, and he must be ever vigilant. He is devoted to an evil end, and therefore must create an evil order. Since the tyrant cannot ever think a good thought or remember or imagine or do things that are not evil, if he does do some good it will be not for his own citizens but for foreigners. He maintains friendships with lords and masters of foreign peoples, for he views his citizens as rivals and is always afraid of them. He tries to use foreigners to strengthen his position at home. He wants his rule to be secret, and to seem not to be governing at all. He says and he makes his henchmen say that he does not want to change the city's form of government but only to preserve it. He wants to be viewed as the preserver of the common good, and therefore he shows mercy in small things, gives audience occasionally to mere boys and girls or to poor people, and often defends such persons even from minor wrongs. He longs to appear as the author of all the honors and dignities that are given to citizens and wants everyone to feel that these come from him. As to the punishments of those who err, however, or of those who are found guilty by his henchmen in order to bring them down or make them less fortunate, these sufferings he blames only on his officials, and excuses himself for not being able to help. Thus he acquires a good reputation and the love of the people, by making the officials bear the hatred of those who do not see through his stratagems.

He also tries to seem religious and dedicated to the service of religion, but he only does certain exterior things, like going to church, giving to certain charities, building or decorating churches and chapels, and other such things, all for ostentation. He even likes to converse with religious persons, and he falsely confesses to those who are really religious, so as to seem to have been absolved. Yet he ruins religion by usurping the benefices and giving them to his satellites and henchmen, as well as wanting them for his sons. Thus he usurps both temporal and spiritual goods. He wants no citizen to do anything fine, to outshine him in building a palace, or giving feasts, or endowing churches, or backing works of government or wars, for he wants to appear unique. Secretly he often ruins great men, and having brought about their downfall, he will appear to exalt them more than ever, so that they themselves may think they are obliged to him, and so that the people generally will think him merciful and magnanimous and give him their support.

He does not leave justice to the courts for he wants to favor and to kill or ruin whomever he pleases. To get wealth he seizes the commune's money and invents new taxes and revenues. With this money he feeds his satellites and pays off princes and other captains, often without regard to any need of the community. He wants to keep the military well off, and to make them his friends, and he can burden the people with taxes more honorably if he says it is needed to pay the soldiers. For this reason he tends to make unnecessary war and to cause others to make war for no purpose. He does not seek or desire victory nor to diminish foreign powers, but he does it just to keep his people lean and to stabilize his position. He often uses the commune's money to build great palaces and churches, and he displays his arms everywhere and feeds men and women entertainers, for he wants to stand in solitary splendor. To men he has raised from a low condition he gives the daughters of noble citizens for wives, both to lower and destroy the name of the noble families and to exalt such low persons as will be loyal to him. These have no generosity of soul, but they need him, being commonly such vain persons as consider his friendship the ultimate beatitude.

He eagerly receives presents in order to collect property, but he seldom gives to other citizens, prefering to bestow his gifts on princes or other foreigners in order to win their friendship. When he sees something that he wants, belonging to a citizen, he praises it and looks at it and makes such gestures as show his desire, so that the person will, for shame or fear, give it to him. He has flatterers around him to urge the person to make the gift. Often he makes people lend him things that he likes, and then does not return them. He despoils widows and orphans, while pretending to be their defender, and he seizes the goods and the fields and the houses of the poor for parks or pastures or palaces or other purposes that will give him pleasure. He promises to pay the owners a just price, but he never pays half what he says he will. He does not pay those who serve in his house as they deserve. He wants people to serve him for nothing. His satellites he tries to pay only with the goods of others, giving them offices and benefices that they do not merit and taking the offices of the city from others for their sake. If any merchant has a great deal of credit, he strives to make him go bankrupt, for he wants no one to have as much credit as he.

He raises bad men to high places, men who would be punished by the law if he did not protect them. These will then defend him because they thus defend themselves. If he occasionally gives a wise and good man a high position, he does it to show the public that he is a lover of virtue. He always keeps a sharp eye on the wise and good, however, and does not trust them. He also makes sure by the way he maintains them that they cannot hurt him.

Those who fail to court him and do not present themselves at his house or come to his public appearances, he considers enemies. He has followers everywhere who try to draw the young to themselves and provoke them to evil, even to oppose their own fathers. These get the young men to come to him and try to implicate all the youth of the country in their evil counsels. They make the youth hostile to all whom he views as opponents, even to their own fathers. He also tries to induce them to consume their goods in feasts and other delights so that they will be poor and he alone will remain rich.

He does not like any office to be filled without consultation with him; or rather, he wants to fill them all with his own choices. Down to the cooks of the palace and the servants of the public officials, he does not want any jobs given without his consent. Often he gives offices to a younger brother, or to the youngest of a family, or to one with less qualifications of skill and character, in order to make the older and better persons envious and angry, thus creating discord. No opinion can be given, nor any praise bestowed, nor any peace arranged without him, for he wants always to favor one party and degrade whichever does not suit him as well.

All the good laws he cunningly tries to corrupt because they are opposed to his unjust government, and he constantly makes new laws to suit himself. In all governmental and administrative positions, within as well as outside the city, he has busy spies to tell him whatever is being done and said, and these give their own laws to such persons as they appoint to lesser offices, so he makes himself the refuge of all criminals and the nemesis of the just. He is supremely vindictive, and tries to avenge even the slightest injuries with great cruelty, so as to make others afraid, for he is afraid of everyone.

If anyone speaks ill of him, that person had better hide, for he will persecute him even to the ends of the earth, seeking revenge by ambush or poison or other means. He is a great murderer, for he wants to remove each and every obstacle to his rule, though he always presents himself as just the opposite, and very grieved by the death of others. He often pretends that he wants to execute some murderer who has been working for him, but secretly arranges his flight and, after a certain amount of time, that person will pretend to seek forgiveness and will be taken back and maintained close to him.

The tyrant wants to be the best at everything, even at little things, such as games, and rhetoric, and jousting, and horse racing, and scholarship. In any field where there is competition, he will always try to be first, and if he cannot win on his own talents, he will cheat and use some stratagem.

To enhance his reputation he makes it hard to see him. He often busies himself about his private pleasures while the citizens stand outside and wait. Then he gives them a brief interview and ambiguous replies. He would like to be understood by mere signs, for it seems he is ashamed openly to desire and demand what is in itself evil or to refuse what is good, so he speaks in broken phrases that sound good but he also wants to be really understood. He often jeers at good men, with words and by the way he treats them. With his close followers, he laughs at them.

He has secret communications with other princes and then, not telling what information he has acquired, he calls a council to discuss what is to be done. Everyone there gives the best answers he can, but the tyrant alone appears prudent and wise in the end, and well-versed in the secrets of the great lords. And for this he alone wishes to judge all men, and a little scrap of paper from him or a word sent by one of his pages counts more with any judge or official than any law.

Under the tyrant, in short, nothing is sure. Everything depends on his will, which is directed not by reason but by passion. Any citizen subjected to him hangs in suspense because of the tyrant's pride, any man's wealth is unsafe because of his greed, any lady's chastity and modesty are endangered by his lust. Especially at great feasts, there are male and female debauchees to corrupt the women and girls for him. There are often secret passages where the women are led away unsuspecting and find themselves caught in a trap. To say nothing of sodomy, which he likes so much that no boy who is at all attractive is safe. It would take a long time to discuss all the sins and wicked actions of the tyrant, but these will do for this treatise, and now we shall consider the particular problems of the city of Florence.

Chapter III

The well being of Florence is undermined by tyranny;
for Florence of all cities, tyranny is especially bad.

If tyranny is the worst form of government in whatever city or province it occurs, this, if we look at it as Christians, seems to me true to the highest degree in Florence. For all governments of Christian men ought to have as their ultimate purpose the salvation promised us by Christ, and this salvation cannot be attained but by good Christian living which (as we have shown elsewhere) is the best of all ways of life. Christians, therefore, ought to make both their local and their universal governments primarily encourage goodness in daily life. Since good living is nourished and fostered by religious institutions, these ought to be cultivated and preserved and expanded. It is not so much a matter of having more ceremonies as of encouraging more truth, and fostering good, holy, and learned clergy, both secular and regular. Bad men should as far as possible be removed from among the city's priests and monks. As the saints teach us, indeed, there are no worse men than these nor men who do more harm to true religion and good Christian living and every kind of good government. It is better to have few and good priests than many bad ones, for the bad ones provoke the wrath of God against the city. The gravity and number of their sins, which lead the majority of the people to sin likewise, and their persecution of good and just men, cause God to withdraw his hand and not let the grace of good government flow, for all good government comes from him. Read and reread the old and new Testament; you will find that all the persecutions of just men have tended to come from evil clerics, and that their sins have brought scourges of God on the people, and that they have always ruined good government by corrupting the minds of kings and leaders and whatever men were in power.

It is of the utmost importance that the city foster good living and that it be filled with good men, especially priests. If religion and morality improve, government is bound to be perfected. This is true, first, because God and his angels give especial care to bring it about. You can read in the old Testament in many places how, when religion flourished and increased, the kingdom of Judea went from good to better. The same is clear in the new Testament concerning Constantine the Great and Theodosius and other religious princes. Second, the prayers offered by those who are religious, and by the good people in the city, and by the whole community gathered at public feasts are efficacious. We read in the old and new Testament that cities have been saved from mortal danger by prayer and endowed by God with abundant spiritual and temporal goods. Third, good counsel is sure to maintain and increase the kingdom, for when the citizens are good, they are given special enlightenment by God, as it is written: *Exortum est in tenebris lumen rectis corde*, that is, in the shadows of trouble of this world, the righteous in heart are illuminated by God. Fourth, there will be unity, for where people live the good Christian life there cannot be discord; since the roots of discord, pride and ambition, greed and sensuality, are not there. Where there is unity, there is bound to be strength, and indeed past experience has shown small kingdoms made great through internal unity, while great ones have been quickly torn apart by discord. Fifth, there will be justice and good laws, which good Christians cherish. As Solomon said: *Iustitia firmatur solium*, that is, by justice the land is strengthened. The land will also attain wealth through good living, for since the people do not spend their wealth on waste, vast sums will collect in the treasury, with which to pay soldiers and officials and to feed the poor. By these means they will make their enemies afraid. Moreover as merchants and other rich men hear about their good government, they will gladly come to the city, while neighboring peoples who have been ill-governed by others will wish to be ruled by them. Their unity and the friendship of their allies will mean that they need few soldiers, and all arts and sciences and achievements will come to the city and vast treasure be gathered there, and its rule will expand in many directions. This will be a good thing, not only for the city, but also for other peoples, because they will be well-governed and because religion and faith and good Christian living will expand. This will be great glory to God and to our Savior Jesus Christ, king of kings, and lord of lords.

This is what tyrannical government prevents, this is what it spoils, for there is nothing the tyrant hates more than the worship of Christ and good Christian living. It is directly opposed to him, and opposite seeks to oust opposite. The tyrant, therefore, tries as hard as he can to remove the true worship of Christ from the city, though it persists secretly. If an occasional good bishop or priest or monk turns up, especially if he makes free to speak the truth, the tyrant tries carefully to remove him from the city or to corrupt his mind with adulation and presents. And he is sure to give benefices to bad priests and to his own churchmen and to his henchmen. He favors the bad clergy who flatter him.

And he seeks always to corrupt the youth and all the good life in the city as something utterly opposed to him. That is a great, even a supreme evil, in any city or kingdom, but it is especially terrible in a Christian city, and Florence seems to me still the greatest Christian city . . . first, because this people is truly religious by inclination, as those who know the city know. It would indeed be very easy to create in this city perfect religious institutions and the best Christian life, if there were good government here. For, as we know by everyday experience, if it were not for the bad priests and monks, Florence would go back to the life of the first Christians and would stand as a mirror of true religion for the world. Even at present, in the midst of such persecutions of those who seek to live rightly and of good men, and with so many internal and external obstacles, excommunications and evil ideas in the air, we see these people living in such a way in this city of the good that (may I say it without offense to any other?) no other city can be named or exists where there is a greater number of righteous people or a greater perfection of life. If amidst persecutions and obstacles, she grows and is fruitful by the Word of God, what would she be if there were a quiet order within, and no opposition from lukewarm and bad priests, monks, and citizens?

The truth of this is confirmed by the well-known subtlety of the Florentines' minds, for we know how terribly dangerous it is if such minds turn towards evil, especially if they grow used to evil from childhood. For then they are hard to heal and will probably propagate a multitude of sins on earth. But if such minds do turn towards the good, it will be hard to pervert their goodness and they will be able to propagate the good in many directions. Florence, therefore, requires great care. It needs good government, and no one must be allowed to become a tyrant here; for we know how much evil tyranny can accomplish here and in other cities. [Florentine] tyrants have often been able cunningly to deceive the princes of Italy and to keep not only neighboring cities but even remote states in a divided condition. This has been all the more possible because the city is so affluent and so industrious. Thus it has repeatedly caused trouble for all Italy.

The rightness of our plea is also confirmed by the fact that, as we have remarked, tyranny, being a violent thing, cannot naturally endure. To express it in Christian terms, tyranny is permitted by God to punish and purge the sins of the people, but once they are purged, such government must cease. Once the cause is gone, the effect must disappear. If such government cannot endure in other cities and kingdoms, it certainly cannot endure in Florence without a fight. So many good minds cannot rest, and we have seen in fact frequent uprisings in Florence against whatever government there was. Such commotions and civil wars have sometimes brought upheaval to all Italy, and caused many evils.

For the reasons I have given, and for many others that I must omit for the sake of brevity, it is fully clear that, if tyranny should be removed from any city and if anywhere any other kind of government can be more readily tolerated in its imperfections than tyranny with its horrendous effects, all this is even more applicable to Florence. Anyone who has really tasted of these things will easily understand that no punishment and no scourge in this world weighs like the sin of the man who tries or even wishes to try to become or to raise another as tyrant in the city of Florence. Any punishment that can be imagined in this present life is light compared with such sin. But the omnipotent God who is a just judge will know how to punish it as it deserves in this life and the next.

THIRD TREATISE

Chapter I

How to found a civil government and make it work.

Having decided that in Florence the best government is civil government, and that in that city of all cities tyranny is the worst kind of government, we must now see how one can be sure that tyranny does not arise in Florence and how civil government can be introduced. Sometimes tyrants gain power by force of arms, and as reason cannot resist force, we cannot in this case give any further instructions. We do intend to show, however, how provision can be made so that one citizen does not, as in the past has happened, take over, coming into power little by little, by cunning and not by arms, with the help of his friends. It may be said that for this purpose we would have to prevent any citizen becoming excessively rich, since money attracts followers and the very rich citizen can easily make himself the ruler. If we wanted to make this provision, however, it would lead to trouble. It is too dangerous a thing to wish to take the property of the rich and too difficult to set a specific limit on the private wealth of citizens. We shall assert, rather, that wealth is not the basic cause of one citizen's becoming a tyrant. A rich citizen possessing wealth alone, in fact, cannot attract the multitude of other citizens needed to support his government. Others have little to hope for from such a rich man. A small amount of money alone would not buy their consent to his tyranny. Each one would want a lot of money, and no citizen, no matter how rich, could actually buy as many citizens as he would need in such a big city. Having been made rich, moreover, the majority would naturally refuse with indignation to become the slave of persons viewed as equals.

Citizens in fact seek more than money status and fame within the city. They know that reputation helps a man grow rich. We must make sure, therefore, that no citizen is able, by any means whatsoever, to distribute benefices, and offices, and positions of dignity in the city. The true root of tyranny in the city is the fact that citizens adore positions of honor and want to be highly esteemed. If they think they cannot get benefices and honors by any other means, they willingly subject themselves to the person they believe can give them these things. Little by little the number of citizens self-subjected to the man with more authority increases, and so he becomes a tyrant. When there is a small group which usurps such authority, the people inevitably divides into factions which finally fight each other, and the one with the greatest following or the one who wins becomes the tyrant. It is necessary, therefore, to institute a system which lets only the whole people distribute offices and honors. One citizen, then, will not need to look up to another. Every man can consider himself the equal of any other. No one can make himself boss.

Because it is too hard to assemble the whole people every day, a cer-

251

tain number of citizens must be chosen to hold this kind of authority from the whole people. Because a small number, however, could be corrupted through friendships and family ties and bribery, this group must be large. Perhaps everyone would want to be in this group, and that could generate confusion. Perhaps the plebeians would want to get into the government, which would quickly lead to disorder. The number of citizens must be limited in such a way, therefore, that those who threaten to bring disorder cannot enter. Yet no citizen should have any reason to complain. Once this large group of citizens is established, which calls itself the Great Council, and which distributes all offices of honor, this group undoubtedly is the lord and master of the city. Hence it is necessary, as soon as the council has been created, to do three things.

First, to stabilize it in the right way and protect it with strong legislation, so that it cannot be deprived of power. Citizens who do not love the city well enough, however, and who care more for their own special interests than for the common good, would not want to join the council (but if they neglected it, the council could lose its power and be destroyed). One must make sure, therefore, that members who fail to attend at the appointed time, with no legitimate excuse, pay a fine, and a larger fine on the second offense, and that on the third offense, they lose their place in the council. Those who are not motivated by love to be active, therefore, though they ought to be so motivated, will be coerced. Everyone should care for the common welfare more than for his private affairs, and everyone ought willingly to risk his property and his life for the community's sake. So many good things, they should realize, proceed from good government and so much evil results, as we have shown, from bad government. Further legislation and penalties should be set up, as men gradually learn how best to make the council secure and to stabilize its control of the city. If that falls, all is lost.

Second, one must also make sure that this lord and master cannot turn into a tyrant. For just as one man who is a natural lord can be corrupted by bad men and become a tyrant, so a good council can, through the malice of bad men, become bad and tyrannical. Since dissolute and frivolous men, when there are a lot of them, are the cause of many evils in government, they must, as far as possible, be systematically excluded from the government. Heavy penalties must be established to prevent people's conniving with others, or asking others for agreement or for votes. If anyone is caught doing this, he must without fail be punished. Without severe penalties, we cannot preserve our state. We must diligently make arrangements that prevent the roots of evil and of flaws that would undermine the honesty of the council. It must not, especially its majority must not, fall into the control of bad men. That would mean instant ruin and tyranny would ensue.

Third, we must make sure that this system is not abused by exaggeration. The citizens must not be asked to assemble for every little thing. The true lords should personally decide only important matters, while minor matters fall to subordinates. The council must, however, preserve always the right to distribute offices and benefices. Everyone must pass through the gates of judgment. This, as I have said, will eliminate the source of all tyranny. The citizens should meet at regular and fairly convenient times to discuss the many things which will have to be done in these days of meeting. They will have to make the elections as quick and as expeditious as possible. We cannot say much about this or go into great detail, but if the Florentine citizens will stick with our principles, and accept what is said in the next chapter, they will be able to manage. As to details of procedure, with the help of God and their own good will, they will learn day by day from experience. Nor do I myself want to overstep the bounds of my condition and to give our opponents grounds for complaint.

Chapter II
What the citizens must do to perfect their system of civil government.

Every Florentine citizen who wants to be a good member of his city and to help her, as everyone should wish to do, must first of all believe that this council and this civil government were ordained by God. This is true, indeed, not only because all good government comes from God, but also and especially because of the providential care which God has recently manifested in preserving the city. No one who has lived here for the past three years and is not blind and devoid of judgment would deny that, but for the hand of God, this government would never have been created against so much and such powerful opposition, nor would it have maintained itself to this day among so many traitors and so few friends. God, however, demands of us that we ourselves use the intellect

253

and the free will he has given us. He has made all that pertains to government imperfect at first, so that with his help we can improve it. This government is still imperfect and has many flaws. We have hardly more than the foundation. Every citizen, therefore, should strive to perfect it. It can be made perfect only if all or at least the majority are blessed with the following four virtues.

First, fear of God. It is known that every government comes from God, for everything does. He is the first cause of all things and he governs all things. The government of things in nature is visibly perfect and stable, because natural things are subject to him and do not disobey. As they submit to all his commandments, he will always guide them to the perfection of their order and show them whatever they must do.

Second, love of the common good. When they hold offices and other dignities, the citizens must put aside all private interests and all the special needs of their relatives and friends. They must think solely of the common good. This concern will illuminate the eye of the intellect. With their own affections put aside, they will not see falsely. With a firm grasp of the true ends of government they will not tend to go wrong in their decisions. They will deserve God's help, indeed, in fostering the growth of the common good. This, it is said, is one of the reasons for the expansion of the Roman empire, that they loved the common good of the city very much, and therefore God, to reward this virtue (for he does not want any good to go unrewarded, and yet their virtue, lacking the sancitification of grace, did not merit eternal life) rewarded them with temporal goods corresponding to their virtue. He caused the common good of their city to grow and extended their empire over the whole earth.

Third, love of one another. The citizens must drop feuds and forget all past offenses. Hatred, bad feeling, and envy blind the eye of the intellect and do not let it see the truth. Sitting in councils and in public offices, anyone who is not well purged in this regard will make many mistakes. For this God will let them suffer, for their own sins and those of others. But when they are well purged of such feelings, He will enlighten them. Beyond this, if they are peaceful and love one another, God will reward their benevolence with perfect government and growing power. This again is one of the reasons God gave such an empire to the Romans, for they loved one another and in the beginning lived in concord. Theirs was not divine charity, but it was good and natural charity, and God therefore rewarded it with temporal goods. If the citizens of Florence love each other with charity natural and divine, God will multiply their temporal and their spiritual goods.

Fourth, justice. Justice purges the city of bad men, or makes them live in fear. The good and just endure in high authority because they are gladly elected to office by those who love justice. They are enlightened by God in legislation and in guiding the city to a happy state. Justice will make the city fill up with goodness because it always rewards goodness; and the good men, wanting to live where there is justice, will congregate there in great numbers. God, for justice also, will increase the city's empire, as he did that of the Romans. Because the Romans exercised strict and severe justice, He gave them imperial power over the whole world. He wanted justice to make his peoples righteous.

The Florentine citizens, if they deliberate and use rational judgment, will see that they require no other government than the one we have described. If they have faith, moreover, that it was given to them by God, and exercise the four virtues we have named, their government will doubtless be soon perfected. They will arrive at good counsels together, in which God will illuminate their minds concerning whatever they seek to do. God will give them special light, moreover, because they are his servants, and they will know many things that they could not have found out for themselves. They will create on earth a government like that of heaven. They will be blessed with many spiritual and temporal blessings. If they will not have faith, however, that this government is given to them by God, and that they must truly fear God and love the common good, and if they follow only their own wills, without love for one another but with factionalism as always before, and if they fail to do justice, the government ordained by God will still remain. Only they and their children will be wholly consumed rather than receive the grace of it.

God has shown signs of his anger already, but they do not want to open their ears. God will punish them in this world and in the next. In this one they will always be restless and full of passions and sadness; in the other they will burn in the eternal fire. For they refused to follow the natural light, and even the divine signs which have been vouchsafed them, and to realize that this truly is their government. Some who failed to act righteously under this regime and were always restless with it are already suffering the pains of hell. Florentines! You have seen that God wants this government and signs have been given you, you know that it has not faltered despite attacks from within and without, and you realize that those who attack it are threatened by God with many punishments. I beg you by the bowels of mercy of our lord Jesus Christ, that you be content now to accept it. If you are not, God will send a greater scourge to assail you than he has done before. You will lose then both this world and the other. But if you support it, you will gain the happiness that I shall attempt to describe in the next chapter.

Chapter III
Those who rule well are happy, and misery afflicts both tyrants and their followers.

This government is made more by God than by men, and those citizens who, for the glory of God and for the common good, obey our instructions and strive to make it perfect, will enjoy earthly happiness, spiritual happiness, and eternal happiness.

First, they will be free from servitude to a tyrant. How great that servitude is we have declared above. They will live in true liberty, which is more precious than gold and silver. They will be safe in their city, caring with joy and peace of mind for their own households and for making an honest profit in business. When God increases their property or their status, they will not be afraid of someone taking these away. They will be free to go to the country or wherever they want without asking permission from the tyrant. They will marry their sons and daughters to whomever they choose. They will be free to have weddings and celebrations and friends and to pursue science or art, whichever they please, and in other ways too, to build for themselves a certain earthly happiness.

Second, spiritual happiness will follow. Everyone will be able to dedicate himself to the good Christian life, and no one will prevent him. No one when in office will be forced by threats not to give justice, because everyone will be free. Nor will a man be forced by poverty to make evil pacts. The government of the city being good, riches will abound and everyone will work. The poor will earn money. The boys and girls will receive a holy upbringing. Good laws will protect the honor of women and girls. Religion especially will flourish, for God, seeing the people's good will, will send them good clergy. As the Scripture says: "God gives priests to suit the peoples." And these priests will be able to govern their flocks without hindrance, and good church officials and good monks too will become numerous. The bad, indeed, will not be able to live here, since contrary expels contrary.

Thus in a short time the city will be filled with true religion. It will be like a paradise on earth. The people will live amidst rejoicing and singing of psalms. The boys and girls will be like angels growing up in both the Christian and the civic life combined. They, in time, will create a government in this city that is more heavenly than earthly. The happiness of the good will be so profound that they will enjoy in this world a certain spiritual beatitude.

Third, not only will this earn the people eternal happiness, but it will raise the level of that happiness by a great deal. Their merits and therefore their reward in heaven will be increased. For God gives to those that govern well the greatest reward, since beatitude is the prize of virtue, and the greater a man's virtue, the greater his actions, the greater the prize. It is certainly greater virtue to rule oneself and others, and especially a community and a kingdom, than merely to rule oneself. It follows that he who rules a community merits in eternal life the greatest prize. Greater reward as we see in all the arts is given to the master who governs the undertaking than to the servants who obey his directions. In the military art, more is given the captain of the army than the soldiers; in building, greater reward is given the master builder and the architect than the manual workers. And so on in all the arts. The better the actions of a man, moreover, the more he honors God and makes himself useful to his neighbors, the more deserving he is. Certainly to govern a community well, especially one like the Florentine, is an excellent action. It will, as we have shown, bring great glory to God and benefit the souls and bodies and temporal prosperity of men. There can be no doubt then, that it merits a high reward and great glory.

We know that one who gives to charity or feeds a few poor is greatly rewarded by God, for our Savior says that in the day of judgment he will turn to the just and say: "Come, blessed of the Father, receive the kingdom prepared for you from the beginning of the world, for when

I was hungry and when I was thirsty and when I was naked and wandering, you fed me and dressed me and took me in. And you came to visit me when I was ill, for what you have done to my little ones, you have done to me also." If God, then, gives great rewards for each man's particular charity, what reward will he give to the man who governs a large city well? Good government feeds many poor, provides for many who are wretched, defends widows and orphans, and takes out of the hands of the powerful and wicked the persons who otherwise could not defend themselves from their power, liberates the country from thieves and assassins, protects the good, and maintains good living and religious practise. Beyond all this it does infinitely more good. Similar loves similar, moreover, and he will love most whoever most resembles him. All creatures are similar to God, and all are loved by him, but because some are more similar to him than others, he loves them more. He who governs is more similar to God than he who is governed, and therefore surely, if he governs justly, is more loved and rewarded by God for this than for private actions when he is not governing. Whoever governs also takes more risk and suffers more weariness of mind and body than he who does not govern, for which again he deserves greater reward.

But the would-be tyrant is unhappy. First, he has no earthly happiness, for though he has riches, he cannot enjoy them because of the affliction of his spirit, his fears and continual worries, and especially because of the vast sums he must spend to remain in power. And though he wants to make everyone else a mere subject, he is the merest subject of all, forced to wait upon everyone in order to win people over. He is deprived of friendship, which is the greatest and best thing a man can enjoy in this world, because he does not want anyone to be his equal, because he is afraid of everyone, and especially because a tyrant is almost always generally hated for the evils he perpetrates. If bad men love him, it is not because they really wish him well, but because they want to profit from him. No true friendship, therefore, can exist among them. Because of the evils he does, he does not have fame and honor. Others always hate and envy him. He can never really be consoled and free of melancholy, because he must always be vigilant and suspicious that his enemies may try something. He is necessarily always afraid. He does not trust even his guards. He is spiritually unhappy also, moreover, for he lacks the grace of God, and all knowledge of him. Surrounded by

sinners and by the perverse characters who make up his assiduous following, he is bound to fall into evil ways. He will, therefore, be eternally
unhappy, for tyrants are almost always incorrigible. The multitude of
his sins means that sin has become a habit with him, extremely hard to
abandon. To give back all the property he has stolen, also, and to offer
reparations for so many evil deeds would mean being left in his under-
wear, a thing one can imagine would be difficult to one accustomed to
a life of such pride and indulgence. He is also prevented by his flatterers,
who make light of his sins and convince him that wicked things are
good, even by the tepid monks who confess and absolve him, showing
him white when they should show him black. Thus he is wretched in
this world and goes to hell in the other, where he is more severely punished than other men. There stands against him the multitude of his
sins and of the sins he has caused others to commit. He is also condemned for the office he has usurped, for, as the good ruler earns God's
greatest rewards, the bad one is most severely punished.

The tyrant's followers all participate in his wretchedness in temporal,
in spiritual, and in eternal things. They lose their liberty, which is the
greatest of treasures, as well as their property and honors and sons and
wives. For all these come into the tyrant's power. They are always
imitating his sins, in order to please him and to be as like him as they
can. In hell, too, therefore, they will participate in his terrible punishment.

The citizens who dislike civil government because it stops them from
being tyrants all participate in the same wretchedness even though they
are not actually tyrants. They lack riches, honors, reputation, and friendship. All the lean ones congregate around them hoping to repair their
fortunes, and all the bad men surround them. They must be always
spending money, and the good people avoid them. They have not a
single real friend, for their followers try to rob them. Their bad companions lead them into a thousand sins which they would not otherwise
commit. They are restless in heart and at all times filled with hatred,
envy, and complaints. Thus they have hell both in this world and the
next.

Since (as we have shown), therefore, those who rule well are happy
and are like God, and those who rule badly are unhappy and like the
devil, every citizen should abandon his sins and his private affections to

strive to rule well. Everyone should work to preserve and increase and perfect this civil government, for the honor of God and for the salvation of souls. God gave this government especially to Florence because of his love for this city. Through this government, it can be happy in this world and the other, by the grace of our Savior Jesus Christ, king of kings, lord of lords, who with the Father and the Holy Spirit lives and rules *in saecula saeculorum*.

Index

(Italicized numbers refer to translated texts.)

Age, *27, 104, 114,* 153–54
Alberti, Leon Battista, 4, 6, 10–11, 15–16, *98–101;* and the Medici family, 98
Aquinas, St. Thomas, 228
Arcadius, Emperor, *45, 50*
Architas, *212*
Arezzo, *30, 44, 64–65*
Argyropoulos, 187
Aristides, Aelius (*Panegyric* of Athens), 189
Aristotle, 22, *121, 134–37, 139–40, 214, 215,* 228
Attila (king of the Huns), *53–55*

Bandini, Bernardo, *173, 181*
Barbarian invasions (Goths, Huns, Vandals, Lombards), *45–46, 48–62*
Baron, Hans, 9
Belisarius, *57*
Bentivoglio, Giovanni (of Bologna), *77–79, 88–90, 180*
Bologna, *76–77*
Bruni, Leonardo, 4, 6, 9–10, 22–25, 169–70, 189

Cataline, *32–33*
Charlemagne, *61–64, 65*
Charles VIII, 226
Childhood, *105*
Cicero, 6, *31, 32, 142,* 189, *201,* 216, *219*

Civil rights, 10, 23, *70–72,* 229–30. *See also* Freedom, Justice, Law
Community, 16, 18, *233–34, 252*
Cusanus, Nicolas, 6

Etruscans, *34–37;* wars with Rome, *36–45*
Eugene IV, Pope, 98, *107, 114*

Falerii, *43–44*
Family, 18, 24, *130–31, 212*
Ficino, Marsilio, 6, 153–54, 168, 187
Fidenae, *37–38*
Fiesole, *30–31*
Florence, 7–8; Bruni's *History of, 27–91, 204, 236–38, 247–50. See also* Imperialism: Florentine
Fortuna, 17, *103*
Frederic II, *67*
Freedom (*see also* Civil rights, Liberty): internal political, 10, 12, 13–14, 18–19, 23, 24; (Roman), *46–47, 68–73,* 151, 189, *227–29, 236–38, 251–53* of peoples, 9, 12–13, 23, *109–10* of speech, 14–15, *70,* 189, *202–3* right to privacy, 15, 18

Galla, Placidia, *52–53*
Garin, Eugenio, 9
Gauls, *36, 44*
Giano della Bella, 10, 23, *68–73*

261

God, *28, 214, 231–33, 253–60. See also*
    Religion
Guelf-Ghibelline conflict, *65–67*
Guicciardini, Vito, 188

Hannibal, *45, 137*
Holy Roman Empire, *62*
Honorius, Emperor, *45, 50–52*
Humanism, 3–9, 22, *28,* 98–99, *118–19,
    121–22,* 152, 169, 187, 190–91, *201,
    214,* 228

Imperialism:
    Florentine, 13, 23, *72–73,* 208–9, 236–37
    Roman, 9, 27, *30, 33–34, 36–45, 60–61,
        254*
Innocent VIII, Pope, 151, *162*
Intoxication, 105–6

Jerome, Saint, 130
Justice, 10, 99, *129,* 189, *219, 258*

Kristeller, Paul Oscar, 5

Ladislas (king of Naples), 27
Landino, Cristoforo, 153
Law, *203. See also* Justice
Leadership, 16, 24, *114,* 153, *258*
Leo I, Pope, *55*
Leo X, Pope (Giovanni de' Medici), 8,
    12, 151, 154, *161–62;* Lorenzo de'
    Medici's letter to, *162–65*
Liberty, 12–17, 189–90, *195–222, 256. See
    also* Freedom
Livy, *35, 36, 37, 39, 137*
Lucian, 6
Luxury, 11, 13, 17, *31–32, 113, 164,* 235.
    See also Wealth.

Machiavelli, Niccolò, 12, 17, 169, 229
Marsh, David, 121, 147, 171
Medici family, 3–4, 8, 10, 11, 22–23; and
    Alberti, 98;
    bank, 152, *157–60, 174–75;*
    individuals:
    Cosimo, *120,* 152, 187
    Giuliano, 169, *176–77, 179, 183,* 187
    Lorenzo (brother of Cosimo), *120, 122–
        25, 129, 134, 138–39, 140, 143–45*
    Lorenzo the Magnificent, 4, 11, 16,
        150–55, 169, *175–76, 179–80,* 187,
        188, 190, *217, 220–21,* 226–27,
        241–50
    Piero di Cosimo, 187

Metrodorus, *121*
Milan, *75, 84–88. See also* Visconti, Gian
    Galeazzo
Military forces (veterans), *32, 72–73, 131–
    32. See also* War
Monarchy, *233–35*

Niccoli, Niccolò, 15, *120;* speaker, *122–47*
Nicolas V, Pope, *107*
Nobility, 118; comparative, *125–28;* con-
    cept of, *132–34;* Poggio's *On Nobility,
    121–47*

Patriotism, 5, 11, 23, 109, *112–13, 113–
    14, 145,* 152, 218
Patronage, 12, 153
Pazzi conspiracy, 8, 16, 151, 168–69,
    171–83, 186, 190, *196*
Pazzi family:
    Francesco, *172–73, 178*
    Galeatto, *181*
    Giovanni, *180*
    Guglielmo, *180, 181*
    Jacopo, 168, 169, *171–72, 177–
        78, 182*
    Renato, 168, *180*
Peace demonstration, *74–75*
Perosa, Alessandro, 168
Pico della Mirandola, 6
Pisa, *27, 64, 75*
Pius II, Pope, 6
Plague, *76,* 188
Plato, 22, *141–42,* 199, 217
Plutarch, 6
Poggio Bracciolini, 4, 6, 15, *118–20*
Poggio, Jacopo di, 168, *173, 178*
Poliziano, Angelo, 4, 16, 153, 168–70
Porcari, Stefano (conspiracy of), 11,
    107–15
Poverty, 17, 18, *98*
Public opinion, 15, 16, *71–72, 104, 251*

Religion (Etruscan), *37, 74–75, 104, 119,
    154, 162–65,* 227, *255. See also* God
Riario, Girolama (duke), *173*
Rinuccini, Alamanno, 168, 186–191
Rinuccini, Alessandro, *193*
Robert, Emperor, *78–88*
Rosamunda (Lombard queen), *59*
Rubinstein, Nicolai, 188
Ruling classes, 10, 17, *118. See also*
    Nobility

Sallust, *31*, 169
Salutati, 9, 22
Salviati, Francesco (archbishop of Pisa), 168, 169, *172*, *173*, *177*, *178*
Savonarola, Girolamo, 4, 11–12, 226–30
Seneca, *142–43*, *180*
Serfdom, 119
Sixtus IV, Pope, 8, *161*, *162*, 169, *220*
Slavery, 16, 17, 99, *103–6*
Stilico, *50*, *52*
Stoics, *141*, *215*
Sulla, *30–31*

Tacitus, 169
Tarquinius, *39–40*
Themistocles, *137*, *139*
Theocritus, *199*
Theodosius, *50*
Thucydides, 17
Tolomeo of Lucca, 228
Totila (king of the Goths), *57*, *63*
Tyranny, 12, *70–72*, 153, 204–7, *217*, *238–50*, *252–53*, *258–59*

Valens, Emperor, *49*
Veii, *38*, *41–43*, *44*
Venice, *82–88*, *90–91*
Vespasiano da Bisticci, 5
Vespucci, Piero, *181*
Virgil, *35*
Virtù, 5, 6, 22, 23, *132*, *143–45*, *146–47*, 189, *200*
Visconti, Gian Galeazzo, *75–76*, *91*
Voigt, Georg, 5
Volterra, 151

War, *115*, 151, *208–10*, *250–51*. See also Barbarian invasions, Etruscans, Frederic II
Wealth, 10, 16, 17, *110*, 119–20, *130*, *140*; Medici bank, 152, *160–61*, *212*, *216*, *251*. See also Luxury
Weinstein, Donald, 228–29

Xenophobia, *113*. See also Patriotism
Xenophon, 190